Best Hikes Sacramento

Best Hikes Sacramento

The Greatest Vistas, Rivers, and Gold Rush Trails

SECOND EDITION

Tracy Salcedo

GUILFORD, CONNECTICUT

FALCONGUIDES®

An imprint of The Rowman & Littlefield Publishing Group, Inc.
4501 Forbes Blvd., Ste. 200, Lanham, MD 20706
Falcon and FalconGuides are registered trademarks and Make Adventure Your Story is a trademark of The Rowman & Littlefield Publishing Group, Inc.

Distributed by NATIONAL BOOK NETWORK

A previous edition of this book was published by FalconGuides in 2012.

TOPO! Maps copyright © 2018 National Geographic Partners, LLC. All Rights Reserved.

Maps © Rowman & Littlefield

All photos by Tracy Salcedo unless otherwise noted

British Library Cataloguing-in-Publication Information available

The Library of Congress has cataloged the previous edition as follows:

Salcedo-Chourré, Tracy.
  Best hikes near Sacramento / Tracy Salcedo-Chourre.
     p. cm.
  Summary: "Featuring 41 of the best hikes in the greater Sacramento area, this exciting new guidebook points locals and visitors alike to trailheads within an hour's drive of the city"—Provided by publisher.
  ISBN 978-0-7627-8090-7 (pbk.)
  1. Hiking—California—Sacramento Region—Guidebooks. 2. Sacramento Region (Calif.)—Guidebooks.
  I. Title.
  GV199.42.C22S237 2012
  917.94'54—dc23

                                                                    2012017911

ISBN 978-1-4930-3026-2 (paperback)
ISBN 978-1-4930-3027-9 (e-book)

Printed in the United States of America

For Alexandera,
A reminder that lovely things can be found in unexpected places

Contents

Canyon View Bridge spans Coon Creek above its confluence with Deadman Creek.

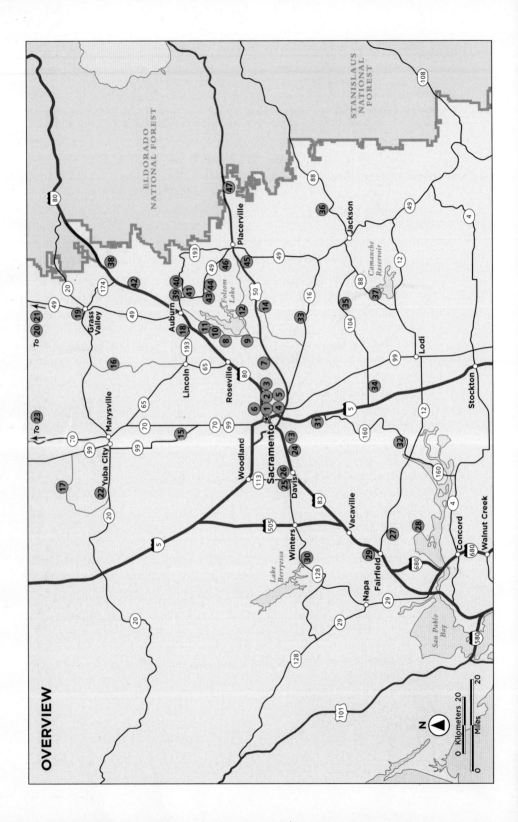

OVERVIEW

Introduction

I knew I had to go back to Hidden Falls. Located just west of Sacramento, tucked in foothills at the foot of the Sierra Nevada, the park had undergone a massive expansion in the years since the first edition of *Best Hikes Near Sacramento* was published, and there was another waterfall to visit.

I knew I had to add North Table Mountain. This park outside Oroville pushes the limits in terms of distance from California's capital city, but it boasts stellar views across the Sacramento Valley to the Yolla Bolly Mountains and a stellar trail leading down to one of its many falls. I got lucky on my hike here: It was spring, and California had abundant winter rain. There was a superbloom.

I knew I had to hike the Sutter Buttes. The Middle Mountain dominates viewscapes in the valley just north of Sacramento. The open space there is preserved by a local land trust, and hiking is restricted. No matter—the walking was also a revelation.

I also wanted to revisit places that had never left my consciousness, but that I hadn't seen since the first time around. The birds of Gray Lodge. Bobelaine on the Feather River, swamped by the winter's record rainfall. The surprise of the Empire Mine. Provocative Rancho Seco.

And downtown Sacramento, where the rivers meet and lengthy urban pathways encourage exploration, gets more vibrant with time.

Sacramento and the smaller satellite cities within a reasonable drive of the state capital, like Davis, Auburn, and Colfax, are no longer hiccups along the freeway that beelines from the San Francisco Bay Area to Lake Tahoe and the shining Sierra. The unexpected beauty of these parklands has been unmasked, like a wallflower coaxed into the lights on the dance floor. Their beauty may be more muted, but they are radiant upon exploration.

This guide includes some urban hikes. Several paved, flat tracks, often following riverbanks, levee roads, or abandoned railroad grades, weave across the sprawling Sacramento metropolitan area. These routes satisfy the varied recreational needs of area residents, accommodating after-work escapes, lunchtime power walks, needed perambulation for cooped-up canines, the walk-and-talks of parents pushing strollers, the marathoner's workout, and Sunday sunset walking meditations.

Suburbia and agriculture form a shifting ecotone around Sacramento, with rivers and streams as the major thruways. An increasing number of parks and preserves have been set aside along these corridors. Not all allow public access or have developed trail systems, but some do, and hiking in these open spaces, particularly in the foothills, offers a glimpse into what the landscape offered when its only inhabitants were tribal hunters and gatherers.

The mighty Sacramento River and its tributaries—the three forks of the American, the Feather, the Yuba, and the Cosumnes—inform nearly every park and trail in this guide. They evolve as they flow out of the mountains and merge on the flatlands, growing from clear, fast-moving streams into navigable waterways that look lazy

Springtime in the Great Valley, especially after a year of record rainfall, brings spectacular wildflower blooms throughout the region.

until the sun highlights the complicated currents that churn below the surface. Trails around the rivers and their levees and sloughs—especially where the Sacramento and San Joaquin Rivers splinter into a complex delta as they reach San Francisco Bay— range through riparian habitats and wetlands that support a wealth of bird, plant, and animal life. You'll be hard-pressed to find a trail in the delta, or in any riverside park, that doesn't ring with birdsong.

History also informs the region's trails. On the landscape, bedrock mortars and scattered arrowheads are the most durable legacy of California's first peoples; coupled with oral histories and the resiliency of modern tribal members, these offer fragile links to lifeways that predate the arrival of the Spanish in the late 1700s. But rem-nants of the state's fabled gold rush and the endeavors of its forty-niners can be found throughout the area, especially in the foothills. Urban hikes through Old Sacramento and down the Capitol Mall to Capitol Park recall the evolution of the city from a flood-plagued frontier outpost to its present-day role as California's political epicenter.

Each hike in this guide is unique for its ecology, history, topography, or natural beauty and represents a sampling of the best hiking that can be found in the region. I hope you will find these treks as satisfying as I have—again. I also hope they will inspire you to explore farther, and will stick with you as they have stuck with me.

Weather

The climate of the Central Valley is essentially Mediterranean, with rainy and dry seasons. Hiking is possible and pleasant year-round, but hikers should remember that each season poses unique challenges.

After four years of extreme drought, California experienced record rainfall and snowfall in the winter of 2016–17, which caused the Sacramento River and its tributaries to swell. This sign in the Bobelaine Audubon Sanctuary on the shores of the Feather River was nearly a casualty. A new nail can set it right, just as a season of good rainfall has done a lot to set right the damage done by the long drought.

The rainy season generally runs from November through March and includes storms that can drop anywhere from a trace to several inches of precipitation in a shot. The occasional atmospheric river (aka Pineapple Express) can bring more drenching downpours. Because the valley lies in the rain shadow of California's Coast Ranges, average monthly rainfall totals in winter are modest, ranging from 2 to 4 inches. Average daytime high temperatures are in the 50s and 60s; average lows are in the 40s, with occasional dips into the 30s.

Winter rains may not be intimidating, but the fog can be. Inversions occasionally trap moisture on the valley floor, creating dense banks of "tule" fog that can reduce visibility, in the extreme, to less than 50 feet. The fog is primarily a hazard for drivers on area freeways, but it also significantly limits the vistas that can be enjoyed from any trail.

Conditions on some trails can degenerate into boot-sucking mud following winter rains. A day or two of dry weather usually hardens most surfaces so they are passable. The occasional cold front may deposit snow on the peaks of the coastal mountains and in the foothills. Usually this does not render the trails impassable, but hikers should be prepared for slick conditions.

In the dry season, April through October, rainy days are sparse to nonexistent. With hot temperatures and warm winds blowing in from the delta to the west, by late July most vegetation has crisped to a crackly crunch, and hikers will crisp up too if they don't carry enough drinking water. Average daytime high temperatures range from the high 80s to the 90s, with heat waves raising the mercury into the 100s. Lows average in the 50s.

The greatest danger a hiker faces on hot summer days is dehydration. No matter the trail's length or the amount of shade along the route, carry plenty of water. When the temperatures soar, avoid hiking in the heat of the day. Morning and evening hours offer lovely light and a greater opportunity to see wildlife, as well as mitigate the risks of heat-related illness that skyrocket when temperatures reach into the high 90s and 100s.

Flora and Fauna

Landscapes traversed by trails within an hour's drive of Sacramento include oak woodlands, grasslands (or savanna), wetlands (both freshwater and saltwater), and lower montane forests.

The most recognizable is the savanna, as that is the primary setting for the city and its suburbs. Supporting annual grasses that green up in winter and dry golden in summer, the terrain is flat or rolling. Springtime wildflower displays, particularly after a wet winter, are spectacular. Vernal pools may also appear in spring, supporting a variety of ephemeral wildflowers and rare fauna, including fairy shrimp.

A pair of Canada geese paddle up the American River beneath a highway overpass in Discovery Park, underscoring the value of urban trails and green spaces for all species.

On the west side of the Great Valley, several trails in this guide venture into the saltwater-infused wetlands of the Sacramento–San Joaquin Delta, characterized by stands of pickleweed and frequented by shore- and waterbirds such as herons, egrets, and many species of ducks.

Freshwater marshes are scattered throughout the region, recharging with winter rains and meltwater from the Sierra Nevada in springtime. The marshes attract numerous birds, including migrating species like sandhill cranes, and are thick with tules, reeds, and cattails, which provide cover for songbirds and other marsh inhabitants such as muskrats and frogs.

Oak woodlands blanket the slopes of the Coast Ranges and the lower slopes of the foothills. California is home to a variety of oaks, some evergreen and some deciduous, including the blue oak, valley (white) oak, live oak, and tanoak. The trees require an expert eye to differentiate, especially since they hybridize. Other trees include bay laurel, buckeye, and, in the foothills, digger pine and other evergreens. Nut-loving critters, such as acorn woodpeckers and gray squirrels, thrive in this habitat.

Venture a little higher into the foothills and you'll encounter the mixed evergreen forest of the lower montane ecosystem. Fragrant incense cedar, a variety of pines, Douglas fir, and black oak provide shade, with manzanita and ceanothus in the understory. This is bear country; it also harbors deer and squawking jays.

Etiquette for Animals

You'll encounter mostly benign, shy creatures on these trails—deer, rabbits, chirping chickadees. More rarely seen (during the daylight hours especially) are coyotes, raccoons, and opossums. Deer in some of the parks are remarkably tame and may linger on or close to the trails. Make noise to alert them to your presence; hopefully they will move along. Do not approach any wildlife; these creatures are safest and healthiest when they are permitted to do whatever they are doing in peace, including walk away. Never offer food to a wild creature. Your food, no matter how delicious to you, is junk food to any wild animal, and does more harm than the picture is worth.

Among the common domestic creatures you are likely to encounter on the trail are cows. They are passive and will usually move away as you approach. If you are uncertain of a cow's intentions, extend your arms and make noise.

Remoter regions of the foothills and coastal mountains are habitat for mountain lions, bears, and rattlesnakes. Encounters are infrequent, but you should be prepared to react properly if you meet a snake, cat, or bear while hiking.

Rattlesnakes generally only strike if they are threatened. You are too big to be dinner, so they don't want to waste venom on you. Keep your distance and they will keep theirs. If a snake doesn't retreat or assumes a threatening posture—coiling up and shaking its rattle in warning—back slowly away and pick another route.

If you come across a mountain lion, make yourself as big as possible. If you are hiking with a child, pick him or her up. This will not only make you appear bigger but also protect your kid. Maintain eye contact and do not run. If you don't act or

Bleached bones rest on a lichen-covered boulder in the Sutter Buttes.

look like prey, you stand a good chance of not being attacked. Make noise and back away slowly, and the animal will most likely retreat. If you are attacked, fight back.

Black bears are generally not a threat, but you don't want to take any chances. If you see a bear, make lots of noise; usually the animal will run away. If the bear appears aggressive or charges, make yourself as big as possible. Bears sometimes charge as a bluff, then veer away, so stand your ground and do not run. You don't want to resemble prey. Retreat slowly. In the event of an attack, again, fight back.

Plants to Avoid

Poison oak is a California native plant that, if touched or handled, coats the skin in urushiol, an oil that can cause a nasty skin rash. When the leaves turn red in autumn, the plant is easy to spot and stay away from. In spring, when it's green, the adage "leaves of three, let it be" will help you steer clear. In winter the plant loses its leaves entirely and becomes indistinguishable from other leafless vines, shrubs, and ground cover. That's when you'll want to employ the best tactic for avoiding poison oak, and one that works year-round: Stay on the trail.

Stinging nettle is another irritating plant that may be encountered along Sacramento-area trails. Upon contact, it produces a stinging sensation that's quite uncomfortable and long-lasting. Common in grasslands and along waterways, the best way to avoid contact is, again, to stay on the trail.

Wilderness Restrictions/Regulations

Most of the trails described in this guide are on public lands. While day-use fees, parking fees, and registration may be required to access certain trails, specialized permits

On occasion you may find yourself sharing the trail with members of the Sacramento Valley's agricultural community.

are usually not required. Fees vary from park to park. In the wake of a funding crisis in 2012, some state parks are operated by nonprofits, so access and services may be subject to change due to funding shortages or lack of volunteer services. Check the official web page of the park you would like to hike in before visiting (supplied as part of the hike descriptions).

A few of the trails cross properties managed by the California Department of Fish and Game. Charged with managing these properties for the benefit of wildlife, and not necessarily for humankind, land managers occasionally restrict access. This can be to accommodate a particular species' breeding season, or to allow seasonal hunts (intended to help keep wildlife populations at healthy numbers). Go to the department's web page for the area you wish to visit (for example, Grizzly Island Wildlife Area) to check on restrictions before you visit. The specific web pages also contain notifications of closures for other reasons, such as flooding.

A couple of trails have limited access, or are accessible only via docent-led hikes. Don't shy away from these. They offer special opportunities to learn more about both the natural and cultural history of the land, and permit you to walk in places that retain an element of the untamed. Contact information for the land manager is provided in the hike description.

Support California's state and local park systems by paying required fees or purchasing seasonal passes. You can also become active in any of the nonprofit volunteer organizations that have stepped up to support many parks.

Green Tips

Given the great beauty of the parks, trails, and wildlands in and around Sacramento, and especially given the heavy use all receive, it's important that we do all we can to keep them clean, lovely, and healthy. The Green Tips scattered throughout this guide will help you do just that.

Getting Around

This guide targets the Sacramento-area hiker as well as the hiker from farther afield. All hikes are within an hour's drive (or so) of greater Sacramento. A few stretch that limit, but in general this limitation precludes the high country of the Sierra Nevada and hikes in popular Coast Range destinations. The focus is, rightfully, on the landscapes integral to California's Great Valley.

Hikes are located in Sacramento, Yolo, Sutter, Placer, and El Dorado Counties. The guide includes hikes in or near Fairfield, Davis, Winters, Marysville/Yuba City, Oroville, Grass Valley, Auburn, Placerville, Galt, and Jackson.

Brimming waterways and ponds in the Gray Lodge Wildlife Area offer sanctuary for a great variety of birds.

Sometimes trailside beauty is man-made.

Several major highways and interstates converge in Sacramento. Directions to trailheads are given from these arteries, which include I-5 (north–south), I-80 (east–west), US 50 (east–west), CA 99 (north–south), and CA 49 (north–south in the foothills, linking Grass Valley, Auburn, and Placerville).

Public Transportation

The Sacramento Regional Transit District offers bus and light rail service throughout the greater Sacramento metropolitan area, with service to suburban cities including North Highlands, Roseville, Folsom, Rancho Cordova, and Elk Grove. Contact information is (916) 321-BUSS (2877); sacrt.com.

How to Use This Guide

My hope is that you'll find this guide thorough and easy to use. Each hike is described with a map and summary information that delivers the trail's vital statistics, including length, difficulty, fees and permits, park hours, canine compatibility, and trail contacts. Directions to the trailhead are also provided, along with a general description of what you'll see along the way. A detailed route finder (Miles and Directions) provides mileages between significant landmarks along the trail.

Hike Selection

The hikes range from short educational excursions perfect for families with small children to challenging all-day adventures. While these trails are among the best, keep in mind that nearby trails, sometimes in the same park or preserve, may offer options better suited to your needs or abilities.

Difficulty Ratings

To aid in selecting a hike that suits particular needs and abilities, each is rated easy, moderate, or challenging. Ratings are based primarily on elevation gain and loss, challenges on the treadway (uneven footing, exposure to steep drop-offs), and trail length. Bear in mind that even the most challenging routes can be made easy by hiking within your limits and taking rests when you need them.

Willows take root in the sandy soil of the hydraulic mining pit at Malakoff Diggins State Historic Park.

- **Easy** hikes are generally short and flat, taking no longer than an hour to complete.
- **Moderate** hikes involve increased distance and relatively mild changes in elevation, and will take one to three hours to complete.
- **Challenging** hikes feature steep stretches, greater distances, and generally take four or more hours to complete.

Ratings are completely subjective. A hike's relative difficulty is entirely dependent upon an individual hiker's level of fitness and the adequacy of his or her gear (primarily shoes). Take both into consideration when selecting a hike. If you are hiking with a group, select a hike with a rating that's appropriate for the least fit and least prepared in the party.

Hiking times are based on the assumption that on flat ground, most walkers average 2 miles per hour. Adjust that rate by the steepness of the terrain and your level of fitness (subtract time if you're an aerobic animal; add time if you're hiking with kids), and you have a ballpark hiking duration. Be sure to add more time if you plan to picnic or take part in other activities like birding or photography.

Trail Finder

Hike No.	Hike Name	Best Hikes for Bird Lovers	Best Hikes for Children	Best Hikes for Dogs	Best Hikes for Great Views	Best Hikes for History	Best Hikes for Lake Lovers	Best Waterfall Hikes	Best Hikes for Nature Lovers	Best Urban Trails	Best Riverside Hikes	Best Long Rambles
Sacramento Metro Area												
1	Old Sacramento and Waterfront Promenade		●		●	●				●		
2	Capitol Mall and Capitol Park					●				●		
3	William Land Park Tour		●							●		
4	Jedediah Smith Memorial Trail / Discovery Park		●							●		
5	Sacramento Northern Bikeway									●		
6	Gibson Ranch Loop Trail		●									
7	Effie Yeaw Nature Loop		●						●		●	
8	Miners Ravine Nature Reserve	●	●									
9	Lake Natoma Loop			●						●		
10	Dotons Cove Trail			●	●		●		●			

Hike No.	Hike Name	Best Hikes for Bird Lovers	Best Hikes for Children	Best Hikes for Dogs	Best Hikes for Great Views	Best Hikes for History	Best Hikes for Lake Lovers	Best Waterfall Hikes	Best Hikes for Nature Lovers	Best Urban Trails	Best Riverside Hikes	Best Long Rambles
11	Sterling Pointe to Rattlesnake Bar				•		•					•
12	Sweetwater Trail				•		•					•
13	Yolo Bypass Wildlife Area Loop	•							•			
14	Mather Nature Loops		•						•			
Honorable Mention												
	Maidu Regional Park					•				•		
North Valley and Foothills												
15	Bobelaine Audubon Sanctuary	•							•			
16	Shingle Falls							•				•
17	Gray Lodge Wildlife Area	•	•		•				•			
18	Hidden Falls Regional Park		•					•				•
19	Empire Mine State Historic Park					•						
20	Malakoff Diggins State Historic Park				•	•						•

Hike No.	Hike Name	Best Hikes for Bird Lovers	Best Hikes for Children	Best Hikes for Dogs	Best Hikes for Great Views	Best Hikes for History	Best Hikes for Lake Lovers	Best Waterfall Hikes	Best Hikes for Nature Lovers	Best Urban Trails	Best Riverside Hikes	Best Long Rambles
21	Independence Trail to Rush Creek Falls							•				•
22	Sutter Buttes					•			•			
23	North Table Mountain Waterfall Hike		•					•				
Honorable Mentions												
	Little Humbug Falls							•				•
	Spring Creek Falls							•			•	
	South Yuba River State Park											
West Valley												
24	Putah Creek Loop Trail	•										•
25	UC Davis Arboretum Trail								•			
26	Covell Greenbelt									•		
27	Rush Ranch		•		•	•						
28	Howard Slough at Grizzly Island Wildlife Area	•			•							•
29	Rockville Hills Regional Park								•			

Hike No.	Hike Name	Best Hikes for Bird Lovers	Best Hikes for Children	Best Hikes for Dogs	Best Hikes for Great Views	Best Hikes for History	Best Hikes for Lake Lovers	Best Waterfall Hikes	Best Hikes for Nature Lovers	Best Urban Trails	Best Riverside Hikes	Best Long Rambles
30	Homestead and Blue Ridge Loop (Stebbins Cold Canyon Reserve)				●				●			●
South Valley												
31	Stone Lakes National Wildlife Refuge	●	●									
32	Delta Meadows River Park								●			
33	Deer Creek Hills Preserve								●			●
34	Cosumnes River Walk	●							●		●	
35	Howard Ranch Trail	●							●			●
36	Indian Grinding Rock State Historic Park		●			●						
37	China Gulch Trail						●					
Foothills South of I-80												
38	Stevens Trail Falls				●			●				
39	Mountain Quarry Railroad Trail		●			●					●	
40	Lake Clementine Trail							●			●	

Hike No.	Hike Name	Best Hikes for Bird Lovers	Best Hikes for Children	Best Hikes for Dogs	Best Hikes for Great Views	Best Hikes for History	Best Hikes for Lake Lovers	Best Waterfall Hikes	Best Hikes for Nature Lovers	Best Urban Trails	Best Riverside Hikes	Best Long Rambles
41	Olmstead Loop								•			•
42	Codfish Falls							•			•	
43	Cronan Ranch Regional Trails Park Loop				•						•	
44	Dave Moore Nature Trail		•								•	
45	El Dorado Trail from Missouri Flat to Forni Road									•		•
46	Monroe Ridge–Marshall Monument Trail Loop				•	•					•	
47	Jenkinson Lake Loop						•					•

MAP LEGEND

Freeway/Interstate Highway		Boat Ramp
US Highway		Bridge
State Highway		Building / Point of Interest
Paved/Improved Road		Campground
Unpaved Road		Cave
Gravel Road		Dam
Railroad		Gate
Featured Trail		Mountain / Peak
Trail		Park Headquarters
Paved Trail		Parking
Levee		Picnic Area
Boardwalk		Restroom
National Forest		Scenic View / Overlook
State / Local Park		Trailhead
Body of Water		Visitor / Information Center
Swamp / Marsh		Waterfall
River or Creek		
Intermittent Stream		

Sacramento Metro Area

TRAILS THROUGH URBAN PARKS AND ALONG RIVERS

Parks and trails are integral to the Sacramento metropolitan area, which includes nationally recognized urban routes. The American River Parkway features a paved path nestled in a greenbelt along the namesake river. The path—the Jedediah Smith Memorial Trail—stretches for more than 30 miles from the confluence of the American and Sacramento Rivers to Folsom Lake State Recreation Area. Other trails in the metro area are also paved, making them accessible to parents pushing strollers and folks who employ wheelchairs and scooters in their outdoor endeavors. Others are short explorations of urban parks perfect for family outings.

The old and the new: Brick and wood storefronts in Old Sacramento are now overshadowed by the glass and concrete structures of modern downtown.

Though the rich lands along the rivers were long inhabited by native peoples, and John Sutter established his famed fort on the banks of the American when Mexico still governed what was then known as Alta California, Sacramento's urban identity originated in the days of California's gold rush. The city at the base of the Sierra Nevada's foothills burgeoned with the wealth of the argonauts. Once the rush was over, Sacramento thrived as California's capital. The beauty of its natural setting, its history, its cultural amenities, and its political relevance continue to draw new residents and visitors to the region.

Growth has been a constant, with urban development stretching in all directions. But like many of the state's metropolitan areas, the Great Valley's greatest city has preserved what all Californians cherish—green spaces and wildlands, and trails that wander through them.

1 Old Sacramento and Waterfront Promenade

A boardwalk and promenade follow the waterfront of the Sacramento River, beginning among the bustling shops and restaurants of historic Old Sacramento, heading down past the eastern foot of the Tower Bridge, and following a scenic promenade to the edge of downtown.

Start: Behind the California State Railroad Museum in Old Sacramento, adjacent to the Sacramento River
Distance: 1.1 miles out and back
Hiking time: 0.5–1 hour (longer if you stop to enjoy the sights)
Difficulty: Easy
Trail surface: Pavement, boardwalk
Best season: Year-round
Other trail users: Cyclists
Amenities: While there are no specific amenities at the trailhead proper, you'll find restrooms, water (and other libations), food, and resources galore in Old Sacramento.
Canine compatibility: Leashed dogs permitted

Fees and permits: None
Schedule: Accessible all day, year-round
Maps: USGS Sacramento West CA. The trail is straightforward enough that no map is needed.
Trail contact: Bicycle Coordinator with the City of Sacramento, 915 I St., Room 2000, Sacramento 95814; (916) 808-8300; www.cityof sacramento.org/Public-Works/Transportation/ Programs-and-Services/Bicycling-Program
Other: Have your wallet handy—an appetite wouldn't hurt either. Old Sacramento encompasses a mother lode of restaurants, shops, parlors, and museums. Clothing, cotton candy, champagne, caviar . . . you can find it here.

Finding the trailhead: The trailhead is in downtown Sacramento. Take the J Street exit from I-5 and follow the signs to Old Sacramento. Both on-street parking and parking garages are available in the area; fees are charged. The closest garage is at the end of J Street, across the street from the railroad museum, which is at 111 I St. **GPS:** N38 35.058' / W121 30.256'

The Hike

Culture and history are the focal points of this short urban route, with great views of fishing and pleasure boats on the Sacramento River adding to the appeal. Sandwiched between the river and a working rail line in the heart of the capital city, the trail serves up restaurants, riverboat rides, tattoo parlors, candy shops, a history lesson, and the chance to see an old-time locomotive cruising on a historic set of tracks.

The route begins in front of the historic Central Pacific Railroad Depot in Old Sacramento. It traces the tracks of the Sacramento Southern Railroad, upon which the California State Railroad Museum runs excursion trains April through September. The railroad dates back to the turn of the twentieth century, when the Southern

The iconic Tower Bridge, which spans the Sacramento River at the west end of the Capitol Mall, is a visual treat along the riverside promenade.

Pacific built the line to facilitate transportation of the bounty of the Central Valley's fields and orchards to port cities in the San Francisco Bay Area.

The Sacramento River, flowing broad and deep alongside the route, also connects Sacramento to San Francisco. The trail offers views down onto boats plying the quick waters, which look deceptively smooth but harbor powerful currents. This is no place for a swim.

A rustic boardwalk leads south past touristy restaurants and the *Delta King* paddleboat, ending at the intersection with the Capitol Mall. The yellow pylons of the Tower Bridge rise on the right (west); the capitol building graces the end of the mall on the left (east). Carefully cross the road and continue south

▶ **William Tecumseh Sherman, who would gain fame during the Civil War by leading a fabled triumphant march through the Confederacy, helped survey and lay out Sacramento's street grid.**

THE ORIGINS OF THE CITY OF SACRAMENTO

The land at the confluence of the American and Sacramento Rivers had long been occupied by the Nisenan, a tribal people who established villages in the bottomlands. But it wasn't until settlers from the United States drifted west into what was, at the time, Mexico's Alta California, that a city was born.

The transformation began with the arrival of John Sutter in 1839. Sutter was awarded a land grant by the Mexican governor and established his fabled Sutter's Fort not far from the riverfront. The fort was more than a frontier outpost; it was the centerpiece of what was essentially a small town. Sutter's Fort accommodated trappers, emigrants, and explorers for years, but it wouldn't gain historical prominence until miners swarmed into California during the gold rush.

The area that is now Old Sacramento was, in those pre–gold rush days, known as Sutter's Embarcadero. Recognizing the prime location of the embarcadero, enterprising businessman Sam Brannan opened a store on the site. Once gold was discovered, Brannan profited mightily by outfitting the thousands of miners who poured down out of the mountains for provisions. A city grid, with numbered streets running north–south and lettered streets running east–west, was imposed on the riverfront, and other businesses catering to the forty-niners were established. Within a couple of years, "Sacramento City" was burgeoning.

In its early days the fledgling city was repeatedly inundated by floodwaters (the American and Sacramento having not yet been corralled by levees) and was also devastated by fire. But it endured. The muddy miners' camp would one day be California's capital city.

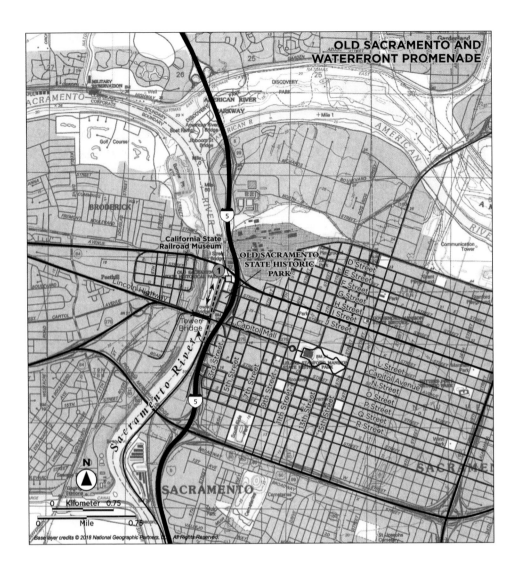

along the wide promenade, lined with lampposts and flower-filled planters bearing plaques that describe Sacramento's colorful history. River travel and locomotives, wharves and warehouses, food-packing plants and laundry houses: You can read all about it. Benches overlook the river, making this the perfect place to rest and digest after a meal in one of the Old Town restaurants. Between the glass-faced high-rises of downtown and the glassy river, the whole scene glows in a sunset.

The end of the promenade is the turnaround point for this short excursion. Retrace your steps back to the trailhead. (**Option:** Finish your walk by looping back through Old Sacramento, following covered boardwalks and passing storefronts that harken back to gold rush times.)

Miles and Directions

0.0 Start on the riverfront levee, heading south between the railroad tracks and the river. You'll pass a few interpretive signs as you ramble beneath the sycamores.

0.1 The wide boardwalk begins. Pass the *Delta King* paddleboat and the railroad depot, with the Tower Bridge looming ahead.

0.4 Arrive at the junction with Capitol Mall. Cross the street and continue on the promenade.

0.5 The promenade ends at Front and O Streets. Retrace your steps to Old Sacramento, looping back through the historic district. The historic area stretches several blocks parallel to the trail's end.

1.1 Arrive back at the trailhead near the railroad museum.

Option: Whether outward bound or returning on the trail, you have the opportunity to venture into Old Sacramento. Historic buildings housing restaurants and shops line the cobbled streets a block from the riverside. This won't add significantly to the mileage, so you really can't justify that caramel apple by saying you took a longer hike.

On the other hand, you can stretch the journey by following the bike trail that continues from the end of the promenade, tracing river and tracks to Marina Park. Another option is to pair this route with an amble on Capitol Mall to Capitol Park, a nice addition.

Hike Information

Local information: Old Sacramento merchants have teamed up with city and state officials to promote the historic district. For listings of events, businesses, and activities, as well as historical information, visit http://oldsacramento.com. You can also call (916) 442-8575 for more information.

Visit Sacramento, 1608 I St., Sacramento, CA 95814; (916) 808-7777 or (800) 292-2334; www.visitsacramento.com.

Local events/attractions: Sutter's Fort State Historic Park, 2701 L St., Sacramento; (916) 445-4422; www.parks.ca.gov/?page_id=485. Located not far from the riverfront, this re-creation of Sutter's Fort contains a museum and hosts living-history days as well as other special events.

Restaurants: Indulge in a gourmet taste of Old Sacramento at the Cafe Americain Champagne and Caviar House, 1023 Front St., Sacramento; (916) 498-9098; www.cafeamericain.info. Be sure to check out the speakeasy saloon downstairs.

2 Capitol Mall and Capitol Park

California's stately capitol building, with its classic dome and columned facade, is the centerpiece of this urban exploration. Begin at historic Tower Bridge, travel through the heart of downtown, and complete your tour amid the roses and statuary of Capitol Park.

Start: Foot of the Capitol Mall at Tower Bridge
Distance: 2.3-mile lollipop
Hiking time: 1-2 hours
Difficulty: Easy
Trail surface: Pavement
Best season: Year-round
Other trail users: Hikers only
Amenities: None at the trailhead. Restrooms, water, and information are available at the state capitol and in various businesses along the route.

Canine compatibility: Leashed dogs permitted
Fees and permits: None
Schedule: Accessible all day, year-round
Maps: USGS Sacramento West CA. There's a map of Capitol Park in front of the capitol building, but no map is needed.
Trail contact: Capital District Office, California State Parks, 111 I St., Sacramento 95814; (916) 445-7373; www.parks.ca.gov

Finding the trailhead: The route begins at the corner of Front Street and Capitol Mall, at the east end of Tower Bridge. Parking, for a fee, is available on city streets and in parking garages near the intersection. The length of the walk will vary depending on where you park (not a bad thing, considering the variety of sights and amenities available in downtown Sacramento). **GPS:** N38 34.809' / W121 30.418'

The Hike

Starting at the evocative Tower Bridge and culminating in a tour of the varied gardens surrounding California's state capitol building, this classic urban walk immerses you in the culture and evolution of Sacramento's historic downtown.

Sacramento is the last in a long list of cities that have been designated the state's capital since the arrival of European colonists in the late eighteenth century. In the era of Spanish exploration and conquest, San Diego and Monterey both claimed the seat. After Mexico won its independence from Spain and Mexican governors took control of Alta California, Vallejo (named for General Mariano Vallejo, a powerful Mexican landowner) and Benicia (named for General Vallejo's wife) were proclaimed capitals. Sacramento got the nod in 1860, more than a decade after California became a state of the Union, and construction on the capitol building commenced. The main building, capped with a dome and grandly styled, was completed in 1874. The East Wing, which contains the governor's suite, was added as part of a remodel and restoration performed between 1949 and 1951.

The walk begins at the east end of Tower Bridge. You can walk up either side of the street, which is divided by a grass median. Banks and investment firms have offices in the glass-walled high-rises along the mall, with restaurants and pubs occupying some of the first-floor spaces, some featuring outdoor patios fronting the mall. Closer to the capitol itself, government offices occupy buildings with stodgy, uninspired architecture.

Cross 9th Street and the business of the mall gives way to formal gardens and the halls of government. The classical architecture of the State Office Building and the State Library are bookends to a plaza with a circular drive, and are buffered by spreading shade trees and flower-bordered lawns. "Bring Me Men to Match My Mountains" is carved into the stone facade over the entrance to the office building—hardly the language of bankers or communists, but rather that of frontiersmen inspired by the formidable Sierra Nevada, which they'd crossed to reach their Golden State and which reluctantly yielded its riches to their enterprise.

▶ **Capitol Park contains more than 800 trees and shrubs, with more than 200 varieties represented. Look for the labels that identify each unique planting, including natives, like the redwood, and exotics, like the Japanese persimmon.**

Cross 10th Street and you are at the foot of the stairs leading up to the capitol itself. A map shows the intertwining paths of the park that stretches several blocks

California's historic capitol building anchors a walk down Sacramento's Capitol Mall.

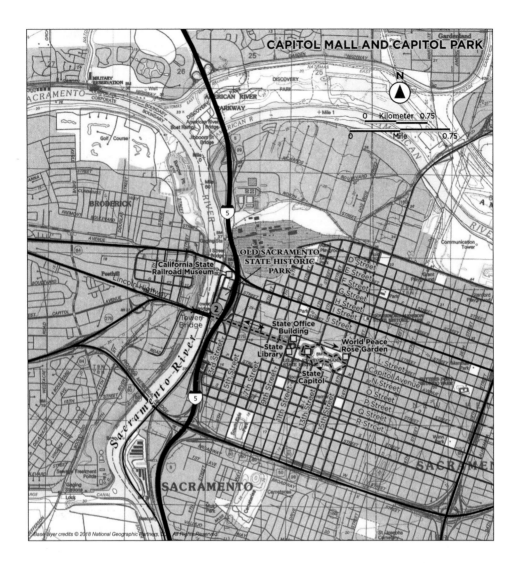

east of the building, with plantings of both native and foreign flora identified. Pick your own route through the park; a clockwise loop through the themed gardens and honorary statuary is described.

Walking around the north side of the capitol, a monument to the Sisters of Mercy, who cared for the children of miners, the sick, and the homeless during the state's early days, shelters in a glade shaded by redwoods. The building itself was built on land that once was the site of the sisters' school.

Heading east along the palm-lined sidewalk, take the asphalt path toward the park's central promenade, passing benches, fruiting Valencia orange trees, and more statuary. The California Firefighters Memorial is at the center of the park on the wide promenade.

Continue east up the promenade to the Vietnam Memorial, inscribed with the names of lost warriors and decorated with provocative sculptures and bas-reliefs. The rose garden is at the eastern border of the park, the blooms accompanied by poetry composed by California schoolchildren.

Heading back west toward the capitol, take time to check out the cactus garden, then continue to the stark obelisk of the Veterans Memorial. Continue along the garden paths to the palm-lined sidewalk that leads back to the front of the building. From here, with the Tower Bridge in your sights, retrace your steps to the trailhead.

Miles and Directions

0.0 Start at Tower Bridge on Front Street, heading up the mall toward the capitol.

0.3 Pass 5th Street. Stay straight on the Capitol Mall.

0.6 At 9th Street the business district gives way to greenscapes and the more classical archi- tecture of the State Office Building and the State Library. Cross 10th Street and head left around the capitol building to access the paths of Capitol Park.

1.1 Reach the International World Peace Rose Garden and the eastern boundary of Capitol Park at 15th Street. Explore the paths and plantings in the other half of the park as you head back toward the capitol.

1.7 Return to the front of the capitol at 10th Street. From here, retrace your steps to Tower Bridge.

2.3 Arrive back at Tower Bridge.

Hike Information

Local information: Sacramento Metro Chamber, One Capitol Mall, Ste. 700, Sac- ramento 95814; (916) 552-6800; http://metrochamber.org.

Visit Sacramento, 1608 I St., Sacramento, CA 95814; (916) 808-7777 or (800) 292-2334; www.visitsacramento.com.

Local events/attractions: California State Capitol Museum, 10th and L Streets (State Capitol), Room B-27, Sacramento; (916) 324-0333; www.capitolmuseum .ca.gov. Housed in the same historic structure as California's legislature, the museum contains portraits of governors, historic artifacts, and collections of artwork. Open daily, year-round, 9 a.m. to 5 p.m.

Hike tours: Tours of the capitol building and museum are conducted daily on the hour, beginning at 9 a.m. and ending at 4 p.m. Call (916) 324-0333 for more information.

To take part in the Take A Hike! City Walks program offered by the state parks department, visit www.parks.ca.gov.

3 William Land Park Tour

Flat, easy paths wind through one of Sacramento's premier city parks, circling ponds, skirting a golf course, and permitting access to family attractions including the Sacramento Zoo and Fairytale Town.

Start: Sidewalk in front of Fairytale Town
Distance: 1.9-mile lollipop
Hiking time: About 1 hour
Difficulty: Easy
Trail surface: Pavement, a bit of grass and gravel
Best season: Year-round
Other trail users: Cyclists, joggers, golfers
Amenities: Restrooms, water, picnic facilities, ball fields, golf course, zoo, amusement park
Canine compatibility: Leashed dogs permitted

Fees and permits: None
Schedule: Open sunrise to sunset year-round
Maps: USGS Sacramento West CA and Sacramento East CA; online at www.cityof sacramento.org/ParksandRec/Parks/ Park-Directory/Land-Park/William-Land
Trail contact: City of Sacramento Department of Parks and Recreation, 915 I St., Third Floor, Sacramento 95814; (916) 808-5200; www .cityofsacramento.org/parksandrec/

Finding the trailhead: From downtown Sacramento head south on I-5 for about 2.5 miles to the Sutterville Road exit (also signed for the Sacramento Zoo and William Land Park). Head left (east) on Sutterville Road for 0.4 mile to Land Park Drive. Turn left (north) on Land Park Drive and go about 0.1 mile to the entrances of Fairytale Town and the zoo. Park alongside the road; the suggested route begins in front of Fairytale Town. **GPS:** N38 32.322' / W121 30.123'

The Hike

William Land Park is one of the first urban parks built in the city of Sacramento. It was conceived in 1911, when former mayor William Land gifted the city a generous sum of money earmarked for a city park. The parcel, called a "swamp" by Land's heirs, according to writer Steven Avella, was secured in 1918, though controversy about its suitability landed the acquisition in court. The dust settled in 1922, the wetlands were drained, a levee was built, and amenities were installed, including fountains, sculptures, plantings of trees and shrubs, a golf course, and eventually a zoo and Fairytale Town, a children's amusement park.

This hike describes a lollipop loop through the eastern portion of the park, but many variations exist and getting lost is virtually impossible. The park encompasses a bit more than 166 acres, roughly divided by Land Park Drive, and is surrounded by city blocks. It is crisscrossed by paved drives, so taking a shortcut or stretching the route is easily accomplished.

Begin by taking the dirt track that heads north, past the entrance to Fairytale Town and parallel to Land Park Drive. Cross 15th Street, skirt a parking lot, and head around the gazebo, then the amphitheater. Cross the grass to the paved path around the shore of the first lake, where geese and ducks float peacefully while youngsters and their parents try their luck fishing.

A quick walk up the gravel track along Land Park Drive leads to 13th Avenue. Turn right and enjoy a long streetside stretch shaded by sycamores and enlivened by the varied architecture of the homes across the avenue. Updated brick ranch-style homes with green lawns and colorful plantings frame the occasional brick facade of a Tudor, which in turn may be nestled against a home with an Art Deco flair, and something colonial may be a couple of doors down. The bulk of William Land Park, shady and green, is on the right.

▶ **In 2011 a private consulting firm conducted a survey of William Land Park's historical and cultural features and determined that the park meets the criteria for inclusion on city, state, and national historic registers.**

At busy Freeport Boulevard, head back into the park. The latter part of the loop links grass and dirt tracks back to 14th Avenue. Roughly parallel 14th back toward Land Park Drive, with the easiest walking on the close-clipped grass of the verge, shaded by redwoods, eucalyptuses, and different varieties of oaks. Looking beneath the canopies, you can watch the golfers play. The kids (or the dog) can scour the grass between the roadway and the fairway for errant golf balls.

Cross the park road at the triangle junction of 14th Avenue and 18th Street, then drop across the grass to the second lake, enjoyed by picnickers and geese alike. Leave

A fine urban stroll explores one of Sacramento's premier, and oldest, city parks.

the lakeside path for the grass again, returning to the corner of 14th Avenue and Land Park Drive. From there, retrace your steps to the trailhead.

Miles and Directions

0.0 Start in front of Fairytale Town, heading north to cross 15th Street.

0.2 Pass the gazebo and amphitheater, cross the grass, and pick up the paved path at the small lake. Follow the path around the lake.

0.3 Cross the lawn to the gravel walking/jogging trail alongside Land Park Drive. Turn right and follow the path north to 14th Avenue.

0.4 Turn right onto the path alongside 13th Avenue.

0.7 Cross a park road and continue on the street-side path.

1.0 Reach Freeport Boulevard and turn right on the gravel path. Go 1 block and turn right again, walking on the grass along the side of 14th Avenue.

1.2 At the junction of 14th Avenue and 18th Street, cross the triangle and drop down across the grass to the side of the small lake. Go left on the lakeside path.

1.6 Cross the grass to the junction of Land Park Drive and 14th Avenue. Retrace your steps to the trailhead.

1.9 Arrive back at the trailhead.

A stretch of paved trail skims one of a pair of small lakes in William Land Park, which also features a golf course, zoo, fairytale park, and other amenities, making this an ideal family excursion.

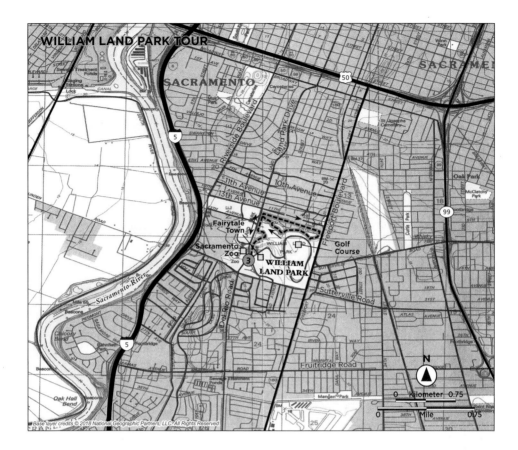

Hike Information

Local information: Sacramento Metro Chamber, One Capitol Mall, Ste. 700, Sacramento 95814; (916) 552-6800; http://metrochamber.org.

Visit Sacramento, 1608 I St., Sacramento, CA 95814; (916) 808-7777 or (800) 292-2334; www.visitsacramento.com.

Local events/attractions: Sacramento Zoo, 3930 West Land Park Dr., Sacramento; (916) 808-5885; www.saczoo.org. Creatures on exhibit include lemurs, big cats, Masai giraffes, and a variety of exotic birds and reptiles. The zoo is open from 9 a.m. to 4 p.m. daily. Admission is charged.

Fairytale Town, 3901 Land Park Dr., Sacramento; (916) 808-5233 (24-hour information line) or (916) 808-7462 (main office); www.fairytaletown.org. A variety of exhibits allow children to act out their favorite fairy tales. Open year-round, weather permitting, Mar through Oct from 9 a.m. to 4 p.m., and Nov through Feb from 10 a.m. to 4 p.m. Closed Thanksgiving, Christmas, and New Year's Day. Admission is charged.

4 Jedediah Smith Memorial Trail / Discovery Park

This sampling of Sacramento's premier cycling and pedestrian trailway begins at the confluence of the American and Sacramento Rivers and stretches east through manicured parklands and strips of riparian woodland.

Start: Boat ramp parking area near the confluence of the American and Sacramento Rivers

Distance: 4.4 miles out and back

Hiking time: About 2.5 hours

Difficulty: Moderate due only to length

Trail surface: Pavement with shoulder of decomposed granite for pedestrian use

Best season: Year-round, though the trailhead area at the confluence may flood in winter or with spring runoff.

Other trail users: Cyclists (lots of them), trail runners, a few in-line skaters and equestrians

Amenities: Large parking lot, restrooms, informational boards, water, picnic facilities, boat launch. There are no amenities at the Northgate Boulevard turnaround. Call boxes are located along the route.

Canine compatibility: Leashed dogs permitted

Fees and permits: A day-use fee is levied at Discovery Park. Fees are charged at other American River Parkway access points, though generally neighborhood access is free.

Schedule: Park is open daily, sunrise to sunset, year-round. Trail may be accessed 24 hours a day, 7 days a week, year-round.

Maps: USGS Sacramento East CA and Sacramento West CA; Jedediah Smith Memorial Bicycle Trail map produced by the Sacramento County Regional Parks Department, available for purchase at various locations along the trail including the Effie Yeaw Interpretive Center in Ancil Hoffman County Park. The map is also available at http://arpf.org/pdf_files/ARPmap.pdf.

Trail contact: Sacramento County Regional Parks Department, 4040 Bradshaw Rd., Sacramento 95827; (916) 875-6961; www.regionalparks.saccounty.net/Pages/default.aspx

Other: The trail is wheelchair accessible.

Special considerations: This trail is extremely popular with cyclists. The speed limit is 15 mph but is not always obeyed. Walk on the parallel gravel path so that cyclists have room to pass. Summertime temperatures can reach into the 100s. If you hit the trail in the heat of a summer's day, bring plenty of drinking water.

Finding the trailhead: Discovery Park is at the confluence of the American and Sacramento Rivers just north of the state capitol. Take the Garden Highway exit from I-5 and follow the Garden Highway east for 0.4 mile to the Discovery Park entrance. The boat ramp and trailhead are at the west end of the park. **GPS:** N38 36.024' / W121 30.455'

The Hike

The American River Parkway, a 23-mile-long linear greenbelt that stretches from downtown Sacramento to Folsom Lake, is without question the most loved open space in the Sacramento metropolitan area. It's also the most well used, with an estimated 8 million people visiting the park each year.

If the American River is the parkway's lifeblood, then the 32-mile-long paved Jedediah Smith Memorial Trail is the artery that connects the river to the hearts of the people. Starting at Discovery Park, the national recreation trail links to local neighborhoods via access paths and staging areas, some with facilities including picnic areas, restrooms, and boat launches. The paved path roughly parallels the route of US 50, and access to the trail and parkway is identified on freeway signs.

The parkway concept dates back to 1915, when mention of an American River Parkway was made in a city plan, according to a Sacramento County Regional Parks fact sheet. Frederick Law Olmsted Jr., son of the legendary landscape architect who designed New York's Central Park, included a parkway along the American River when he surveyed California for potential park sites in the late 1940s. Land acquisitions started in 1960 and weren't completed until 2008, but by then the Jedediah Smith Memorial Trail, and many of the other 82 miles of trail in the parkway, were in place.

▶ Homeless encampments along the American River Parkway have grown more numerous in recent years, and hikers should be aware that people live along the riverside in tents and other improvised shelters. Efforts are under way to secure permanent housing for the region's growing homeless populations, and to mitigate impacts of the camps on the environment and recreational uses.

To explore the length of the memorial trail on foot would require days, a feat worthy of the route's mountaineering namesake, Jedediah Smith, who hiked across the Sierra in the early 1800s and camped along the river. Taken in segments, however, the trail easily accommodates six to eight fun day hikes. You could explore the confluence of the Sacramento and American Rivers at Discovery Park one day, move upstream to check out the protected area at Cal Expo next, then spend another day on the riverfront in Pond and River Bend (formerly Goethe) Parks. Farther upstream the trail passes through the Lower and Upper Sunrise areas and rambles through oak woodlands with wonderful river views to the Nimbus Dam and Fish Hatchery. A circuit of Lake Natoma makes a nice daylong outing. And then there's a link along the shoreline of Folsom Lake.

The trail through Discovery Park, easy to access and remarkable because of its location at the confluence of the Sacramento and American Rivers, makes for a pleasant out-and-back hike. The park is busy in spring, summer, and fall, with boats launching, families throwing parties in the picnic grounds, anglers casting lines from the riverbanks, hikers and cyclists heading out on the trail, and archers practicing at the nearby archery range. It's a hustle and bustle start, but the trail enters a mellower environment by the 0.5-mile mark.

Interpretive signs are sprinkled along the path as it meanders through a relatively quiet stretch of the river's floodplain in the shade of oaks and sycamores.

A trail sign in Discovery Park indicates the distance between the confluence of the American and Sacramento Rivers and the Nimbus Dam at Lake Natoma.

The signs offer insights into the nature of the riparian habitat and the creatures that live there.

The trail breaks away from the river at about the 1-mile mark, separated by a wetland that is flooded in winter and spring and dries by late summer. The marshland is populated by a variety of birds, and kites may perch on the power lines overhead, scanning the reeds for prey. The trail is not shaded along this stretch, though the Natomas East Main Drainage, a water-filled channel that parallels the trail on the north side, supports a thick riparian ribbon that includes blackberry brambles and wild grape.

The turnaround point is Northgate Boulevard, but you can continue on . . . and on . . .

Additional options along the trail include a 4-mile out-and-back hike between Watt Avenue (where you'll find parking) and the Guy West pedestrian suspension bridge (a scaled-down Golden Gate Bridge). This segment of path is bordered by quiet residential neighborhoods on one side and the river on the other. A dirt track runs parallel to the paved path at the foot of a levee; you can also walk on the levee-top path. Or . . .

Pick up the trail in the William B. Pond Recreation Area and head east, across the scenic Jedediah Smith pedestrian bridge, into River Bend Park. Both parks offer all kinds of amenities, including picnic areas, playing greens, and river frontage. This is a little more than 2 miles out and back. If you want to add something a bit wilder to this outing, continue east into the more undeveloped areas of River Bend Park,

JEDEDIAH SMITH

Born in New York State in 1799, Jedediah Smith would become one of the premier mountain men of the early nineteenth century. His expeditions in the American West included first-time explorations of some of the most forbidding landscapes in the region, including the Salt Lake basin and the Great Basin, and forging a new route through the Rocky Mountains.

Smith's journeys were financed by the fur trade, with beaver pelts in high demand and a symbol of wealth at the time. He ventured into California twice, where he and his party were detained by Spanish authorities who suspected Smith was up to no good. The Spanish governor later allowed Smith to survey and hunt in the territory, and the mountain man spent some time during his second trip hunting in the Sacramento Valley.

Though Smith, reportedly a deeply religious man, survived serious challenges on his expeditions, including a mauling by a grizzly bear that left him with distinctive scars, he was destined to die young. On his last adventure, he led a supply party along the Santa Fe Trail to the trail's namesake city in 1831. The story goes that while scouting alone for water, Smith disappeared. It's assumed he was killed by Comanche Indians, but his body was never recovered.

where the route traverses oak woodlands and savanna. The grasses support a nice wildflower bloom, but this area can be hot and exposed in summer. Or . . .

Take in the scenic gorge, the Fair Oaks pedestrian bridge, great river views, riverside beaches—all from beneath the shade of overhanging oaks—on the 4-mile out-and-back trail segment between the Upper Sunrise access point and the Nimbus Fish Hatchery at Hazel Avenue.

Miles and Directions

0.0 Start near the boat launch and the I-5 overpass, where yellow posts mark the trailhead. Pass under the freeway and head east along the American River past lawns and picnic areas.

0.4 Noise from the freeway fades as fields and parking lots open on the left (north).

0.6 Pass the archery range.

0.8 Pass an interpretive sign about habitat restoration.

1.3 Reach a stop sign where the Jedediah Smith Memorial Trail meets a paved access trail. Continue straight (east) on the Jedediah Smith Memorial Trail. The river is out of sight to the right (south), separated from the route by the grassy floodplain.

1.9 A hedge of blackberry shields a utility yard on the right (south), then the floodplain opens again. The paved route is shadowed by a gravel track.

2.2 Reach the Northgate Boulevard trail junction and the turnaround point. Retrace your steps toward the confluence.

4.4 Arrive back at the trailhead.

A bridge spans the American River just before it meets the Sacramento River in Discovery Park.

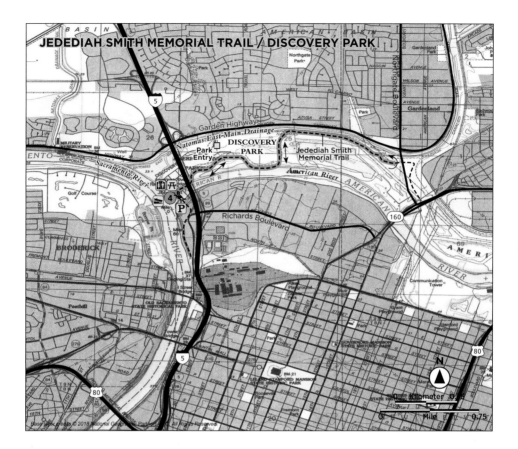

Hike Information

Local information: Sacramento Metro Chamber, One Capitol Mall, Ste. 700, Sacramento 95814; (916) 552-6800; http://metrochamber.org.

Visit Sacramento, 1608 I St. Sacramento, CA 95814; (916) 808-7777 or (800) 292-2334; www.visitsacramento.com.

5 Sacramento Northern Bikeway

This rail trail, mostly flat and paved, runs north from downtown Sacramento into the suburbs of Rio Linda and Elverta. A short section is described here, illustrating the provocative dilemmas that urban trails strive to bridge. The route begins amid industry and runs through the strip of riparian parkland along the American River at the border of Discovery Park.

Start: Archway between 19th and 20th Streets, next to the almond-packing plant
Distance: 3.4-mile lollipop
Hiking time: About 2 hours
Difficulty: Easy
Trail surface: Asphalt
Best season: Year-round
Other trail users: Cyclists, dog walkers, joggers
Amenities: On-street parking
Canine compatibility: Leashed dogs permitted
Fees and permits: None
Schedule: Accessible all day, year-round
Maps: USGS Sacramento East CA; online at www.cityofsacramento.org/Public-Works/

Transportation/Programs-and-Services/Bicycling-Program
Trail contact: Bicycle Coordinator with the City of Sacramento, 915 I St., Room 2000, Sacramento 95814; (916) 808-8300; www.cityofsacramento.org/Public-Works/Transportation/Programs-and-Services/Bicycling-Program
Other: The paved portion of the trail is wheelchair accessible.
Special considerations: When the American River runs high in spring, the trail section between CA 160 and the intersection with the Jedediah Smith Memorial Trail may be flooded.

Finding the trailhead: From the westbound lanes of the Capitol City Freeway (US 50), take the 15th Street (CA 160) exit (the 16th Street exit if you are headed eastbound). Go north on 16th Street, a one-way road, to D Street. Go right (east) on D Street to 20th Street. Turn left (north) on 20th Street to reach C Street. The trail, denoted by an archway, is located between 19th and 20th Streets, on the north side of the road. Parking is street side. **GPS:** N38 35.052' / W121 28.575'

The Hike

The complexities of downtown Sacramento are in evidence along this section of the Sacramento Northern Bikeway. The paved path links the graceful Victorian homes of a tree-shaded neighborhood, industrial yards, railroad tracks, and the greenbelt that runs alongside the American River, offering a snapshot of the heartland city's diverse urban landscape.

The trail follows the former Sacramento Northern Interurban Electric Rail line, which carried passengers between the bustling agricultural communities of Sacramento and Chico. Trains stopped running in the mid-1940s, and the rail line was eventually abandoned. Construction of the rail trail, which has been upgraded through the years, began in 1980.

The trail begins on C Street between 19th and 20th Streets, at the edge of a charming old neighborhood with sycamore-lined streets. To borrow a word most often applied to the edges of natural habitats, the trail straddles the "ecotone" between industry and residential community, with the Blue Diamond Almond factory complex on one side and the neighborhood on the other. An archway marks the entry point.

The trail runs north, passing first through a tunnel under the bridge of the active Union Pacific Railroad tracks. Narrow strips of greenery line the path on either side, but they are not dense enough to hide the rail yards and shipping containers to the east.

▶ Almost a ton of garbage was removed from a stretch of river between the Tower and Pioneer Bridges on a single day in 2016.

Industry is history by the 0.5-mile mark, where the trail reaches a junction with a path leading into a neighborhood. Go right, and climb gently to the star attraction: the trestle bridge spanning the American River. Take a

The Sacramento Northern rail trail crosses the American River near downtown.

break mid-span, as all your fellow hikers and cyclists will do, and gaze down on the seemingly passive waters of the American River, wide and green and deepening before its confluence with the even mightier Sacramento River just a few miles downstream.

From the trestle the trail drops into the riparian greenery along the riverbank. You are briefly enveloped in a pocket of green space, but this is not wildland: The cottonwoods, willows, blackberries, and wildflowers that flourish along the river's edge have found a way to thrive between the columns supporting CA 160, which soars overhead. The clash of concrete and thicket is paradoxical enough, but there's another juxtaposition that becomes apparent as you travel toward the junction with the American River Parkway and Jedediah Smith Memorial Trail. Modern-day hobos have beaten tracks into

THE MAGIC OF A RAIL TRAIL

Rail trails are an urban ideal. The Sac Northern rail trail is a perfect example of what they do best, linking neighborhoods to businesses, parks, schools, public transportation, and other neighborhoods.

Beyond the greenery of Discovery Park, the Sac Northern takes on a distinctly urban demeanor. Industry hitches up against homes and retail outlets. Arches mark the borders of different towns and neighborhoods along the route: Noralto, Robla, Del Paso Heights. Paths break from the trail both right and left, giving access to quiet residential streets. At times the trail is strictly urban; elsewhere it has a more suburban feel, broadening and featuring gazebos that offer shade and benches that offer respite.

Busy Rio Linda Boulevard and the I-80 overpass mark where the Sac Northern abandons an urban setting for a more rural one. The trail enters country proper as it continues north, stretching between green pastures that bleach blond after the long, hot summer. The canopies of broad-leafed trees shade the route and insulate it from the few signs of the metro area that it remains part of, including the Rio Linda Airport. The community park at Rio Linda, which the trail passes through, offers a tot lot, broad lawns, and the Rio Linda Depot, an open, gazebo-like structure housing picnic tables.

The route ends on Elverta Road, providing still more access to neighborhoods and green space. In the span of little more than 10 miles, the trail has linked central city with industry with parkland with suburbia with farmland. It's a remarkable passage. If there's something about a train that's magic, the same can be said for the rail trail that follows in its tracks.

the greenery under the freeway and along the river, and have set up camps in the brush. Some tents are visible; others are out of sight. Some of the inhabitants are also visible, sometimes as fellow travelers on the route, sometimes as spectators watching you pass by.

The Sac Northern merges briefly with the Jedediah Smith trail at the next trail intersection, at an old raised wooden trestle. Head left (north) on the merged trails, across Del Paso Boulevard and into Discovery Park.

The bottomlands of the American River, which cradle the trails at this juncture, may be flooded in spring when the river runs full with snowmelt from the Sierra Nevada. Ponds form amid thickets ringing with birdsong. In summer the ponds may dry up, but the wetland atmosphere, including the flutter and chatter of hidden wildlife, remains. The paved paths split, with the Sacramento Northern trail taking the high road, climbing onto a raised bed from which you can look down upon the ponds.

At the 1.7-mile mark, the rail trail drops across the railroad tracks and then continues north. Just before the tracks, a gravel road switchbacks sharply to the left. Take this gravel track, dropping onto a wide dirt pathway that parallels the rail trail, but along the base of the raised bed. On the right, the wetlands and ponds of the bottomlands press close (indeed, if the water is high, you may be forced to retrace your steps on the elevated path). Side paths lead into the tangled undergrowth of wild grape, scrub oak, and blackberry. The walking is easy along the pathway, which leads back to the Sac Northern–Jedediah Smith trail junction near Del Paso Boulevard.

From the junction, retrace your steps to the trailhead.

Miles and Directions

0.0 Start at the archway on C Street, adjacent to the almond packing plant.

0.5 At the trail junction with a paved path leading into a neighborhood, go right on the Sacramento Northern trail (no sign).

0.7 Cross the trestle bridge over the American River.

1.0 Pass under CA 160.

1.1 Reach the junction with the Jedediah Smith Memorial Trail. Go left on the merged trails. Cross Del Paso Boulevard and enter Discovery Park.

1.2 At the junction just inside Discovery Park, go right on the Sac Northern trail (again, no sign), climbing onto the raised bed.

1.7 Turn left onto the gravel road just before the Sac Northern rail trail leaves the raised bed and crosses the railroad tracks. Pick up the wide dirt track that runs parallel to the rail trail at the base of the levee.

2.2 The dirt path ends at the junction with the Jedediah Smith trail on the north side of Del Paso Boulevard. Retrace your steps toward the trailhead.

3.4 Arrive back at the trailhead.

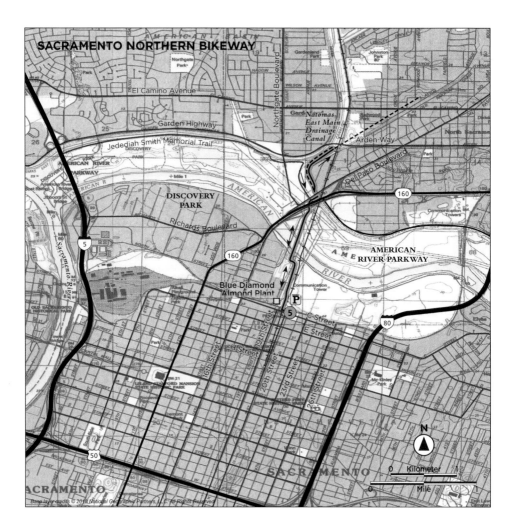

Hike Information

Local information: Sacramento Metro Chamber, One Capitol Mall, Ste. 700, Sacramento 95814; (916) 552-6800; https://metrochamber.org.

Visit Sacramento, 1608 I St., Sacramento, CA 95814; (916) 808-7777 or (800) 292-2334; www.visitsacramento.com.

6 Gibson Ranch Loop Trail

The riparian corridor along Dry Creek serves as a shady start to a hiking tour through Gibson Ranch County Park. Between the creek and the park's wetland area lie picnic areas and playing greens, as well as the paddocks and pastures of boarded horses.

Start: Northeast corner of the park on the bank of Dry Creek
Distance: 3.0-mile loop
Hiking time: About 1.5 hours
Difficulty: Moderate
Trail surface: Dirt singletrack and ranch road; a short stretch along the paved park road
Best season: Year-round
Other trail users: Equestrians, trail runners
Amenities: Restrooms and water at nearby parking areas
Canine compatibility: Leashed dogs permitted
Fees and permits: Day-use fee
Schedule: Open daily, 7 a.m. to sunset, year-round

Maps: USGS Rio Linda CA; park map available at the entry kiosk
Trail contact: Sacramento County Regional Parks Department, 4040 Bradshaw Rd., Sacramento 95827; (916) 875-PARK (7275); www.regionalparks.saccounty.net/Parks/RegionalParksDetails/Pages/GibsonRanch .aspx or www.gibsonranchpark.com
Other: The park accommodates a number of activities, including picnicking, trail rides, animal husbandry, and fishing. While you are welcome to explore all facets of the ranch, please do not feed the animals.

Finding the trailhead: From I-80, the Capitol City Freeway, or US 50, take the Watt Avenue exit. Head north on Watt Avenue to Elverta Road (about 5 miles from the I-80 exit). Turn left (west) on Elverta Road and follow it 0.7 mile to the park entrance, on the right (north). The park road leads 1.3 miles, past pastures, paddocks, the park store, and residential facilities, to the parking lot in the northeast corner of the property. The trailhead is marked by a couple of yellow posts at the base of the creek levee. **GPS:** N38 43.644' / W121 23.912'

The Hike

A circumnavigation of Gibson Ranch distills, in just a few miles, the complex interface of Sacramento's natural, agricultural, and suburban worlds. The richness of the riparian zone along Dry Creek backs up to pastures; the pastures back up to the fenced-off backyards of neighboring homes; a birdsong-filled marsh backs up to farm roads and a radio tower. The park's perimeter trail travels through this diversity.

The route begins in Dry Creek's riparian corridor, a 6-mile-long greenbelt in northern Sacramento County that is part of a planned 70-mile regional greenway loop. Contrary to its name, Dry Creek runs year-round. Preserving its floodplain, which includes wetland and riparian habitats, is an objective of parkway planners.

In Gibson Ranch the creek is an inviting waterway bordered by oaks, cottonwoods, buckeyes, and tangled figs. Side trails drop to sandy beaches where you can wade or skip stones. On the park side of the path, fenced pastures can be seen through breaks in the trees and thick brush.

Reach the front of the park, and the suburban interface takes center stage. The trail bumps against a golf course and Elverta Road, then traces the park access road along the fences of a neighboring subdivision. Suburbia ends at the pastures and paddocks where the ranch's horses are boarded. The horses have consumed anything living within their fenced enclosures, leaving only dirt, and some hug the fences, leveling big-eyed gazes on passersby. They, and the cows found elsewhere in the valley, are part of a long legacy of ranching in the Sacramento Valley, and in California as a whole.

Spanish colonizers, and later Mexican dons, ran cattle on vast ranchos throughout what was then known as Alta California. Fattened on the abundant grasses growing on the slopes of coastal mountains and on inland valley floors, the animals provided hides, tallow, and meat for their owners. Though the gold rush and California's eventual inclusion in the United States resulted in huge cultural changes, ranching stayed constant, with European immigrants from Italy, Switzerland, and other nations securing holdings that stayed in families for generations. The gold came and went, the railroads came and went, but through it all, the ranchers remained.

Old farm equipment rests along a portion of the ramble through Gibson Ranch.

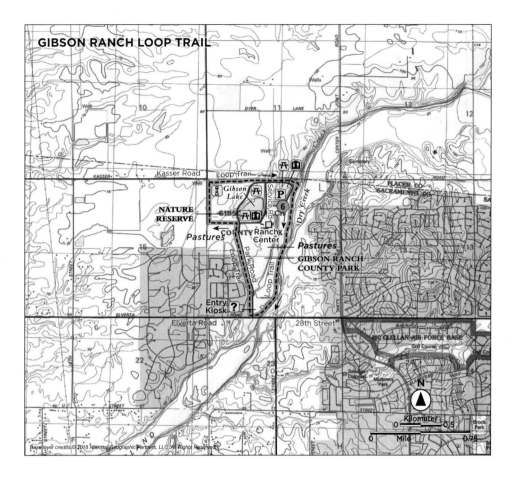

GIBSON RANCH LOOP TRAIL

Beyond the paddocks the trail arcs northward again, into an expanse of reeds, cattails, willows, and cottonwoods that resounds with birdcall. Hugging the park's western boundary, the route extends toward the radio tower in the park's northwest corner. Oaks provide shade from what can be an unrelenting sun, and algae-covered pools give way gradually to meadows that bloom with wildflowers in season.

Following the trail back east toward the trailhead, the final stretch skirts Gibson Lake, surrounded by playing greens, picnic sites, and barbecues.

The park also hosts weddings, concerts, athletic events, birthday parties, and group picnics. It can be a busy place, but early mornings and weekdays offer the possibility for some solitude along the loop trail.

GREEN TIP
Carry a reusable water container that you fill at the tap.
Bottled water is expensive, lots of petroleum is used to make
the plastic bottles, and they are a disposal nightmare.

Miles and Directions

0.0 Start by heading right (south) on the shady elevated trail along Dry Creek. Social trails drop to the creek, and park amenities are visible through riparian thicket on the right (west) side of the path.

0.2 At the trail junction stay straight (south) on the obvious creekside route.

0.5 At the intersection continue straight (south) on the creek trail, passing a shelter at the edge of a fenced pasture.

0.8 The trail curves west to another trail junction. Continue straight on the loop trail.

1.0 The path meets Elverta Road. Head west alongside the pavement to Gibson Ranch Road (the main park road), then turn north, following the edge of the park road past the entry kiosk. Hook up with a grass or dirt track (depending on the season) that runs parallel to the pavement.

1.5 Pastures border both sides of the road and trail.

1.7 Arrive at the stop sign at the junction of Gibson Ranch Road. Go left (west) on the dirt road that passes between pastures 16 and 10. Horse paddocks border the track.

2.0 Reach the park boundary and turn right (north) on the ranch road that skims the edge of the marsh.

2.2 A radio tower and a fence mark the park's northwest boundary. Go right (east) on the dirt road toward the ranch buildings and pastures.

2.6 The trail reaches the park road, then parallels it past the picnic grounds and tot lots bordering the lake.

2.7 Pass an intersection of park roads at a picnic area.

2.9 Pass a gate and climb onto the Dry Creek Trail at the park's northeastern boundary. Go right (south) on the trail.

3.0 Arrive back at the trailhead and parking lot.

Hike Information

Local information: The Rio Linda–Elverta Chamber of Commerce and Civic League; www.rlechamber.org. Information about community businesses and events are listed on the website.

7 Effie Yeaw Nature Loop

Interpretive trails wind through oak woodlands along a scenic stretch of the American River. The area supports an abundance of wildlife, including deer, wild turkeys, an abundance of waterfowl, and a chattering collection of songbirds.

Start: Effie Yeaw Nature Center in Ancil Hoffman County Park
Distance: 1.7-mile lollipop
Hiking time: About 1 hour
Difficulty: Easy
Trail surface: Dirt singletrack
Best season: Year-round, though summertime heat and winter storms may preclude pleasant hiking.
Other trail users: Hikers only
Amenities: Information board and plenty of parking. Restrooms are in the Effie Yeaw Nature Center.
Canine compatibility: No dogs allowed

Fees and permits: Parking fee; donations also gratefully accepted
Schedule: Open daily, sunrise to sunset, year-round
Maps: USGS Carmichael CA; online at http://cms.capitoltechsolutions.com/ClientData/Effie Yeaw/uploads/EYNC-trail-map-2015.pdf; free trail maps available at Effie Yeaw Nature Center
Trail contact: Sacramento County Regional Parks Department, 4040 Bradshaw Rd., Sacramento 95827; (916) 875-6961; www.regionalparks.saccounty.net/Pages/default.aspx. To contact the Effie Yeaw Nature Center, call (916) 489-4918 or visit www.sacnaturecenter.net.

Finding the trailhead: From US 50 take the Watt Avenue exit. Go north for 1.8 miles on Watt Avenue to Fair Oaks Boulevard. Turn right (east) on Fair Oaks and go 4 miles to Van Alstine Avenue. Go right (east) on Van Alstine for 0.4 mile to California Avenue and turn left (north). Follow California Avenue for 0.1 mile to Tarshes Drive and the entrance to Ancil Hoffman County Park. Follow Tarshes Drive for 1 mile, through the golf course, to San Lorenzo Way. Go left (north) on San Lorenzo Way for 0.2 mile to the interpretive center parking area and trailhead. **GPS:** N38 37.015' / W121 18.758'

The Hike

Walk this trail with the web of life in mind. Everything is connected: the river to the shore, the shore to the trees, the trees to the wind, the wind to the wings of the hawk that flies overhead. A quote from Chief Seattle, posted in the Effie Yeaw Interpretive Center, helps set the tone:

> Man did not weave the web of life;
> He is merely a strand in it.
> Whatever he does to the web, he does to himself.

Any hike on these trails should begin with a visit to the interpretive center, which houses a bonanza of information about the natural and human history of the

American River basin. The main hall of the center is full of interactive stations that describe the ecology and natural history of the area, including hands-on displays. Resident animals, which cannot be released into the wild, include a great horned owl, a saw-whet owl, a kestrel, and a pair of hawks, as well as snakes, frogs, and western pond turtles. You can pick up guidebooks to help you identify these creatures, and more, wherever you walk.

The center and trails are named for teacher and environmentalist Effie Yeaw, who, among other endeavors, made it her mission to show local schoolchildren the wonders of nature by leading them on guided walks through what was then known as Deterding Woods. She also spearheaded efforts to preserve the American River Parkway, recognizing its potential

▶ **Naturalist John Muir echoed the thoughts of Chief Seattle regarding the web of life when he wrote: "When we try to pick out anything by itself, we find it hitched to everything else in the universe."**

as both a natural and a cultural landmark. Her legacy shines along these trails, which interpret the human and ecological history of the river. The inspirational educator died in 1970; her namesake interpretive center was completed in 1976.

Paths intertwine on the nature center property, enabling hikers to vary the route to suit their whims. A clockwise loop around the nature study area is described, beginning with a tour of the Nisenan village, where tule huts, a granary, and other native California artifacts have been replicated and a garden of native plantings has been nurtured. The route then heads north along the Main Trail to the banks of the American River, with interpretive signs along the path documenting the human history of the area. Follow the river south on the Riverview Trail, skimming the interface between its cobbled banks and the oak woodlands that thrive on its shores. The Discovery Trail, with interpretive signs describing inhabitants of the preserve's wildlands, leads back north toward the

A cairn has been cobbled together on the bank of the American River.

Trails surrounding the Effie Yeaw Nature Center branch onto the banks of the American River.

interpretive center, passing a nature study pond that offers hikers the opportunity to sit and watch the ducks paddle about. Interpretive signs along the trails offer insights into the history and natural diversity of the 100-acre parcel.

Though interpretive signs delineate the formal routes, informal trails may intersect. If you get confused, stay on the well-marked interpretive trails. Using informal trails is generally discouraged given the impacts on habitat, so hikers should avoid wandering at will.

The interconnectedness of the place to surrounding suburbia is hard to ignore. This isn't wildland, as evidenced by the park's fearless deer, foraging the annual grasses with little or no regard for walkers on the trails. Standing close to these wild creatures, with the boundaries of predator and prey broken by familiarity, is a perfect demonstration of how changes on one strand in the web of life affect those on another strand.

Miles and Directions

0.0 Start by exploring the Nisenan village cultural demonstration area. Native plantings line the gravel path.

0.1 The Main Trail and other paths in the park begin adjacent to the interpretive center. Head east on the broad dirt path, which is lined with interpretive signs.

0.3 At the cluster of trail intersections, stay left (northeast) on the broad Main Trail, heading toward the river.

0.5 Turn right (east) on the narrow track that leads down to the singletrack Riverview Trail; there is a bench at the intersection. Turn right (south), heading downstream along the riverside in the shade of the riparian zone. Social trails lead down onto the cobbled floodplain (if the river is low); stay high on the well-trod trail.

0.8 At the trail junction continue straight ahead (south and parallel to the river), heading into the woodland.

1.0 Pass a bench and stay left (south), along the river. The trail enters an open grassland.

1.1 At the signed junction for trails to the nature center and the nature study pond, go right (north) on the pond route (the Discovery Trail).

1.2 Turn left (west) to the reed-rimmed pond, where you'll find a couple of benches and an interpretive sign. When you've finished watching the ducks, head north on the signed trail to the nature center.

1.3 Pass a bench and trail sign.

1.4 Stay left (north) at the trail junction, passing interpretive signs.

1.5 Arrive back at the junction near the interpretive center. Go left (west) to return to the trailhead.

1.7 Arrive back at the trailhead.

Tules, used by the native Nisenan people to weave baskets and build houses, grow in the native garden fronting the Effie Yeaw Nature Center.

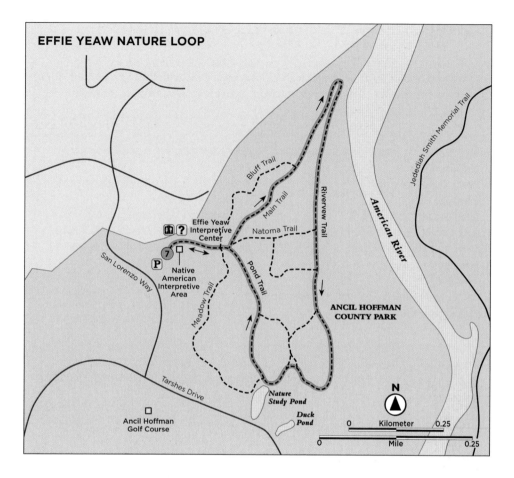

Hike Information

Local information: Carmichael Chamber of Commerce, 6241 Fair Oaks Blvd., Ste. K, Carmichael 95608; (916) 481-1002; www.carmichaelchamber.com.

Local events/attractions: The Effie Yeaw Nature Center houses informative displays that are both adult and kid friendly and is well worth a visit. The center is operated by the nonprofit American River Natural History Association. The center is open Tues through Sun from 9 a.m. to 5 p.m. Feb through Oct; from 9:30 a.m. to 4 p.m. Nov though Jan. It is closed Monday but open on Monday holidays, except if Christmas or New Year's Day. The center is closed on Thanksgiving, Christmas, and New Year's Day.

8 Miners Ravine Nature Reserve

Two short loops link archaeological and historic sites, including a grinding stone once used by local Native Americans, with natural features including a stream, riparian woodlands, and granite boulders.

Start: Southern trailhead on Discovery Trail
Distance: 0.8-mile double loop
Hiking time: 0.5–1 hour
Difficulty: Easy
Trail surface: Dirt singletrack
Best season: Spring and late fall
Other trail users: Hikers only
Amenities: Parking, trash cans, information signboard
Canine compatibility: Leashed dogs permitted
Fees and permits: None

Schedule: Open daily, sunrise to sunset, year-round
Maps: USGS Rocklin CA; map on information signboard in parking lot
Trail contact: Placer Land Trust, 11641 Blocker Dr., Ste. 220, Auburn 95603; (530) 887-9222; www.placerlandtrust.org/project/miners-ravine-preserve/
Special considerations: Please stay on trails to preserve natural and historic artifacts.

Finding the trailhead: From I-80 in Roseville, take the East Douglas Boulevard exit. Go 5.3 miles east on Douglas Boulevard to Auburn Folsom Road. Turn left (north) on Auburn Folsom Road and go 4.2 miles to the Miners Ravine parking area, on the left. The park address is 7530 Auburn Folsom Rd. in Granite Bay. **GPS:** N38 45.300' / W121 10.020'

The Hike

Once the site of Hiram and Elizabeth Allen's ranch house, as well as a food preparation site for the native Valley Nisenan and Southern Maidu people, tiny Miners Ravine Nature Reserve is packed with both historical and natural values.

The Allens ranched and farmed more than 400 acres in the Miners Ravine area, including the 24 acres now part of the reserve, beginning in the 1860s. By then the native tribes that had used granite boulders along the creek as bedrock mortars were long displaced, though they left behind permanent reminders of their industry— nearly perfectly circular grinding holes where they once prepared acorns, a staple of their diet.

The Allens prospered on the site, providing food and goods for miners and other workers traveling between the gold fields in the Sierra foothills and Sacramento. In 1909 a railroad station was planned for the area, and in anticipation of the business this would bring to their ranch, the Allens "incorporated" their enterprise into Allentown. The station never was built, and Allentown faded from history.

Wedged between Auburn Folsom Road and perennial Miners Ravine, the reserve boasts two short trails. This exploration of the reserve begins on the Discovery Trail, which winds through scrub oak past the unsigned site of the Allen farmhouse to a split at the start of the loop. Travel the loop in a clockwise direction, starting to the left. Road noise from busy Auburn Folsom Road is constant, but the roadway is mostly screened by the understory.

Cross a little bridge over a seasonal streamlet, and then reach the bedrock mortar site, marked by an Archeological Resource Area sign. One of the prettiest little outdoor food-prep counters you'll ever see, look carefully along the top of the low, moss-covered rock for the grinding holes. Remain on the trail, and don't disturb the site.

> Poison oak, which thrives in woodlands throughout California, can cause a debilitating rash. Folktales recommend using soaproot, which often grows near the irritating plant, as a salve for the rash. Soaproot was a multipurpose resource for indigenous Californians, who also used the fibrous bulb cover as a comb.

There are no trail signs marking the route where it intersects a dirt roadway, but turn right on the broad path to continue the loop. At the post about 50 yards beyond, go right again on the narrower path. If you take the path heading straight (left), you'll wind down to the ravine's stream, where water pools behind small rock dams adjacent to a neighborhood. The path dead-ends here, but it's worth a visit, especially if it's a hot day and you'd like to cool your heels.

Now in dense foliage, the trail is littered with leaves and noise from the roadway is muffled. Pass a bench and over another little bridge spanning a seasonal streamlet. Squirrels and jays chatter and yell, warning

Easy trails lead to bedrock mortars within the Miners Ravine natural area.

neighbors that walkers have arrived. A side path to the left leads down to the creek, with large sunny rocks on the banks. Another side path leads to an underground utility riser. Stay right to close the loop, passing blackberries that ripen in August and poison oak that'll give you a nasty rash year-round if you touch it.

The signed North Loop begins across the parking lot from the Discovery Trail. Take the right fork, again launching into an oak woodland peppered with black-berries and humming with road noise. Snake through an open area and climb up and over a berm, then pass a smooth granite outcrop and drop into a clearing. Another wonderful place for a family picnic, the sprawling limbs of an oak tree (as well as the rock itself) are perfect for young climbers (or climbers who are young at heart). Memorial benches dedicated to Michelle Short and Tom Thompson, "Placer County's Tree Guy," provide ideal opportunities to sit and relax. Trails collide in the clearing, but stay left, curling around the benches and the rock outcrop, to stay on the loop. Pass through a cool bower of oaks and brambles before emerging at the trailhead and parking lot.

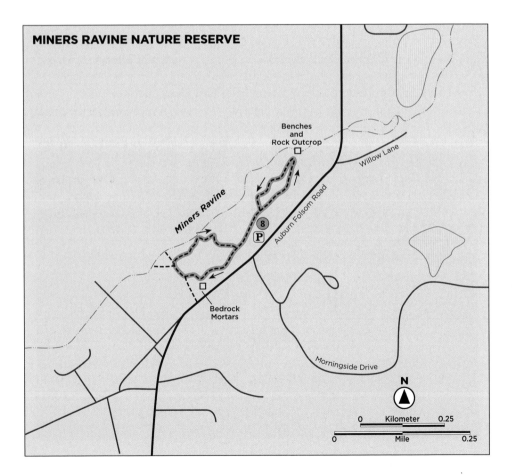

Off the beaten path: These pools lie down a side path off the nature trail in Miners Ravine.

Miles and Directions

0.0 Start on the signed Discovery Trail. Where the trail splits after 500 feet stay left, traveling the loop clockwise.

0.1 A small bridge spans a seasonal stream. Reach the bedrock mortars.

0.2 At the junction with a wider path/roadway, go right. A post marks the next junction, about 50 yards beyond. Go right on the path.

0.3 A side trail leads down to the Miners Ravine creek. Continue on the loop by staying right.

0.4 Close the loop and retrace your steps to the parking lot.

0.5 Cross the parking lot to the beginning of the North Loop. Start off by going right, traveling counterclockwise.

0.6 Reach a clearing with benches, a rock outcrop, and an oak with sprawling limbs. Several side trails splay out utility sites and dirt roads. Stay left on the unsigned path.

0.8 Arrive back at the parking lot and trailhead.

Hike Information

Local information: Roseville Chamber of Commerce, 650 Douglas Blvd., Roseville 95678; (916) 783-8136; www.rosevillechamber.com.

Visit Sacramento, 1608 I St., Sacramento, CA 95814; (916) 808-7777 or (800) 292-2334; www.visitsacramento.com.

Local events/attractions: Folsom Lake State Recreation Area, 7755 Auburn Folsom Rd., Folsom; (916) 988-0205; www.parks.ca.gov/?page_id=500. Boating, fishing, hiking, and camping are all available in the recreation area.

9 Lake Natoma Loop

This daylong hike circumnavigates the lower of two reservoirs on the American River. Lake Natoma is smaller, narrower, and mellower than Folsom Lake, with the paved circuit trail never straying far from the shady shoreline.

Start: Nimbus Flat entrance station for the Folsom Lake State Recreation Area on Hazel Avenue
Distance: 11.6-mile loop
Hiking time: 6-8 hours
Difficulty: Challenging due to trail length
Trail surface: Pavement
Best season: Year-round; unshaded portions of the trail should be avoided on hot summer days.
Other trail users: Cyclists, in-line skaters, dog walkers, trail runners
Amenities: Large paved parking lot, restrooms, trash cans, picnic sites, information kiosks and interpretive signs, boat launch (for nonmotorized vessels), swimming beach

Canine compatibility: Leashed dogs permitted
Fees and permits: Day-use fee
Schedule: Open daily, year-round. Hours for Nimbus Flat staging area change with the season. The recreation area is typically open 6 a.m. to 9 p.m. in summer (daylight saving time) and 7 a.m. to 7 p.m. in winter (standard time). Check the website for current times.
Maps: USGS Folsom CA; online at www.parks.ca.gov/?page_id=500 (click on park brochure link); available at park entry stations
Trail contact: Folsom Lake State Recreation Area, 7755 Folsom-Auburn Rd., Folsom 95630; (916) 988-0205; www.parks.ca.gov/?page_id=500

Finding the trailhead: From Sacramento, take US 50 east for 19 miles to the Hazel Avenue exit. Go left (north) on Hazel Avenue, over the freeway and through the intersection, to the signed entrance on the right (before the Sacramento State Aquatic Center parking lot). If you go over the Hazel Avenue bridge, you've gone too far. **GPS:** N38 38.049' / W121 13.025'

The Hike

Though better known as a cycling circuit, this long ramble around Lake Natoma is perfect for walking, talking, getting a great workout, and enjoying some of the best lakeside scenery Sacramento has to offer.

Though far from little, Lake Natoma is dwarfed by its larger neighbor to the east, Folsom Lake. Nimbus Dam forms a slender barrier across the American River; below the dam the river flows free, and anglers congregate in the current to see what they can catch. It's likely they'll have some luck, as the Nimbus Fish Hatchery is just below the dam. Chinook salmon and steelhead, which spawned in the American River before it was dammed, are raised at the hatchery and released into the river. They swim downstream to mature at sea, and return to their natal waters when they are grown and ready to spawn—and/or be transformed into somebody's dinner.

On Lake Natoma itself, kayakers, rowing teams, and paddleboarders ply the quiet waters, especially on warm days. Motorized watercraft are permitted on the lake north of Negro Bar but are restricted by a 5-mile-per-hour speed limit, so even if they are present, they coexist peacefully with human-powered watercraft. A swimming and wading beach runs along the linear picnic ground and the parking lot at the trailhead, so you're likely to see people enjoying a dip in the warm months of spring, summer, and fall.

The trailhead proper is in the southeast corner of the 0.4-mile-long parking area, near restrooms and the last picnic area. This is an urban trail, and at this point noise from nearby US 50 is obvious, though it will fade as you proceed. The route winds through chaparral and beneath broad-leaved sycamores, with a gravel path for walkers running parallel to the paved trail. There is plenty of room for cyclists to pass slower foot traffic—and for oncoming traffic as well—but you can avoid potential close calls by sticking to the dirt. If you're on the pavement, be prepared to step off to let speedier travelers pass.

The winding trail loops to join the main American River Parkway trail, passes an access road for a private residence, then arcs across a pedestrian bridge. The narrower gravel track winds through thickets of blackberries that ripen in late summer, and offers easy access to the shoreline for rest and refueling stops. In some areas, small beaches and sunny rocks offer respite. The dirt track features some ups

The Folsom-Auburn Bridge spans Lake Natoma at the turnaround.

and downs, and sometimes is boggy and overgrown, so keep that in mind as you choose your route.

After about 1 mile the parallel dirt track ends on the paved trail. Follow the pavement, past a couple of junctions with access routes, staying left on the obvious primary route. The Willow Creek staging area, at 2.4 miles, makes a nice turnaround point for those seeking a shorter hike.

> Mining camps and towns were built along the river between 1842 and 1862 and named for the groups that established them: Texas Hill by Texans, Mississippi Bar by Mississippians, Negro Bar by African Americans.

Cross another pedestrian bridge. Again, you'll have the chance to pick up a parallel dirt track between the paved route and the lake—but if you do, you'll miss mounds of river cobbles bordering the trail, tailings from hydraulic mining operations worked by gold miners in the gravels of the American River in the late 1800s. The lake is mostly out of view along this stretch, screened by a thick understory of scrub (including blackberry and poison oak) beneath the oaks. Pass several paved paths that lead into adjacent neighborhoods and commercial areas; no worries about taking the wrong route—the parkway trail, with its stripe of yellow separating opposing flows of traffic, is obvious.

A stone marker and plaque, placed by an Eagle Scout in 1996, identifies a spot significant in several eras of Sacramento history. Though not exact, it designates a

THE FOLSOM DAM PROJECT

Folsom Lake and Lake Natoma are recreational byproducts of the transformative hydroelectric and flood control project harnessing the power of the American River. Folsom Dam was completed in 1955, with Folsom Lake filling behind it, extending 15 miles into the forks of the river. Nimbus Dam and Lake Natoma were completed at about the same time and help regulate releases from the larger Folsom reservoir. Both dams and reservoirs provide flood control, serve as water supplies for households and agriculture, and generate electrical power.

The Folsom Powerhouse, located on the shoreline of Lake Natoma east of the Folsom-Auburn Bridge, was built in the last decade of the nineteenth century. Incorporating the original Folsom Dam and a canal, water from the river was converted into electrical power via massive "dynamos," or generators, powered by turbines. The power was transmitted to Sacramento, a feat that was unprecedented in 1895 and was front-page news even in San Francisco.

The Folsom Powerhouse, a landmark listed on the National Register of Historic Places, is the center of a state historic park located at 9980 Greenback Lane in Folsom. For more information call (916) 988-0205 or visit www.parks.ca.gov/?page_id=501.

Looking down Lake Natoma on the way back to the dam.

corner boundary of Rancho Rio de los Americanos, a land grant dating back to the days when Mexico controlled Alta California. It's also near the sites of two mining camps, Negro Bar and Texas Hill, which date back to the gold rush. And it marks the northwest corner of the modern-day city of Folsom.

Whether you follow the main trail or the narrowing dirt track, you'll end up under the Folsom-Auburn Bridge. The dirt track in this final section can be very muddy and overgrown, depending on the season; but with its tangled bowers of blackberry and little rustic wooden bridges, it feels quite wild.

To cross the bridge and continue the loop on the other side of the lake, climb up a flight of stairs and follow the long sidewalk to the signalized intersection of Greenback Lane and Folsom-Auburn Road. Drop down paved switchbacks to the paved path at the Negro Bar Park Access. There are lots of amenities here, including restrooms and parking. If you want to do a shorter hike (about 5.6 miles) and have arranged a shuttle, the Negro Bar staging area is the perfect pickup spot. You can also extend the walk by continuing east to Rainbow Bridge and taking in the sights at Folsom Powerhouse State Historic Park.

Now on the north shore of the lake, headed back west on the return leg, you'll pass through more Negro Bar amenities, including restrooms, parking areas, lawns, picnic grounds, and a boat launch. The Pioneer Express Trail intersects the paved path just beyond the picnic area, offering yet another parallel dirt-track option for hikers, but it's nice to stay on the paved trail, which drops to lakeside and passes below high bluffs composed of clay, sandstone, and river cobbles. As explained on the interpretive signs along the path, the bluffs were exposed by hydraulic mining operations. Other interpretive signs describe area fauna, including birds living along the shorelines and fish plying the depths, as well as flora, including the makeup of an oak woodland.

Beyond the bluffs the trail climbs a hill (the first and only), passing a horse trail and a pond on the right. Then it flattens out and pulls away from the lake, winding through an open landscape of annual grasses, widespread oaks, and wildflowers in season. At the signed trail junction with the spur to Main Avenue, stay straight, toward Hazel Avenue. River cobble tailings again border the trail, and a pair of horse trails (available for pedestrian use as well) intersect the path.

By the time you reach the junction with the western end of the Pioneer Express Trail at the 10.2-mile mark, the Nimbus Dam and trail's end are in sight. Follow the paved path around the fenced-off maintenance structures and climb to the Hazel Avenue Bridge. Turn left on the bridge, and follow the sidewalk down to where the path resumes in front of the Sacramento State Aquatic Center. The paved path winds around the center and back into the Nimbus Flat staging area and trailhead.

Miles and Directions

0.0 Start in the southeast corner of the parking lot / picnic area, following the paved path east into the greenbelt.

0.7 At the stop sign go left on the American River Parkway trail. Stay on the trail at the drive for a private residence less than 0.1 mile beyond.

0.9 Cross a pedestrian bridge. You can opt to follow the dirt and gravel path that parallels the main trail by heading left on any of the side trails connecting the two.

2.1 Stay left at the junction with an access trail. Stay left again where another trail intersects less than 0.1 mile farther on.

2.4 Reach the Willow Creek staging area, with a parking lot. Stay right, crossing the access road.

2.5 Cross a pedestrian bridge. Again, you have the option to take a narrower dirt trail to the left (lakeside) of the paved path.

3.3 Where an access path intersects, stay left.

4.3 Pass an access trail, then a historical marker.

5.0 Pass under the Folsom-Auburn Bridge. Take the staircase up onto the sidewalk alongside Folsom-Auburn Road and proceed across the bridge to the north side and the junction with Greenback Lane.

5.6 Cross to the east side of Greenback Lane and, at the sign for the Negro Bar Park Access, descend to the trail intersection above the parking lot and restroom. Go right on the paved path, beginning the return trip down the north shore of Lake Natoma.

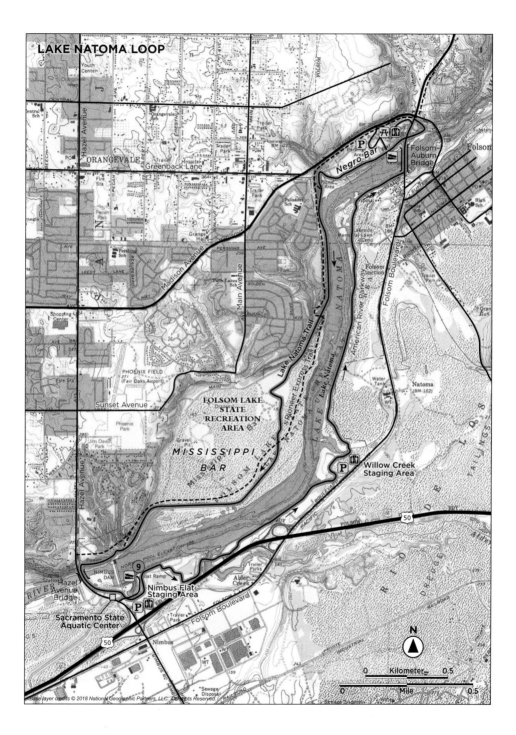

LAKE NATOMA LOOP

6.1 Pass the boat ramp (with a restroom) and head uphill to the parking area. Pick up the paved trail (or a broad, parallel dirt track) heading west from the parking area toward the picnic grounds.

6.7 Just beyond the picnic area, you'll reach the junction with the Pioneer Express Trail. Another nice option for hikers, this path leads back to the Nimbus Dam, running roughly parallel to the paved parkway trail. The route described here remains on the paved trail.

7.1 The trail is wedged between high bluffs and the lakeshore.

7.8 Pass the horse trail and a pond on the right, then climb a short hill.

8.5 At the signed junction with the side trail to the Main Avenue staging area, stay straight, toward Hazel Avenue (3.2 miles farther).

8.7 Pass a junction with a horse trail, staying on the paved path.

9.6 Pass a second horse trail junction, again staying on the main thoroughfare.

10.2 The Pioneer Express Trail merges into the American River Parkway trail. Stay on the paved path.

10.5 Pass another trail junction, again staying on the main parkway trail. The trail to the right (Middleridge) leads to the Snowberry Creek Assembly Area.

10.9 The trail splits below the dam. Take the right-hand path, climbing to the Hazel Avenue Bridge. Go left on the bridge, and drop back into the Nimbus Flat staging area.

11.6 Arrive back at the trailhead.

Hike Information

Local information: Folsom Chamber of Commerce, 200 Wool St., Folsom 95630; (916) 985-2698; www.folsomchamber.com. Check the website for information on area recreation, businesses, and restaurants.

Visit Sacramento, 1608 I St., Sacramento, CA 95814; (916) 808-7777 or (800) 292-2334; www.visitsacramento.com.

Local events/attractions: Nimbus Fish Hatchery, 2001 Nimbus Rd., Ste. F, Gold River; (916) 358-2884; www.wildlife.ca.gov/fishing/hatcheries/nimbus. In addition to instructive exhibits in the visitor center, you can also check out the raceway ponds, where salmon and steelhead are raised until ready for release. The hatchery visitor center is open Mon through Fri from 8 a.m. to 2:30 p.m., and Sat and Sun from 9 a.m. to 2:30 p.m. It is closed Christmas Day.

Sacramento State Aquatic Center, 1901 Hazel Ave., Gold River; (916) 278-2824; www.sacstateaquaticcenter.com. The aquatic center offers a variety of activities on Lake Natoma, including rowing classes (kayaks, stand-up paddling, or paddle-powered vessels), team-building seminars, and sailing lessons.

Organizations: Friends of Lakes Folsom and Natoma (FOLFAN) assists with trail maintenance and development at Folsom Lake State Recreation Area. The group also promotes trail etiquette and recreational and educational opportunities. Contact the organization at www.folfan.org.

10 Dotons Cove Trail

The oak woodland ecology of Folsom Lake frames this short interpretive trail along the shoreline of a relatively isolated bay.

Start: Dotons Cove Trailhead, located 3.8 miles from the Granite Bay entrance station to Folsom Lake State Recreation Area (SRA)
Distance: 1.0 mile out and back
Hiking time: About 1 hour
Difficulty: Easy
Trail surface: Dirt and gravel singletrack
Best season: Spring for wildflowers; fall and winter for cool temperatures. In summer, hike in the morning or evening to avoid the heat of the day. Wait a few days after a heavy winter rain for the trail to dry out.
Other trail users: Hikers only, though tracks in the dirt indicate that mountain bikers might occasionally sneak onto the trail.
Amenities: Parking, restrooms, trash cans
Canine compatibility: Leashed dogs permitted
Fees and permits: Day-use fee

Schedule: Recreation area open 6 a.m. to 10 p.m. in summer (daylight saving time) and 7 a.m. to 7 p.m. in winter (standard time). Check the Folsom Lake SRA website for specifics, as hours change seasonally.
Maps: USGS Rocklin CA; Folsom Lake State Recreation Area map available at park entry stations and online at www.parks.ca.gov/?page_id=500 (click on park brochure link)
Trail contact: Folsom Lake State Recreation Area, 7755 Folsom-Auburn Rd., Folsom 95630; (916) 988-0205; www.parks.ca.gov/?page_id=500
Special considerations: The loop option is only available when the lake level is low. Avoid contact with poison oak, a staple of the woodland ecology, by staying on the trail.

Finding the trailhead: From I-80 in Roseville, take the Douglas Road exit. Go 5.3 miles to the intersection of Douglas Road and Auburn Folsom Road; continue on Douglas Road for 1 mile to the Granite Bay entrance station. From the entrance station, follow the park road for 3.8 miles to its end at the Dotons Cove Trailhead parking area. The trailhead is in the southeast corner of the parking area, near the information boards. **GPS:** N38 46.150' / W121 7.957'

The Hike

In the height of the summer season, Folsom Lake attracts recreationalists like the bell of an ice-cream truck attracts children. Boaters and swimmers, campers and picnickers, horseback riders and mountain bikers—they all relax and play on the water and along the shoreline, savoring the expansive scenery and whatever is cooking on the outdoor grill.

Hikers may be challenged to find peace and quiet on even the remotest of the park's 95 miles of trail during summer, and the nature trail that begins at the Beeks Bight parking area is no exception. But in the off-season, when temperatures cool and the boats are stored, they stand a good chance of being downright isolated on this short, wooded excursion.

Interpretive panels along the route have faded over the years, but offer insight into the human and natural history of the oak woodland ecosystem you'll travel through. They describe how native tribes used the resources of the woodlands: Oak trees, for example, not only provided acorns, a primary element of the native diet, but components could also be used in medicine and dye. Soaproot had a variety of uses, including, of course, as a cleanser. Other signs address aspects of ecology, such as how fire benefits the environment. You'll also find benches along the path, perfect spots for rest or a snack. Numbered interpretive posts line the trail, but guides were not available at either trailhead in 2017.

A "bight" is a bay or cove—in this case a cove named for miller Joe Beek. The bight may be empty or full, depending on the lake level. When the bight off Dotons Point at the end of the trail is dry (which is most likely the case, regardless of the season, and certainly during drought years), hikers can traverse a grassy swale linking the nature trail with the park road to make a loop. If the bight is inundated (which might be the case in spring, when meltwater from the Sierra fills the reservoir, as well as during years with heavy rainfall and snowfall), you'll have to turn around at Dotons Point Road and return as you came.

The path begins by wandering through the oaks that line the edge of the bight. Birds flit in and out of the scrub, and wildflowers bloom in season in pockets of grasslands between thickets of blackberry and scrub. Benches line the path, offering the opportunity to rest in the quiet and shade. A couple of picnic tables have been placed near the far end of the trail, overlooking the bight—another nice respite.

A picnic table overlooks Beeks Bight on the Dotons Cove Trail.

After a winter of abundant snowfall, Folsom Lake brims.

Emerge from the woodland in a clearing with views of Folsom Lake and Folsom Dam. The path hooks into a bike trail near the mouth of the bight, climbing gently to trail's end at a small gravel parking area on Dotons Point Road. To get views of the lake, or to visit the lakeshore, cross the paved roadway and drop down dirt paths on the opposite side to the shoreline. To return to the trailhead, retrace your steps.

Miles and Directions

0.0 Start behind the information board, heading right (south). A mountain biking route departs to the left. Cross a bridge and head into the woodland.

0.1 Cross Dotons Point Road. Continue straight (south) on the nature trail.

0.3 Pass a bench and some interesting rock outcrops.

0.4 Picnic tables overlook a lovely meadow studded with granite outcrops. Continue south, enjoying views of the lake and dam.

0.5 The nature trail merges with a multiuse singletrack. Go left (southeast) on the blended trail, climbing to trail's end at Dotons Point Road. A small parking area and trash cans are available here. Return as you came.

1.0 Arrive back at the trailhead.

Option: If the bight is dry, you can return to the trail junction in the meadow and go left, following the trail across the bottom of the empty bay. Pass a trail marker on the far side of the inlet. The path then climbs to the park road. Keep in mind that

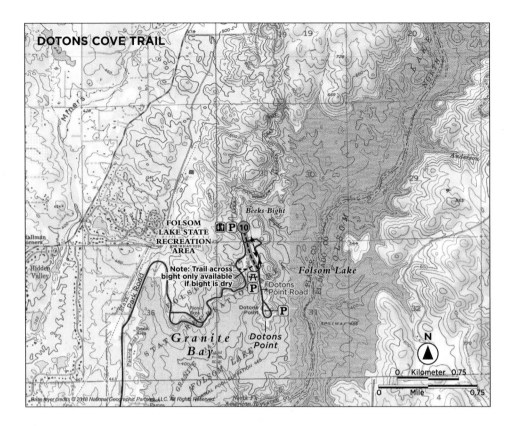

this option is frequented by mountain bikers. Turn right (north) onto the road, and follow it back to the trailhead. Total mileage for the loop is 1.1 miles.

Hike Information

Local information: Roseville Chamber of Commerce, 650 Douglas Blvd., Roseville 95678; (916) 783-8136; www.rosevillechamber.com.

Visit Sacramento, 1608 I St., Sacramento, CA 95814; (916) 808-7777 or (800) 292-2334; www.visitsacramento.com.

Local events/attractions: Folsom Lake State Recreation Area offers a variety of outdoor activities including boating, windsurfing, paddleboarding, swimming, fishing, camping, picnicking, cycling and mountain biking, horseback riding, and lounging on the beach. Much more information is available on the park website at www.parks.ca.gov/?page_id=500; or call (916) 988-0205.

Camping: Folsom Lake has three developed campgrounds plus two hike-in environmental campsites. The closest camp to Beeks Bight is at Beals Point, open year-round. Make reservations by calling (800) 444-7275 or (916) 988-0205, or at reserveamerica.com.

11 Sterling Pointe to Rattlesnake Bar

Follow a remote stretch of Folsom Lake's shoreline to a beachhead with lovely lake views. The route is part of the Pioneer Express Trail, used by equestrians for endurance rides, but those on foot endure nothing more strenuous than a few mellow ups and downs.

Start: Sterling Pointe staging area off Auburn Folsom Road

Distance: 6.8 miles out and back

Hiking time: 4–5 hours

Difficulty: Moderate due to distance

Trail surface: Dirt singletrack, some dirt road

Best season: Spring, late fall, and winter

Other trail users: Equestrians

Amenities: Parking; restrooms; water for humans, horses, and dogs; picnic tables; trash cans; information signboards

Canine compatibility: Leashed dogs permitted

Fees and permits: None

Schedule: Open daily, 8 a.m. to sunset, year-round. The route runs through the Folsom Lake State Recreation Area, but the staging area is not part of Folsom Lake SRA. Recreation area hours change with the season; check the website for current hours.

Maps: USGS Pilot Hill CA; online at www.parks.ca.gov/?page_id=500 (click on park brochure link); available at park entry stations. A map of the Sterling Pointe trails, including the Peregrine Trail and Lake Forest Trail, is posted on an information signboard at the trailhead.

Trail contact: Folsom Lake State Recreation Area, 7755 Folsom-Auburn Rd., Folsom 95630; (916) 988-0205; www.parks.ca.gov/?page_id=500

Finding the trailhead: From I-80 in Roseville, take the East Douglas Boulevard exit. Go 5.3 miles east on Douglas Boulevard to Auburn Folsom Road. Turn left (north) on Auburn Folsom Road and go 5 miles to Lomida Lane. Turn right (east) on Lomida Lane and drive for about 0.8 mile; Lomida becomes Lake Forest Drive and then Sterling Pointe Court. Signs in the neighborhood point the way. Continue for 0.3 mile on Sterling Pointe Court to the road's end at the staging area. **GPS:** N38 48.092' / W121 06.666'

The Hike

The hike from Sterling Pointe to Rattlesnake Bar begins in a ritzy neighborhood, where the manicured backyards of expensive homes back up to the serenity of an arm of Folsom Lake. Following this route, hikers can tap into the appeal of the area—priceless views across the blue-green water, fragrant oak woodland, a sense of well-being enhanced by exercise—and it won't cost them a penny.

The Sterling Pointe Trail, followed down to the Western States Pioneer Express Trail, is part of a hiking and equestrian trail system that offers shorter loops if the longer trek to Rattlesnake Bar is not appealing. The Sterling Pointe path drops past signed junctions with the Peregrine and Lake Forest Trails before reaching the Pioneer Express Trail, with Folsom Lake hidden by a thick screen of scrub. The abundant foliage

The Western States Pioneer Express Trail skirts the shoreline of Folsom Lake as it stretches from Sterling Pointe to Rattlesnake Bar and beyond.

of the understory emerges supple and green in the spring, leaves glossy with moisture from the rainy season, and turns brittle and crispy as the dry season progresses.

The Pioneer Express Trail, an endurance equestrian and trail-running route that runs from Sacramento to Auburn, and then up into the Sierra Nevada, traces the shorelines of both Lake Natoma and Folsom Reservoir. It can be traveled in either direction from Sterling Pointe; you'll be headed toward the foothills. Mile markers along the trail testify to its length; you hop on at about mile 42. Turn left (north and then east) to reach Rattlesnake Bar (and beyond).

▶ **The term "bar," as in Rattlesnake Bar and Horseshoe Bar, was given to bends in the river where forty-niners were likely to find placer gold.**

At Long Bar, a small, overgrown picnic area, social trails branch to picnic sites. Though still out of sight, the drone of boat motors drifting through the trees is a reminder that the lake is below. Once past Long Bar and its cluster of use trails, route-finding simplifies. The well-traveled singletrack weaves northward along the lakeshore, tucking in and out of ravines where black-berries thrive even after the streamlets that nourish them have dried up. Generally ripe in August, the berries are a delicious trailside snack.

By the 1-mile mark, lake views open. Side trails drop to the shoreline, which rises and falls based on rainfall, snowmelt in the Sierra, and releases from Folsom Dam. Glitters of sunlight reflecting off the windows of homes in the wooded hills on the opposite shore catch the eye, as do the boats zooming by on the water.

The trail fractures again at Horseshoe Bar, with unsigned use paths branching right to the lakeshore and to overlooks. Stay left, hooking up and over a short, steep hill and past the gated access point from Horseshoe Bar Road (follow the horse poop and hoofprints if you are uncertain). Continue on the broad dirt road as it arcs around a cove then narrows to singletrack and continues north.

The trail roller-coasters through the scrub and is deeply grooved in sections, chiseled by horse hooves. A large power-line tower sits atop one hill, then the route drops, bending right at a trail junction, to cross one of several little bridges that make negotiating stream gullies easy. The landscape opens to meadow as you approach Rattlesnake Bar, with springtime wildflower displays a lovely addition to widening lake views. Stay right at the trail junctions beyond the meadow—the route is identified with trail markers—until you reach the signs, picnic areas, and parking lot at the eastern edge of Rattlesnake Bar.

Popular and sometimes busy, you can follow paved Rattlesnake Road to the developed areas of Rattlesnake Bar, including the boat launch. A web of dirt roads knots around the lakeshore, and the small point that juts into the lake. Find a quiet spot along the shoreline to rest and have a snack, enjoying expansive views south across the blue waters of the lake. When you are ready, return as you came.

Miles and Directions

0.0 Start at the signed trailhead at the Sterling Pointe staging area, taking the Sterling Pointe Trail.

0.1 Pass the junction with the Peregrine Trail. Stay straight on the Sterling Pointe Trail.

0.25 At the intersection with the Lake Forest Trail, stay left on the Sterling Pointe Trail. After about 500 feet, meet the lower end of the Peregrine Trail. Stay right and downhill, passing a couple of fences as you drop.

0.4 Reach the signed Pioneer Express Trail. Go left toward Rattlesnake Bar.

0.6 The trail splits before reaching the signed Long Bar picnic area. Stay left (on the high road) to skirt the picnic area.

0.8 Pass endurance trail mile marker 43.

1.3 Pass endurance trail mile marker 43.5.

1.5 Arrive at Horseshoe Bar. Stay left (up and over the hill) on the unsigned, broad, road-like track to continue on the Pioneer Express Trail. On the other side of the hill, the broad track bends around a cove.

2.0 Pass endurance trail mile marker 44; the trail begins to climb.

2.3 Pass a section of chain-link fence, then endurance trail mile marker 44.5.

2.4 Pass a power-line tower.

2.5 At the trail junction, stay right, passing a trail signpost. Cross a little bridge over an inlet stream.

2.7 Cross a meadow.

2.8 Pass endurance trail mile marker 45 and a side road that leads left. Stay right on the Pioneer Express Trail.

3.1 Cross a bridge over a year-round stream. Pass another trail marker and stay right.

3.4 Reach Rattlesnake Bar. Take a break, then head back the way you came.

6.8 Arrive back at the Sterling Pointe staging area.

Hike Information

Local information: Roseville Chamber of Commerce, 650 Douglas Blvd., Roseville 95678; (916) 783-8136; www.rosevillechamber.com.

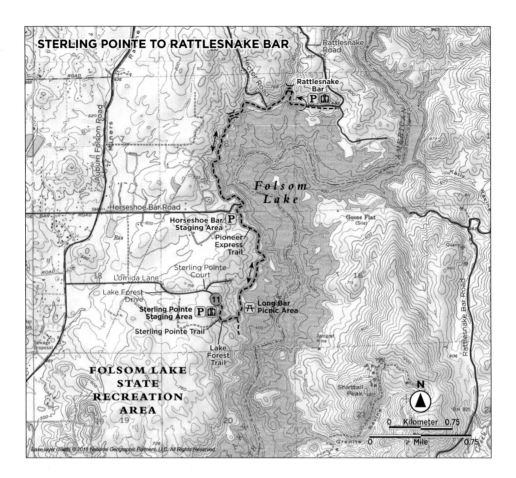

STERLING POINTE TO RATTLESNAKE BAR

Visit Sacramento, 1608 I St., Sacramento, CA 95814; (916) 808-7777 or (800) 292-2334; www.visitsacramento.com.

Local events/attractions: Folsom Lake State Recreation Area offers a variety of outdoor activities including boating, windsurfing, swimming, fishing, camping, picnicking, cycling and mountain biking, horseback riding, and lounging on the beach. Much more information is available on the park website at www.parks.ca.gov/?page_id=500; or call (916) 988-0205.

Camping: Folsom Lake has three developed campgrounds plus two hike-in environmental campsites. Make reservations by calling (800) 444-7275 or (916) 988-0205, or at reserveamerica.com.

Other resources: The Western States Trail Foundation, 150A Gum Lane #103, Auburn CA 95603; (530) 823-7282; www.teviscup.org. The Wendell & Inez Robie Foundation, PO Box 714, Foresthill 95631; (530) 367-4332; http://robiefoundation.org. The Western States Foundation, the Robie Foundation, and others are dedicated to preserving and maintaining historic trails for equestrians and hikers, including the Pioneer Express Trail.

12 Sweetwater Trail

A popular route with mountain bikers and hikers alike, the Sweetwater Trail follows the southern shoreline of Folsom Lake below the inflow of the South Fork American River. Mostly shaded, the trail winds through oak woodland and small meadows, with side trails leading waterside.

Start: Signed trailhead in Salmon Falls raft takeout parking lot
Distance: 5.6 miles out and back
Hiking time: 2-3 hours
Difficulty: Moderate due to distance
Trail surface: Dirt singletrack
Best season: Spring for wildflowers; late fall for cooler weather
Other trail users: Mountain bikers
Amenities: Parking, restrooms
Canine compatibility: Leashed dogs permitted
Fees and permits: Day-use fee
Schedule: Open daily, year-round. The trail is in the Folsom Lake State Recreation Area, and hours of operation change with the season, roughly opening near sunrise and closing at sunset. Check the website for current hours.
Maps: USGS Pilot Hill CA; online at www.parks.ca.gov/?page_id=500 (click on park brochure); available at park entry stations
Trail contact: Folsom Lake State Recreation Area, 7755 Folsom-Auburn Rd., Folsom 95630; (916) 988-0205; www.parks.ca.gov/?page_id=500
Special considerations: This trail is popular with mountain bikers. While trail etiquette requires bikers yield to hikers, it is often easier for a hiker to step off the trail to let a cyclist pass. Be courteous, and use common sense.

Finding the trailhead: From Sacramento, head east on US 50 about 25 miles to Eldorado Hills. Take the Eldorado Hills Boulevard exit. Go north on Eldorado Hills Boulevard for about 4.2 miles to the junction with Green Valley Road, where the name changes to Salmon Falls Road. Continue north on Salmon Falls Road for 5.6 miles to the Salmon Falls raft takeout parking lot, on the left. If you reach the Salmon Falls Bridge, you've gone too far. **GPS:** N38 46.284' / W121 02.583'

The Hike

The Sweetwater Trail's greatest asset is its setting—it winds through a healthy oak woodland, sports views through the trees across a long arm of the South Fork American River as it feeds Folsom Lake, and includes passage through moist, shady drainages and across open meadowlands. But the successful comingling of diverse trail interests is also highlighted on this route.

Conflicts between mountain bikers and other trail users, arguably more stridently with equestrians than with travelers on foot, have been an issue on public lands since the 1970s, when the popularity of fat-tired bikes boomed. No multiuse route has been immune, but nowadays sharing trails is commonplace. Cooperation among the diverse user groups—hikers, horseback riders, trail runners—also extends to building and maintaining trails, and mountain bikers have stepped up in the case of the

Sweetwater, helping create an immaculate, winding, roller-coaster singletrack that is superlative. Go forth with gratitude when you venture onto this path.

Fortunately there are enough mountain biking routes in this neck of the woods to thin out the wheeled population, so unless you hit the trail at the same time as a pack of cyclists (during an organized ride, for example), you are unlikely to cross paths with anyone other than hikers.

Beginning near the Salmon Falls Bridge, where the South Fork American River broadens into the lake, the dirt singletrack heads into scrub and dips through the first of several stream crossings—this one little more than a trickle in late season. Tangles of brush thrive along the waterway, including poison oak. Stay on the path and you should be able to avoid contact with this native plant's leaves and stems, which carry a rash-producing oil.

Ups and downs, twists and turns, and flickering views of the lake through a thick chaparral of ceanothus, scrub oak, and burgundy-skinned manzanita characterize the

The Sweetwater Trail offers tree-filtered views of Folsom Lake.

A small stand of oaks marks a great picnic site near the edge of Folsom Lake, and a possible turnaround point for those seeking a shorter hike.

first mile of trail. Though the walk is generally quiet and remote in feel, noise from boats is constant on busy summer days and more intermittent in spring and fall. Pass trails that lead lakeside as you proceed, with the views improving the farther you head down the path.

Broader vistas open at the halfway point of the outward leg. A bit farther along, side trails lead down to a cove that makes a nice stopping point for a snack or to wet your feet. A stand of oaks provides shade on the otherwise exposed stretch of shoreline.

Beyond the cove the trail curls around a finger of the lake. After crossing a culvert in the shade of more oaks, you'll border a tributary of Sweetwater Creek, which has dug a trench into soft sediments. As the path nears its junction with Salmon Falls Road, noise from passing cars becomes noticeable.

Cross a metal bridge spanning the Sweetwater Creek tributary. Sedges, discernable by the edges on their stalks, line the path. At 2.5 miles the trail empties onto a dirt roadway at a junction; a Sweetwater sign marks the spot. Head left to complete the outbound portion of the hike at the gate and small parking area off Salmon Falls Road. If you don't want to make the last short hitch to the roadside endpoint, you can bear right at the sign and follow any of several trails / old dirt roads (one is signed for use by bikes and horses) that lead across an open, grassy area. Pick a rest spot in the sun or shade, depending on the season, and then retrace your steps to the trailhead.

Miles and Directions

0.0 Start at the signed trailhead in the southernmost corner of the parking area. Cross a seasonal stream.

0.6 Cross a second stream, dry in late season.

1.1 Pass a trail post. A side trail breaks right to the shoreline. Stay left on the obvious main track.

1.2 Cross the first of a pair of seasonal stream drainages. The second is at 1.3 miles.

1.6 Lake views open.

1.8 Buoys mark a cove where a large oak provides the only shade. This is a nice spot for a snack or picnic and can be the turnaround point for a shorter hike.

2.1 Cross a culvert in an oak grove.

2.4 Cross a metal bridge spanning a Sweetwater Creek tributary.

HOW TO SHARE A TRAIL

Growing up in Fairfax, California, I was lucky enough to be part of mountain biking's first wave. We were a motley crew, riding in jeans and tennis shoes instead of padded Lycra bike shorts and specialized footwear, and rocketing down now legendary downhill runs including the iconic Repack (so named because you'd have to repack the bearings in your brakes after you burned through them on the descent).

In those early days there were no trail restrictions, and mountain bikers rode where they pleased. But the hills had long been the territory of horseback riders and hikers, who were startled and upset by the new, speed-fueled use. We were unwelcome upstarts, a mostly silent surprise that spooked horses and hikers when we suddenly appeared. Some of us exacerbated the culture clash by being rude, ignoring hikers who asked us to slow down when we approached, and horseback riders who asked us to dismount so we wouldn't startle their animals.

The conflicts that sometimes erupted—usually shouting matches but sometimes worse—led to mountain biking bans on many of the singletrack paths that inspired wheeled trailblazers in the first place. But most mountain bikers realized the impacts they were having on fellow outdoorspeople and began to abide by the commonsense rules now ingrained in the trail-use credo. With the exception of a few hardheads, most mountain bikers agreed to a trail etiquette dictating cyclists yield to all other trail users. It's not always possible, but in my experience, even the intent goes a long way toward peaceful encounters with other users—no matter mode of travel—on the trail.

To this day mountain bikers are dispelling the bad feelings engendered by arrogant cyclists who wouldn't (and won't) compromise for the benefit of all. Organizations such

2.5 Reach the end of the singletrack at a Sweetwater sign. Bear left to head up to the small parking area at Salmon Falls Road.

2.7 Arrive at the turnaround at the small parking area off Salmon Falls Road. A gate spans the trail. Retrace your steps to the last junction, at the Sweetwater sign.

2.8 Bear left to explore the meadow if you choose. Otherwise, go right on the Sweetwater Trail to return to the trailhead.

5.6 Arrive back at the trailhead.

Hike Information

Local information: Eldorado Hills Chamber of Commerce, 2085 Vine St., Ste. 105, El Dorado Hills 95762; (916) 933-1335; www.eldoradohillschamber.com. The chamber provides information on community activities and businesses.

as IMBA (International Mountain Biking Association) were formed to educate all trail users about trail etiquette once it became apparent that mountain biking was here to stay. Mountain biking clubs, like FATRAC on the Sweetwater and other popular trails in the Sacramento region, have adopted trails and maintain them for all users. Their goodwill has slowly been mending the breach.

Mountain bikers bear the responsibility to let hikers know where they are, and to travel at reasonable speeds when they know hikers (and horseback riders) share a route. With years on the trail, and hundreds (thousands) of miles under my wheels and feet, I can honestly say I've encountered only a handful of rude riders. Trail users—regardless of their mode of travel—are a peaceful bunch by nature. We new kids in the sandbox were rabble rousers at first, but now we all play nicely together.

Sharing the trail begins with a kind word and an understanding that we're all out there for the same reason.

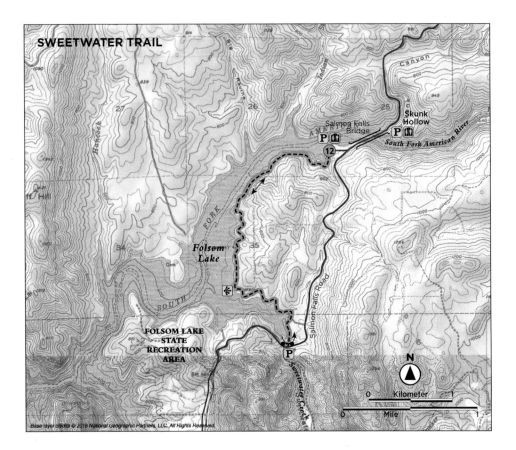

Camping: Folsom Lake has three developed campgrounds plus two hike-in environmental campsites. The closest camp to the Sweetwater Trail is the Peninsula Campground, at the end of Rattlesnake Bar Road. Make reservations by calling (800) 444-7275 or (916) 988-0205, or at reserveamerica.com.

Organizations: The Sweetwater Trail was built by, and is maintained by, the Folsom-Auburn Trail Riders Action Coalition (FATRAC). Visit www.fatrac.org to learn more about this cycling organization.

13 Yolo Bypass Wildlife Area Loop

Follow elevated thruways on a leisurely loop through the 16,600–acre Yolo Bypass Wildlife Area on Sacramento's west side, sharing viewscapes of wetlands, grasslands, and rice fields with countless birds.

Start: Trailhead in parking lot F
Distance: 4.0-mile loop
Hiking time: About 2 hours
Difficulty: Easy
Trail surface: Elevated dirt and mown roadways
Best season: Year-round
Other trail users: Hikers only on the trail. Cyclists are permitted on the causeway located in the northern part of the wildlife area, between I-80 and the railroad tracks.
Amenities: Gravel parking area, restrooms, picnic table
Canine compatibility: Dogs not permitted; leashed dogs allowed on the trails between I-80 and the railroad tracks
Fees and permits: None
Schedule: Open daily, sunrise to sunset, year-round. Seasonal daylight hours are posted at the entry.

Maps: USGS Sacramento West CA; online at www.yolobasin.org or on the California Department of Fish and Games' Yolo Bypass Wildlife Area page: www.wildlife.ca.gov/lands/places-to-visit/yolo-bypass-wa
Trail contact: California Department of Fish and Game, Yolo Bypass Wildlife Area Headquarters, 45211 Yolo CR 32B (Chiles Road), Davis 95618; (530) 757-2461; www.dfg.ca.gov/lands/wa/region3/yolo/index.html
Other: This route is closed during hunting seasons. Trails in the wetlands area accessed from lots B, C, and D are accessible during hunting seasons.
Special considerations: There is little shade on this route, so avoid hiking during the heat of a summer's day.

Finding the trailhead: From downtown Sacramento, head west on I-80 for about 8 miles, through West Sacramento and toward Davis. Take the E. Chiles Road / Yolo CR 32A exit. Head under the freeway to the signed Vic Fazio Yolo Bypass Wildlife Area entrance. Climb atop the levee, then drop right onto the signed auto tour route at parking lot A. Follow the unpaved auto route south, past lots B and C, for about 1.6 miles to the T junction near parking lot D, with a hunter check-in station. Turn left onto the dirt road and head east toward parking lots H and F, driving up and over the slough. Parking lot F and the trailhead are at the end of the dirt road, 1.4 miles from the hunter check-in station. **GPS:** N38 31.790' / W121 35.397'

The Hike

For decades the levee-bound rice fields and remnants of wetlands on the south side of the interstate on metro Sacramento's western edge were little more than a curiosity for motorists speeding by. Now, the Yolo Bypass Wildlife Area's seasonal and permanent wetlands, grasslands, and riparian zones are known as a destination for birdlife of all descriptions, from the commonly seen mallard duck and red-winged blackbird to the more exotic peregrine falcon, great blue heron, and Swainson's hawk.

The wildlife area has also become a destination for hikers, birders, and hunters. It is a major waypoint on the Pacific Flyway, so no matter the season, venturing into the open space will involve bird watching, birdcall, and bird wonder.

The levees encasing the wildlife area's ponds and fields were originally designed for flood control, and their primary purpose remains containment of overflow from the Sacramento River, Putah Creek, and other streams feeding into San Francisco Bay's sprawling and highly developed delta region. In California's 2016–17 winter season, during which the north state was inundated with record-breaking rainfall and snowfall, the Sacramento River weirs were opened for the first time in a decade, and what had been a parched floodplain was transformed into a lake.

Wildlife and habitat management is the other primary focus, and includes agricultural uses, restoration of wetlands, and limited permitted hunting. The refuge's last priority encompasses recreational and educational uses, including hiking trails and guided tours.

Viewed from atop a levee, scudding clouds threaten rain, which would add water to the lowland Yolo Bypass.

The wildlife area, which was established by President Bill Clinton in 1997, is operated by the state Department of Fish and Game. Congressman Vic Fazio, for whom the preserve is named, worked to ensure the wetlands restoration project came to fruition—no small feat considering the divergent interests of the hunters, hikers, flood-control management agencies, businesses, educators, and environmentalists that were (and still are) interested in the project.

Begin by crossing the concrete bridge over the slough. Go right on the wide track, traveling the loop in a counterclockwise direction; you'll return on the path to the left. With sloughs and ponds all around, the foliage is lush, even if it dries brittle and blond at the end of the dry season. Wildflowers, weeds, and willows crowd the margins, with stands of sunflowers reaching nearly 5 feet tall in late summer.

▶ It's a good idea to steer clear of all wildlife, to avoid disturbing their natural habitats and behaviors. Take it a step further and go out of your way to avoid birds and animals that are mating, resting, or taking care of their young.

The birds are always present, with songbirds, bitterns, and great blue herons camouflaged in the brush; ducks paddling on the ponds; and the occasional raptor surveying the scene from above. The snowy egret and great white egret don't hide so well, their white plumage stark against the muted earth tones of the landscape. Crickets and dragonflies, as well as peskier blackflies, bees, and wasps, also may be present.

The route is flat and easy to travel, following mown roadways perfect for walking and talking. While signage is scarce, given the wide-open nature of the area, it's fairly simple to stay on track. Several paths break left from the slough-side track, offering links to shorter loops around the three ponds that form the centerpieces of the longer loop. Heading north toward the barely visible interstate, the low hum of cars on the freeway is a constant, but the birds do a great job of drowning it out. The vistas are expansive, stretching over the open spaces, while signs of civilization—power lines, farm buildings, the straight-line humps of levees—are confined mostly to the horizon (though at the apex of the loop you'll come in close contact with a pump station and power pole, and an industrial complex dominates the eastern skyline).

The return leg of the loop brings you in closer contact with the ponds and seasonal wetlands. Watch for ducks on open water and a variety of songbirds and shorebirds sheltering in the reeds on the shorelines. At one point the route slides between the willow-lined shores of two of the ponds, with the foliage offering a natural blind for birding. The route ends by curling back toward the parking lot alongside the access road.

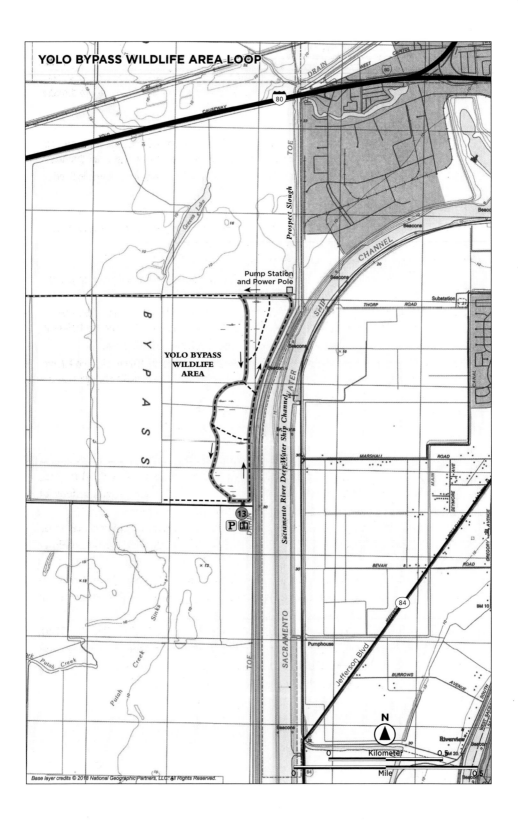

YOLO BYPASS WILDLIFE AREA LOOP

Miles and Directions

0.0 Start by crossing the concrete bridge. Turn right on the path, traveling the loop in a counterclockwise direction. A wide slough is on the right, and a pond is barely visible through the brush on the left.

0.5 At the trail junction, stay right on the mown path alongside the slough.

0.9 At the second trail intersection, stay right again. Two trails branch left, on either side of a waterway that may be dry in late season, presenting an opportunity to shorten the hike.

1.5 Reach a pump station and power pole. Turn left here on the gravel road, which is lined with willows.

1.8 Pass a junction with a mown path, staying straight (right) on the roadway.

2.0 At a large willow (the only shade in the area), leave the roadway and go left on the old mown roadbed that heads south, back toward the trailhead.

2.5 Trails merge at a junction. Stay right on the more traveled path.

2.7 Reach a T junction at a slough. Go right on the doubletrack into the willows, with ponds on either side.

2.9 Several roads converge at the edge of a field. Go left along the field's edge, then stay right at the junction about 50 yards beyond, continuing southbound toward the trailhead.

3.2 At the trail junction, go left on the unsigned doubletrack headed southeast.

3.3 Reach another junction and stay straight, continuing south. At the "Blind" sign, go left on the two-track roadway, with the slough running alongside on the right. The bridge across the slough and the trailhead are visible ahead.

4.0 Arrive back at the trailhead.

Hike Information

Local information: Visit Sacramento, 1608 I St., Sacramento, CA 95814; (916) 808-7777 or (800) 292-2334; www.visitsacramento.com. The site provides plentiful information about activities and services in the Sacramento region.

Local events/attractions: California Duck Days is a festival of educational tours and presentations. Contact the Yolo Basin Foundation (see "Organizations" below) for more information.

Hike tours: Wildlife-viewing tours are organized by the Yolo Basin Foundation on the second Saturday of each month from Sept to June. For more information call (530) 757-3780 or visit www.yolobasin.org.

Organizations: Yolo Basin Foundation, PO Box 943, Davis 05617; (530) 757-3780; www.yolobasin.org. This nonprofit foundation is dedicated to the stewardship and preservation of Yolo Basin wetlands. It publishes a newsletter, available online, highlighting the people and events that make the basin great.

14 Mather Nature Loops

A pair of short loops ramble alongside Mather Lake, offering hikers a chance to stretch their legs, learn about the local habitat, and visit vernal pools in spring.

Start: Trailhead near the dam in Mather Regional Park
Distance: 1.5-mile double loop
Hiking time: About 1 hour
Difficulty: Easy
Trail surface: Wide dirt and gravel trails
Best season: Winter and spring to view the vernal pools; fall for color; spring for birds
Other trail users: Hikers only
Amenities: Parking, restrooms, water, tot lot, lawns, trash cans, fishing pier
Canine compatibility: Leashed dogs permitted
Fees and permits: Parking fee

Schedule: Open daily, sunrise to sunset, year-round
Maps: USGS Carmichael CA. Trails are short and straightforward, so no map is needed.
Trail contact: Sacramento County Regional Parks Department, 4040 Bradshaw Rd., Sacramento 95827; (916) 875-6961; www .regionalparks.saccounty.net/Parks/Regional ParksDetails/Pages/MatherRegionalPark.aspx
Other: Mather Lake is stocked with black bass and trout. No motorized boats are allowed. The vernal pools fill in winter, bloom in April and early May, and are gone by late May.

Finding the trailhead: From US 50, take the Sunrise Boulevard exit. Head south on Sunrise Boulevard to Douglas Road and turn right (west). Follow Douglas Road for 1 mile to Zinfandel Drive and turn left (south). Follow Zinfandel Drive for 0.3 mile to the signed park entrance on the left (east). Start the first walk on the south side of the dock, behind the gate on the dam; the interpretive loop begins to the left, behind the picnic pavilion. **GPS:** N38 33.415' / W121 15.572'

The Hike

The sprawling grasslands that insulated the former air force base at Mather Field, which was a local military facility during World Wars I and II, are now part of a compact regional park. The meadowlands, along with the lake and its surrounding wetlands, provide space for migrating and resident birds to nest and feed, support rare and fragile creatures in vernal pools, and allow appreciative hikers to walk and observe.

Though suburbia encroaches on all sides, and the roar of aircraft engines and freeway traffic nixes this as a wilderness experience, the abundance of color and wildlife makes a walk here more than worthwhile. It's the perfect outing for a family. Mix a short hike with fishing, a picnic, a romp on the tot lot . . . or, for older "kids," perhaps a round of golf.

Ducks and geese abide on the lake year-round, but visit during spring or fall if you are interested in species that migrate along the Pacific Flyway. Autumn is lovely, as the foliage of willows, cottonwoods, and other riparian plants around the lake turns to gold. Spring is even more colorful. That's when the vernal pools bloom, blankets of meadowfoam and goldfields thrown across depressions in the grasslands. The display is short-lived, however; the blooms fade away within weeks.

Vernal pools appear late in the rainy season as water accumulates in shallow depressions. A unique and precious environment, in many cases the plants and animals inhabiting the pools are rare and endangered. These include fairy shrimp, which survive the long dry season as cysts, then hatch and reproduce in the brief time the pool is full.

Named for World War I test pilot Carl Mather, the airfield at Mather Air Force Base dates back to 1918. It didn't stay open very long initially; the facility was shuttered when the war ended. The advent of World War II prompted the base's revival, and this time it operated for decades. The airfield operated through the Cold War and the Vietnam War as a training facility for navigators and as a Strategic Air Command base. Military downsizing resulted in closure of the facility in 1995; nearby McClellan Airfield also shut down in the late twentieth century. The Mather property was divided into a county airport and parkland. Work on the 1,600-acre park is ongoing, with a coalition of community groups, including the Audubon Society and the Rotary Club, balancing preservation of open space with more intensive uses like ball fields.

The tour of trails around Mather Lake is described beginning with the unimproved loop on the south shore, then with the nature trail on the northwest shore.

An interpretive path winds along the shoreline of the small lake at Mather Regional Park.

The first loop explores the riparian zone and grasslands on the south side of the lake, with access to waterside picnic sites. The second loop follows a short interpretive trail, where signs describe the area's creatures, from frogs to rodents, and the habitat that nurtures them.

Miles and Directions

0.0 Start behind the gate that blocks vehicle access to the dam. Follow the dam south, with the lake on your left and meadowland to the right.

0.1 At the end of the dam (which borders the Mather Golf Course), go left (east) on the dirt track, dropping through a picnic site.

0.3 The trail splits; stay right (east). At the second split stay right (east) again, heading into the meadow.

0.5 Swing north as the trail approaches the fence that separates the golf course from the natural area. Marshland thick with cattails, reeds, and birdcall borders the route.

0.7 The trail loops back along the lakeshore. Retrace your steps to the trailhead.

1.0 Arrive at the parking area. Pick up the self-guided nature trail on the northwest shore of the lake, passing the fishing pier and a series of benches set in the trees at waterside, as well as an interpretive kiosk detailing the history of Mather Field.

1.1 The nature trail splits. Go right on the lakeside track, following the line of interpretive signs through the riparian thickets.

Mather Lake attracts swans and other birdlife.

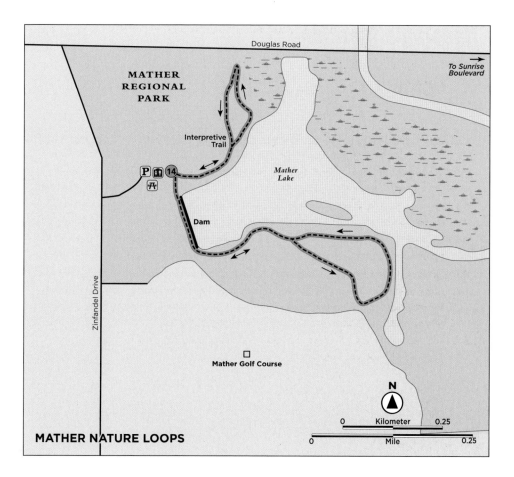

MATHER NATURE LOOPS

1.3 The trail merges onto a wider track near a gate that bars access to Douglas Road. Turn left (south) on the gravel road, heading back toward the picnic area through a grassland dotted with adolescent oaks and sycamores.

1.4 Reach the split in the nature trail and retrace your steps toward the trailhead.

1.5 Arrive back at the trailhead and parking area.

Hike Information

Hike tours: Sacramento Splash offers tours of the Mather Field vernal pools during the peak of the wildflower bloom. Visit www.sacsplash.org/our-programs/public-programs/vernal-pool-tours for more information.

Organizations: Sacramento Splash, 4426 Excelsior Rd., Mather 95655; (916) 364-2437; www.sacsplash.org. This nonprofit organization is dedicated to helping Sacramento's schoolchildren better understand their environment.

Honorable Mention

Maidu Regional Park

Another pocket green space in the midst of suburbia, 152-acre Maidu Regional Park is geared toward the ball player, whether soccer or baseball or basketball, with grass fields, batting cages, basketball courts, and plenty of parking for spectators. It also sports a skate park, tot lots, and picnic areas. The Maidu Museum & Historic Site features exhibits on the native Nisenan people. But hikers are accommodated at the park too. Venture between the museum and the ball fields to explore the compact trail system that winds through grasslands and oak groves. A paved path links the soccer complex to the surrounding neighborhood, and dirt tracks reach into woodlands alongside a stream. The park is located off Rocky Ridge Drive in Roseville. Call (916) 774-5200 or visit www.roseville.ca.us/parks/parks_n_facilities/parks_in_roseville/maidu.asp.

North Valley and Foothills

TRAILS TO WATERFALLS, ALONG RIVERSIDES, AND TO HISTORIC MINES

The region north of the Sacramento metropolitan area is mostly rural, with small towns separated by sprawling agricultural parcels: orchards, sunflowers, rice, and more. The defining landmark is the Sutter Buttes, an anomalous eruption of peaks that juts from the valley floor and forms a spectacular backdrop to the open space and ranchland that surround them. Visible for miles, the buttes are on private land and are accessible to hikers only via docent-led hikes.

The watershed streams of the Yuba and Feather Rivers wind through the region, all eventually emptying into the mighty Sacramento. The twin towns of Yuba City and Marysville straddle the confluence of the Feather and Yuba, and offer a variety of amenities, including historic downtown districts that date back to the gold rush. Yuba City has been the Sutter County seat since the mid–1800s.

Trails in this part of the Sacramento Valley are tightly hitched to the area's water-ways, from the braided Feather as it flows through the Bobelaine Audubon Sanctuary

Fiddlenecks are among the first blooms in meadowlands surrounding Sacramento in springtime.

Hollow Falls spills into its basin on North Table Mountain.

to the ponds of the Gray Lodge Wildlife Area. Dry Creek belies its name, flowing year-round and spilling spectacularly into a deep pool. In the foothills the historic mining town of Grass Valley offers up Empire Mine State Historic Park. Here the big water is underground, flooding hundreds of miles of shafts and tunnels after the famed gold mine closed. Grass Valley and neighboring Nevada City are gateways to scenic foothills hiking as well as good eats and other services.

Directions to trailheads in this region are given from the Sacramento metro area. Marysville and Yuba City are approximately 41 miles (50 minutes) north of Sacramento via CA 99 and CA 70. You can access the trails at Bobelaine, Gray Lodge, and Shingle Falls from these routes. Empire Mine State Historic Park and Malakoff Diggins State Historic Park are in the foothills northeast of the metro area and are reached via scenic CA 49. It takes a bit longer to reach these sites, but CA 49 is a gorgeous drive.

15 Bobelaine Audubon Sanctuary

Rustic paths lead through a wildlife sanctuary on the banks of the Feather River, where you'll share the trail with foxes, deer, and an Audubon guidebook of birds.

Start: Signed trailhead in the small sanctuary parking lot

Distance: 4.6-mile double loop

Hiking time: About 3 hours

Difficulty: Moderate due to trail length and route-finding challenges

Trail surface: Mowed trails, dirt pathways

Best season: Winter, spring, and fall for birding; spring for wildflowers; fall for color

Other trail users: Hikers only

Amenities: Small parking area, information kiosk

Canine compatibility: Dogs not permitted

Fees and permits: None

Schedule: Open daily, sunrise to sunset, year-round

Maps: USGS Nicolaus CA; Bobelaine Audubon Sanctuary map available online at www.sacramentoaudubon.org/bobelaine sanctuary.html

Trail contact: Sacramento Audubon Society, PO Box 160694, Sacramento 95816-0694; www.sacramentoaudubon.org

Other: Bring drinking water. Groups of 10 or more are asked to contact the Sacramento Audubon Society before hitting the trail.

Special considerations: Remain on trails to avoid contact with poison oak and to protect fragile wildlife habitat.

Finding the trailhead: From downtown Sacramento, take I-5 north to the CA 70/99 junction. Go right (north) on CA 70/99 for 19.3 miles toward Marysville and Yuba City, staying left on CA 99 where it diverges from CA 70. Pass over the Feather River bridge and continue to Laurel Avenue. Turn right (east) on Laurel Avenue and drive 0.9 mile (the last 0.1 mile is unpaved) to the trailhead parking area. **GPS:** N38 55.852' / W121 35.441'

The Hike

Bobelaine Audubon Sanctuary encompasses a linear strip of riparian habitat and oak woodland on the western banks of the Feather River. About 2.5 miles in length, a third of a mile wide, and totaling 430 acres, the ecological preserve is small; but with frontage on the river and a wildlife population of amazing variety, it packs a scenic wallop.

Since this is an Audubon Society site and located on the Pacific Flyway, you should expect to see a huge number of both resident and migratory birds—shorebirds, songbirds, and waterbirds, as well as raptors. And, given its location amid the cultivated farm fields north of the Sacramento metro area, the wilderness atmosphere of the place is unexpected and appealing.

The Feather River runs broad and unfettered along the boundary of the sanctuary, weaving through sandbars and deposits of river rock when not in flood, skimmed by bleached-white great egrets and clusters of diving ducks. The bigleaf maples and sycamore trees of the riparian zone sport leaves of prehistoric size, large enough to wear as a mask. Fields of sinuous tule crowd sections of the route and erupt from the trail beds themselves, a bounty that would have kept local Native Americans well stocked with basket-weaving materials.

You'll share the trail with birders carrying binoculars and scopes. Whether you're an enthusiast or not, you'll be hard-pressed not to be charmed by the kinglets, purple finches, and California towhees that jitterbug through the brush; the green herons that hunker on the riverbanks and on bare tree limbs; and the hawks riding thermals overhead. Deer and squirrels scurry through the scrub, and on hot days lizards practice push-ups on the paths.

Most of the trail intersections in the sanctuary are marked with signs, but some are not. Coupled with intertwining social trails—stay on the main routes to avoid damaging the ecology and coming into contact with poison oak—the sparse signage can render route-finding a challenge. To stay on track, keep this guide handy, print a trail map off the website, or snap a picture with your phone of the map on the information board at the trailhead to reference on the route. Keep the river to the east and stay on the clear, mowed tracks—you may stray from your planned route, but you won't get lost.

The tour describes a double loop circling counterclockwise around the sanctuary, incorporating sections of the Oak, Grassland, North, and Center Trails. Begin by climb-

The trail leading into Bobelaine Audubon Sanctuary is framed by oaks and a levee.

CITIZEN SCIENTISTS FOR THE BIRDS

Birds are bellwethers of a healthy environment. Whether by climate change, the use of pesticides, or the transformation of a wetland into a shopping mall, the decline of avian populations is a harbinger that environmental and habitat degradation may be far-reaching, affecting the health and well-being of other species, including those on the top tier, like humans.

Tracking bird populations through time in annual bird counts is key to determining whether populations are flourishing or diminishing and, by extension, whether the environments they rely on are healthy. Citizen scientists are crucial to gathering data during bird counts. You don't need to be a birder to help out. Minimum requirements are the ability to count and the willingness to stay outdoors for the better part of a day.

A pair of annual bird counts—the Christmas Bird Count and the Great Backyard Bird Count—offer hikers and others the chance to be citizen scientists and to help ensure that the environment remains healthy for those on the wing as well as those on foot. Learn more about the Christmas Bird Count at http://birds.audubon.org/christmas-bird-count. More information about the Great Backyard Bird Count is available at http://gbbc.birdcount.org.

ing over the levee, which offers views down onto an orchard on the right (west) and the undeveloped sanctuary, a tangle of wild grape, willow, and oak, on the left (east). A parallel trail runs along the foot of the levee; slide down onto this and head right. As you near the 0.5-mile mark, pick up the trail that leads into the sanctuary at a signed gate.

Meet the South Trail just inside the sanctuary; the trail passes through a gully and meadow before reaching the intersection with the Oak and Center Trails. Follow the Oak Trail through the woodland, then branch off onto the Center Trail. The bigleaf maples along this track sport preternaturally large leaves, and a broad meadow opens to the right (east).

As you near the 2-mile mark, take the side path that branches right toward the Feather River. The trail stretches across a meadow to a bluff overlooking the waterway, which runs brown and furious when flush with runoff and, in late season, is broad, funneled into channels, and curdled with current. When you have taken in the views, retrace your steps to the main trail and turn right to meet the Grassland Trail.

The Grassland track narrows as it passes through stands of tule then curves away from the river through a thicket of encroaching coyote bush. Meet up with the North Trail, which you'll follow to the Otter Trail, which leads back to the Center Trail, which in turn leads back to the levee.

Climb onto the levee and follow the trail back toward the trailhead, enjoying great views across farmlands on the right (west) and placid Lake Crandall on the left (east). The Levee Trail leads back to the parking area and trailhead.

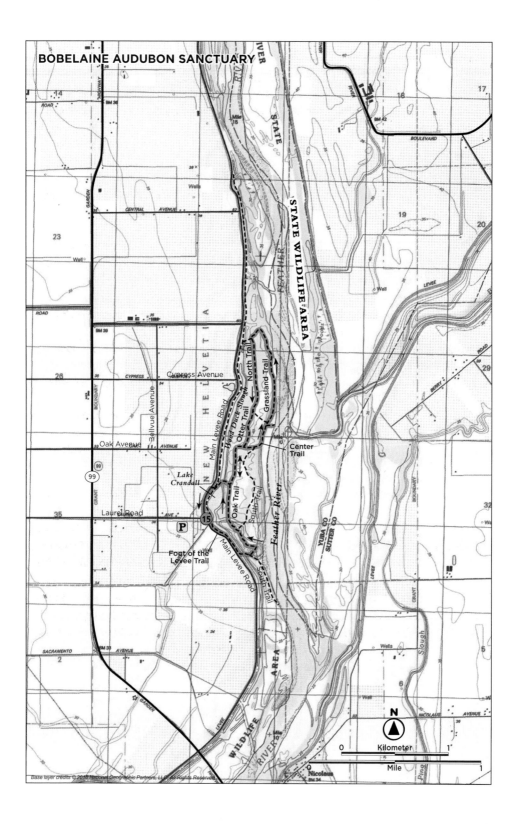

BOBELAINE AUDUBON SANCTUARY

Miles and Directions

0.0 Start by climbing onto the levee and heading right (south).

0.4 Reach a junction with a trail that drops off the levee and a singletrack trail that breaks left (east) into the preserve proper. Go left (east), around a gate, then right (south) on a singletrack trail.

0.5 At the trail intersection, go left (east) on the South Trail. Ignore side trails that wander into the brush.

0.9 Reach the intersection with the Oak Trail. Go left (north) on the Oak Trail.

1.4 Arrive at the junction of the Oak and Center Trails. Stay straight (northeast) on the Center Trail.

1.6 At the unmarked trail junction, stay right (east) on the Center Trail.

1.9 Take the side trail that branches right (east) to the riverside. Check out the river, then return to the main trail and turn right (north).

2.2 Meet the Grassland Trail. Go right on the Grassland Trail.

2.7 The Grassland Trail curves away from the river.

2.9 Reach the junction with the North Trail. Go left (south) on the first trail (the second trail is in a large clearing and leads to the Foot of the Levee Trail).

3.6 Arrive at the junction with the Otter Trail. Go right (southwest) on the singletrack Otter Trail.

4.0 Arrive at the junction of the Otter Trail and the Center Trail. Go right (south) on the wide Center Trail.

4.2 At the trail intersection stay right (west) on the Center Trail. The levee rises ahead.

4.3 Pass the gate and climb onto the levee. Turn left (south), heading back toward the trailhead. A parallel trail runs along the foot of the levee, but the high road offers better views.

4.6 Drop off the levee to the trailhead and parking area.

Hike Information

Local information: Yuba–Sutter Chamber of Commerce, 519 D Street, Marysville 95901; (530) 743-6501; www.yubasutterchamber.com. Find information about the Yuba City / Marysville area and local events through the chamber.

Hike tours: The Sacramento Audubon Society offers periodic tours of the Bobelaine sanctuary and other birding sites in the Sacramento Valley and beyond. Check out www.sacramentoaudubon.org for more information and a schedule of field trips.

16 Shingle Falls

Ramble through rolling woodlands in the foothills east of Marysville to a vigorous waterfall in a small gorge on Dry Creek. A swimming hole and sunny rocks below the falls are perfect for a swim and sunbathing on a hot summer's day.

Start: Gated bridge at the end of Spenceville Road

Distance: 5.2-mile lollipop (including exploration of trails around falls)

Hiking time: 2–3 hours

Difficulty: Moderate

Trail surface: Well-maintained gravel road, dirt singletrack

Best season: Spring for wildflowers; summer and early fall for swimming

Other trail users: Equestrians; hunters in season

Amenities: Parking

Canine compatibility: Leashed dogs permitted

Fees and permits: None

Schedule: Open daily, sunrise to sunset, year-round

Maps: USGS Camp Far West CA and Wolf CA; online at www.dfg.ca.gov/lands/wa/region2/spenceville.html

Trail contact: Oroville/Spenceville Wildlife Area, California Department of Fish and Game, 945 Oro Dam Blvd. West, Oroville 95965; (530) 538-2236; www.wildlife.ca.gov/Lands/Places-to-Visit/Spenceville-WA#1179590-recreation

Special considerations: Hunting is allowed in the Spenceville Wildlife Area from Sept 1 to Jan 31. If hiking in hunting season, be sure to wear bright colors, such as blaze orange. Check with the fish and game department about hunting seasons for wild turkey, generally from late Mar to early May, and other game; it might be best to avoid the area in the opening days of any hunting season.

Finding the trailhead: From Sacramento, head north on I-5 to CA 99. Continue north on CA 99 for about 12 miles to CA 70. Make a slight right onto northbound CA 70 toward Marysville. Travel another 22 miles to the Feather River Road exit. Go right (east) on Feather River Road to the first intersection, then right again onto North Beale Road. Travel 0.2 mile to a signalized arterial, and go left to continue on North Beale Road. Go another 0.8 mile on North Beale to Hammonton-Smartville Road. Go left onto Hammonton-Smartville Road, staying right at the signalized Y intersection with Simpson Lane, which leads to downtown Marysville. Drive for about 15 miles to the intersection with Chuck Yeager Road. Go right on Chuck Yeager Road for about 4 miles to Waldo Road. Go left on Waldo Road, a graded dirt road, for nearly 2 miles, across the single-lane bridge, to Waldo Junction and the signed intersection with Spenceville Road. Go left on Spenceville Road, traveling about 2.3 miles to the parking area on the left, past the camping area and near the road's end. The trailhead is at the yellow gate at the old stone bridge; a small sign identifies the Fairy Falls Trail. **GPS:** N39 06.824' / W121 16.245'

The Hike

They are Shingle Falls according to the US Geological Survey, Fairy Falls on trail signs, and Beale Falls in some printed and online guides. Being "also known as" may create some confusion, but no matter what you call it, this waterfall is a stunning destination.

No worries about confusion getting to the falls, which are reached via well-maintained wildlife area service roads, perfect in width and grade for family outings, with the option of taking an engaging singletrack for the last mile. A web of social trails leads from the access road to the top of the falls—and to the creek below the spill, where a swimming hole awaits. These smaller trails are steep and the footing can be rocky, but standing at the overlook and watching the whitewater dive into the inkwell is ample reward for the effort.

The trail begins at the site of the Spenceville mine. For more than fifty years, copper and other mineral resources were removed from the site. After the mine became part of the Spenceville Wildlife Area, the California Department of Fish and Game (DFG) and the California Department of Conservation (DOC) worked to reclaim the land so that its residual toxicity would not pose significant danger to the fish populations in Dry Creek—or threaten the well-being of other critters in the area, including humans. The result is what you see today: essentially nothing except

Shingle Falls tumbles into an inkwell.

the stone bridges that aid stream crossings at the trailhead, a chain-link fence, and low-key signage that indicates the area is closed. The mitigation was so successful that the DOC earned the Governor's Environmental and Economic Leadership Award for its work.

As with other wildlife areas under the purview of the DFG, hunting and fishing are permitted in the area, as is grazing. The terrain is ideal for both. Rolling hills support a healthy blue oak–gray pine woodland, home to deer, wild turkeys, and other game. Open meadows provide forage for cattle. The grasslands are often cropped close, but where they aren't (and even after they've been grazed), wildflowers bloom in profusion. Encompassing almost 12,000 acres, there is plenty of space for all users to enjoy the wildlife area without bumping into one another.

The trail begins by crossing the stone bridge over Dry Creek, then heads right at the fence line on the dirt roadway, crossing two smaller bridges over side streams.

Follow the road up into the hills. A couple of prominent side trails diverge from the main trail in the first 0.5 mile—the first heading north through a gate, the second dropping south from the roadway into the creek drainage. Stay on the dirt roadway at both. Beyond, the route is straightforward and marked with signs for Fairy Falls; there is no chance of straying.

After a long, gentle climb, with scattered oaks offering scanty shade on hot summer days, the trail hooks sharply right at a white gate. Pass a second white gate,

A scenic stretch of trail leads through remote pastureland on the way to Shingle Falls.

then climb through a sloping meadowland, with views stretching down into the Dry Creek drainage and north across more rolling pastureland.

A cattleguard spans the road at the hilltop. You have a choice here: Follow either the trail to the right or the road to the left. Both meet within sight at the edge of the woods. At the second signed trail junction, you again have a choice. The described route heads up on singletrack into the oaks and returns via the roadway to the right. The road may be signed Upper Falls and the trail Fairy Falls, but the falls are one and the same. Take the trail, climbing into the woodland.

The singletrack is mildly challenging, with occasional downed trees forcing hikers to skirt the obstacles. It dips through several drainages, then traverses a grassy hillside before hitching up with the dirt roadway. Go left on the road, walking alongside Dry Creek in its rock-bottomed bed. A riparian corridor shades the waterway, thick with brambles, poison oak, and maples that fire yellow and orange in late fall.

After passing a streamside clearing, the roadway hitches uphill. A use trail breaks right just before a gate, down to a large swimming hole fed by two short falls, each no higher than 3 feet.

A web of use trails climbs the hillside between the swimming hole and the falls themselves. These are steep and winding, with rocky footing, but are easy to follow. The paths merge onto a narrow track running alongside the edge of the Dry Creek gorge, with a 100-foot drop into the steep-walled chasm below the falls. Though a long jump into the chocolate waters of the inkwell may look inviting to an adventurous soul, it's better to approach from below and simply observe from above.

The falls themselves are a stair-step spill and run year-round, though they are fullest in spring, when swollen with snowmelt, or after rainstorms begin in the fall. The second drop is the longest, at least 50 feet and perhaps more. The inkwell gives the impression of bottomlessness, which makes it as mysterious as the falls are invigorating.

Once you've cooled your heels in the swimming hole, return to the roadway and follow it back to the trailhead. Stay on the roadway where the route meets the narrow Fairy Falls path, making a gentle climb to the cattleguard on the hilltop. From there, retrace your steps to the trailhead.

Miles and Directions

0.0   Start by crossing the stone bridge with the yellow gate. On the far side of the bridge, turn right and follow the dirt roadway over two smaller bridges.

0.1   Pass a singletrack trail behind a gate on the left. Stay right on the roadway.

0.5   At the junction, stay left on the roadway. The path to the right drops into a blackberry hedge along a tributary stream.

1.2   At the first white gate, a Fairy Falls trail sign directs you right. Pass a second white gate and head up through the meadowland.

1.5   Reach a cattleguard and go right on the trail. You can also follow the roadway down to the next trail junction.

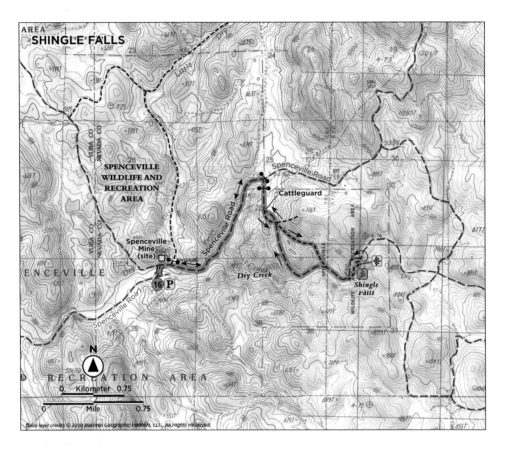

1.7 At the five-way junction, a trail sign indicates that Fairy Falls is 1 mile ahead via a single-track path and Upper Falls is 0.9 mile distant via the roadway. Take the trail.

2.2 The trail ends on the dirt road. Go left on the broad track.

2.4 Take the well-worn use trail that breaks right, toward the creek, just before a twisted open gate. This leads down to the swimming hole.

2.6 Wander up via social trails to the falls overlook. Check out the falls and basin below, then pick up a social trail back to the service road. Retrace your steps to the junction with the Fairy Falls singletrack; stay left on the service road, which winds up to the cattleguard on the hilltop. From here, retrace your steps to the trailhead.

5.2 Arrive back at the trailhead.

Hike Information

Local information: Yuba–Sutter Chamber of Commerce, 519 D Street, Marysville 95901; (530) 743-6501; www.yubasutterchamber.com.

Camping: A rustic campground is about 0.5 mile from the trailhead. Camping is permitted from Sept 1 through the end of the spring turkey-hunting season. Visit www.wildlife.ca.gov/Lands/Places-to-Visit/Spenceville-WA for more information.

17 Gray Lodge Wildlife Area

Thousands of migrating and resident waterfowl forage, rest, and nest in the restored wetlands of Gray Lodge Wildlife Area, on the north side of the Sutter Buttes. These two trails, both featuring observation blinds, wind through a complex of ponds and marshes that offer the birds shelter and sustenance throughout the year.

Start: Wildlife area's parking lot 14
Distance: 2.25-mile loop
Hiking time: 1–2 hours
Difficulty: Easy
Trail surface: Gravel levee roads, wheelchair-accessible paved path
Best season: Spring and fall, during migration seasons
Other trail users: Hikers only
Amenities: Parking, restrooms, information signboard, picnic tables, self-serve fee station
Canine compatibility: Leashed dogs permitted
Fees and permits: Parking fee
Schedule: Open daily, sunrise to sunset, year-round
Maps: USGS Pennington CA; maps and nature trail guides available at information kiosk at trailhead
Trail contact: California Department of Fish and Game, Gray Lodge Wildlife Area,
3207 Rutherford Rd., Gridley 95948; (530) 846-7500; www.wildlife.ca.gov/Lands/Places-to-Visit/Gray-Lodge-WA
Other: In the tiny exhibit room near the entrance to parking lot 14, you'll find fine examples of taxidermy—birds of the marsh great and small, as well as other residents, including beavers, muskrats, and weasels. A 3-mile auto tour route also begins at parking lot 14.
Special considerations: Travel lightly and quietly so you don't startle the wildlife. Additional options are open to hikers during spring and summer; the refuge contains about 70 miles of roadways accessible to hikers and cyclists. Trail closures are subject to the needs of wildlife, which change with the season, food availability, and local conditions. Check online or call for more information about whether longer routes are open at the time of your visit.

Finding the trailhead: From Sacramento, head north on I-5 to CA 99. Go 44 miles north on CA 99 to Live Oak, where a sign for the Gray Lodge Wildlife Area directs you onto Pennington Road. Follow Pennington Road for 8.1 miles to the signed junction with Almond Orchard Road (also Pennington Road) and turn right. Follow Almond Orchard / Pennington Road for 1.6 miles to the signed entrance to the wildlife area on the left. Turn left on Rutherford Road (the park road) and go 2.4 miles to parking lot 14. The trailhead is in the southeast corner of the lot.
GPS: N39 19.400' / W121 50.319'

The Hike

On a sunny day in early November, the marshes of Gray Lodge Wildlife Area clamor. Rafts of ducks paddle on the ponds, too many to count. When they take off, their wings thump the surface, sounding like an old motor turning over. In the reeds the songbirds sing, but they are well camouflaged—ubiquitous little brown birds whose identities may elude the amateur birder. Acres of wetland north of the interpretive trail observation deck are blanketed with hundreds—maybe thousands—of geese, ducks, swans, and cranes, a gray and brown and white patchwork of wings and water.

Walk slowly and silently, and the resting birds won't be disturbed. Many are making a long migration along the Pacific Flyway, some traveling thousands of miles from summer territories in the far north to winter grounds down south. Gray Lodge, with its abundant water and forage, is the perfect way station.

The birds are easily spooked. One group of ducks, sunning on a sandy island amid the reeds, senses danger and takes flight, squawking warnings into the clear blue sky. Those ducks set off another collection of ducks, which sets off another, which sets off the geese, which sets off the cranes . . . and then the air is turbulent with wing beats and cries of alarm—and, quite possibly, scolding. The cacophony takes a while to subside, but eventually it does, the winged ones settling once again on the water and in the brush.

This tour of the wildlife area, which takes in two of its trails, begins on the Flyway Loop Trail. A good gravel levee-top road, bordered by a slough and edged with reeds and sedges, stretches south toward the Sutter Buttes, an island of distinctive peaks

The wide trail heads back toward the ponds, with the Sutter Buttes looming behind.

The quiet waters of Gray Lodge Wildlife Area, sheltered by the rugged Sutter Buttes, are calming for migratory fowl and hikers alike.

stranded in the flats of the Sacramento Valley. Near the 0.5-mile mark, trail signs direct you west, along a second levee road and past the Betty Adamson Observation Hide, a cement-block structure with a bay of windows looking out over the wetlands. Benches and counters inside allow birders to view the wildlife, make notes, and refer to field guides without creating a distraction. The birds remain undisturbed, chirping and quacking and crowing and singing like schoolkids on a playground at lunchtime.

Cross the auto tour road to reach a second blind, this one named for Harry Adamson. The same amenities await, only with a different aspect over a different pond. From the second blind, the levee-top trail continues north to a hub where levees and sloughs meet. Follow the signed Flyway Loop Trail to the east, again bounded by water on both sides, and with great Sutter Buttes views to the right (south).

The Flyway Loop Trail intersects the paved, wheelchair- and stroller-accessible interpretive Wetland Discovery Trail amid towering cottonwoods. Two more informal viewing platforms can be accessed from the interpretive trail. The first is atop a little rise, and the blind consists of reeds that have been woven together. The second is the viewing platform that faces north, open to the birds, where being careful and quiet is paramount.

Returning to parking lot 14 from the last blind, a triad of benches offers one last opportunity to gaze out over a pond before arriving back at the trailhead.

Miles and Directions

0.0 Start on the Flyway Loop Trail, following the gravel levee-top road.

0.4 At the signed junction, go right on the Flyway Loop.

0.75 Arrive at the Betty Adamson Observation Hide. Duck inside to check it out, then continue on the levee-top trail.

0.9 Reach parking lot 18, and cross the auto tour road. The Harry Adamson hide is on the other side, down a side trail to the left. Visit, then continue north on the straight-shot levee road.

1.25 Several levee roads meet at slough gates clustered in a circle. The auto tour route crosses here. Follow the signs around the hub to a levee road signed as the hiking trail, heading northeast. About 20 steps beyond, go right again.

1.6 Meet the paved Wetland Discovery interpretive trail near post 7. Go left.

1.7 Take a short unpaved detour to the Cowan Mound viewing blind, reached via a short flight of stairs. The unpaved trail loops back to the paved route.

Ducks take flight from a pond in Gray Lodge Wildlife Area, with the Sutter Buttes forming a smoky backdrop.

1.9 Go left onto the short trail that leads to the viewing platform. Check out the show, then return to the Wetland Discovery Trail and go left. The trail is now dirt.

2.0 Meet a levee road and go right.

2.1 Rejoin the paved trail. Go left, back toward the trailhead parking area.

2.25 Pass benches overlooking a last pond, then arrive back at the trailhead.

Hike Information

Local information: Yuba-Sutter Chamber of Commerce, 519 D Street, Marysville 95901; (530) 743-6501; www.yubasutterchamber.com.

Local events/attractions: The Sutter Buttes, those tempting mountains just south of the Gray Lodge Wildlife Area, can only be explored as part of guided hikes offered by the Middle Mountain Interpretive Hikes. Call (530) 671-6116 or visit www.middlemountainhikes.org for more information.

Hike tours: Guided tours are offered on weekends throughout the year. No reservations are necessary. Rain cancels. Contact the Gray Lodge Wildlife Area's naturalist office at (530) 846-7505 or visit www.wildlife.ca.gov/Lands/Places-to-Visit/Gray-Lodge-WA for more information.

18 Hidden Falls Regional Park

Waterfalls and cataracts on two streams that run through Hidden Falls Regional Park are the focal points of this loop hike. Hidden Falls drops 75 feet or so over stair-step cliffs, with an overlook platform offering easy access to the view. Just upstream, another overlook provides views of the falls and swimming holes on Coon Creek. The Seven Pools can be seen from a high rock outcrop, water spilling from basin to basin within a rock–walled hollow.

Start: Signed Poppy Trail to the right (east) of the restrooms
Distance: 5.4-mile loop
Hiking time: 3–4 hours
Difficulty: Moderate due to stiff climbs out of Deadman Canyon
Trail surface: Dirt singletrack, gravel roadway
Best season: Spring, when wildflowers are in bloom, water flows in the falls, and cataracts are full
Other trail users: Equestrians, mountain bikers
Amenities: Restrooms, trash cans, picnic sites, information signboards with park maps
Canine compatibility: Leashed dogs permitted
Fees and permits: The park has initiated a reservation-only fee parking system for peak times (weekends, holidays, and some Fridays during spring, early summer, and fall). Visitors must obtain reservations before arriving at the park via an online calendar linked to the park's website.
Schedule: Open daily, sunrise to half-hour after sunset, year-round

Maps: USGS Gold Hill CA; online at www .placer.ca.gov/departments/facility/parks/ parks-content/parks/hidden-falls
Trail contact: Placer County Facilities Services, 11476 C Ave., Auburn 95603; (530) 886-4901; www.placer.ca.gov/ departments/facility/parks/parks-content/ parks/hidden-falls
Other: The Hidden Gate Trail offers a short, paved, wheelchair-accessible option to Hidden Falls park visitors. Expanding recreational opportunities at the park are in the works, including the addition of another 30 miles of trail within the 1,200-acre property and linkages to other open-space parcels.
Special considerations: This park is extremely popular with all trail users. All trail traffic yields to equestrians; step to the downhill side of the trail to allow horses to pass. Swimming holes in the park are popular destinations on hot summer days, but avoid hiking when temperatures soar—climbing out of the creek drainages can be brutal in the heat.

Finding the trailhead: From Sacramento, head east on I-80 for about 25 miles to the exit for CA 49 to Grass Valley and Placerville in Auburn. Go north on CA 49 toward Grass Valley. Drive 2.5 miles to the junction with Atwood Road and turn left onto Atwood. Follow Atwood Road for about 1.7 miles to where it becomes Mount Vernon Road, then follow Mount Vernon Road another 0.5 mile (2.2 miles total) to a T junction with Joeger Road. Go left, continuing on Mount Vernon Road for another 2 miles to the intersection with Mears Road on the right. Turn right on Mears Road and drive 0.5 mile to Mears Place. Turn right on Mears Place and go 0.2 mile to the signed park entrance. The park address is 7587 Mears Place, Auburn. If no parking is available at the time of your visit (reservations required during peak times), plan to return another time. No parking is permitted along the access roads. **GPS:** N38 57.516' / W121 09.830'

The Hike

Hidden Falls, flush with spring runoff, spills through Deadman Canyon with enough force and noise to wake the ravine's namesake. Up the trail and around the bend, Coon Creek tumbles over two-tiered Canyon View Falls, and then runs under the gentle arc of a pedestrian bridge before reaching its confluence with Deadman Creek. A pair of overlook platforms affords visitors the perfect viewpoints from which to enjoy the waterfalls, which remain vigorous year-round. The platforms also act as social gathering places along a loop through this popular regional park where families can settle down with a picnic, dog walkers can allow their furred friends to meet, and hikers can share tales of the trail with their comrades.

Farther upstream on Coon Creek are the reclusive Seven Pools. It would take a feat of bushwhacking down a steep slope through tick- and snake-infested brush to reach them from the rocky overlook on the Seven Pools Vista Trail; better to watch the waterway spill through its steep-walled canyon and overflow basin after basin in short bursts of whitewater from yet another overlook along the route.

The trails that link these highlights cruise through the stream canyons via slopes shaded by a variety of oaks, the occasional digger pine, bay laurel, and manzanita, with bracken fern, blackberry, toyon, poison oak, and wildflowers enlivening the understory.

The loop begins by dropping away from the parking area on the Poppy Trail, a well-maintained path broad enough to allow hikers—or horses—traveling in opposite directions to pass without having to step off the track. The trail drops into Deadman Canyon via a few switchbacks, then runs creekside down to a convergence of trails at a bridge spanning the waterway.

From the bridge, pick up the trail to the Hidden Falls overlook, which traces the creek downstream. Stay right where a social path leads down to the creek, though on a hot day, the shady stream presents a nice rest stop.

Canyon View Falls spills from one pool to another on Coon Creek.

Views of the creek below, flowing through rock-lined pools that form perfect swimming holes, open as the trail switchbacks. Pass a stone staircase on the right that leads down to the swimming holes before reaching the wooden deck overlooking Hidden Falls. The deck offers a great vantage of the stepped spill, which is most spectacular (and loudest) in spring, when the creek is flush with meltwater from the Sierra.

From the platform you can retrace your steps to the trailhead for an easy 3-mile out-and-back hike. But the rest of the park awaits, including two more cascades. To reach Canyon View Falls, retrace your steps to the overlook junction and go left, following the singletrack to the scenic Canyon View Bridge, which spans Coon Creek above its confluence with Deadman Creek. On the other side of the bridge, climb

SNAKEBIT

In the years I've spent wandering in the woods, I've startled and retreated from black bears, hopscotched around tarantulas and newts, won (and lost) stare-downs with coyotes and raccoons, nearly been bowled over by deer erupting from the brush, and frozen mid-step as bobcats and foxes have scurried down or across the trail. The only time I've seen a mountain lion was from the safety of my car, and, the hiking gods permitting, that's as close as I ever want to get.

But close encounters with snakes? Well, that's a different story.

I've been snakebit. Not by a rattlesnake, thankfully. This was a gopher snake, and it was on a little path that led from a paved trail alongside a creek to a soccer complex in the middle of suburbia. My dog stepped over the snake, and startled it. My husband stepped over the snake, and pissed it off. I stepped over the snake, and it sunk its little fangs into my shin.

I launched skyward, kicking and flailing, launching the snake outward into the brush. My husband pursued the poor terrorized creature, quickly determining it was not a rattler.

the short but steep access trail to the covered viewing platform, where you can look down on two-tiered Canyon View Falls and the swimming hole above.

To reach the Seven Pools viewpoint, retrace your steps across the bridge and head uphill on North Legacy Way, a gravel road, toward the crest of the ridge. As you near the high point, go left to pick up the Quail Run Trail, which meets up with the Seven Pools Loop. The loop, in turn, drops around switchbacks into the Coon Creek canyon, passing through thickets of manzanita, poison oak, and scrub oak along the way. Continue parallel to the stream for a distance, passing a junction with the Pond Turtle Trail (an option back to the trailhead), then climb away from the waterway. As you ascend, the trail is bordered by toyon, with its bright red fruits glowing in the autumn sunlight. Below, the creek tightens into cataracts.

But not quite quickly enough, because in the meantime I stood, also terrorized, waiting for the venom to start coursing through my veins. Nothing happened of course. Nothing, that is, except that I now see snakes wherever I go.

Which is not a bad thing. It's good to be aware of the creatures you share the trail with, whether they are big enough to make an obvious ruckus, like a bear or a deer, or camouflaged in the brush at your feet. Rattlesnakes, king snakes, gopher snakes, and garter snakes—as well as fence lizards and alligator lizards, newts, and a plethora of insects and butterflies—creep and crawl through the oak woodlands and grasslands surrounding Sacramento, integral components of a complex ecosystem. They may startle you when you come upon them suddenly, but they are enlivening and, if you can calm what might be an instinctive fear, beautiful and fascinating to observe.

We are taught, and perhaps hard-wired, to fear and defend ourselves from perceived threats posed by bears, snakes, big cats, big dogs like coyotes and wolves—even spiders. But unless we threaten them, or behave inappropriately when we encounter them, they really don't want to mess with us. We are not on the regular menu. Watch and be watched; live and let live.

Hiking down into the Coon Creek drainage in Hidden Falls Regional Park on a cool November afternoon, I saw the rattlesnake before it saw me. It had just poked its distinctive triangle-shaped head out of the grass alongside the trail. I stopped . . . and, no, I did not start screaming and flailing, or reach for a weapon. I observed from a safe distance, even took a picture. I didn't bother it, and it didn't bother me. It wasn't until some equestrians came down the track that the reptile slithered into the shelter of the grass. We continued on our separate ways, mutually respectful and, I assume, mutually hopeful that our paths wouldn't cross again.

Hidden Falls is sapped by the summer sun, but when it's on, it's a spectacular whitewater tumble of about 30 feet.

When you arrive at the next trail junction, take the Seven Pools Vista Trail. This leads up to a rock outcrop that offers a bird's-eye view of the Seven Pools, spilling through the rocky, brush-choked canyon. The pools are all but inaccessible, with nary even a social trail ferreting down through the tangle of brush and rocks.

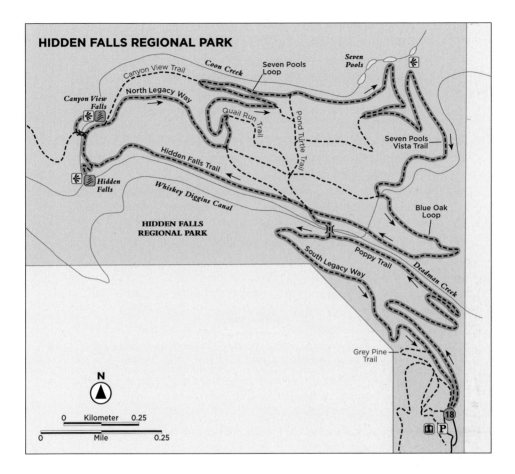

HIDDEN FALLS REGIONAL PARK

From the overlook the vista trail climbs back onto the ridge separating the Deadman and Coon Creek drainages. Pick up the Blue Oak Loop on the other side of North Legacy Way, and descend via sweeping traverses and a switchback into Deadman Canyon. The Blue Oak Loop ends at the bridge and the junction with the Poppy Trail, South Legacy Way, and Hidden Falls Trail. Climb back to the trailhead via South Legacy Way—a gravel road wide enough for horses to travel side by side and still leave plenty of room for a hiker to pass. Look for bracken fern and wild grape on the hillside above and below the roadway as you climb, giving way to grassland above.

Miles and Directions

0.0   Start by passing the restrooms and information signs. Where South Legacy Way, the paved Hidden Gate Trail, and the singletrack Poppy Trail meet, take the Poppy Trail to the right.

0.1   At the trail junction, stay right on the Poppy Trail.

0.6   After the third switchback, the trail follows Deadman Creek downstream.

0.8 The Poppy Trail ends at the bridge, where it meets South Legacy Way. Cross the bridge to the trail junction on the other side, and go left on the signed trail to the Hidden Falls overlook.

1.3 Reach the junction with the hikers-only trail down to the falls. Stay left on the path, keeping right where a social trail breaks left toward swimming holes in the creek.

1.5 Arrive at the observation deck overlooking Hidden Falls. Enjoy the views and visit the swimming holes, then retrace your steps to the junction. Go left to continue to the Canyon View Falls overlook.

1.8 Cross the Canyon View Bridge, then climb the side trail to the overlook of the falls. When you've taken it all in, cross back over the bridge and pick up North Legacy Way, turning left and climbing toward the ridgetop.

1.9 Pass the junction with the Canyon View Trail, remaining on North Legacy Way. A bit higher, you'll pass the junction with the Bobcat Trail, again remaining on the broad track.

2.3 Go left on the singletrack Blue Oak Loop.

2.4 Arrive at the junction with the Quail Run Trail. Go left on Quail Run, which arcs into the woods.

2.6 At the junction, go left on the Seven Pools Loop.

3.1 At the junction with the Pond Turtle Trail, stay straight on the Seven Pools Loop.

3.3 Round a switchback, then cross a little bridge over a seasonal stream.

3.5 At the signed trail intersection, go left on the Seven Pools Vista Trail.

3.7 Arrive at the rock outcrop that serves as the Seven Pools overlook. Check out the views, then continue up the Seven Pools Vista Trail.

4.0 The Seven Pools Vista Trail ends on North Legacy Way. Cross the gravel road to the Blue Oak Loop, and descend via Blue Oak into Deadman Canyon.

4.3 A small bridge spans a seasonal stream.

4.6 Reach the bridge and junction with the falls overlook trail. Go left, across the bridge, then right on South Legacy Way.

5.4 Arrive back at the trailhead.

Hike Information

Local information: City of Auburn, 1225 Lincoln Way, Auburn 95603; (530) 823-4211; www.auburn.ca.gov. The city site offers information for residents as well as visitors. Further information about Auburn and its environs can be found at the Auburn Visitor Center and through the Old Town Auburn Business Association. Call (530) 451-6822 or visit https://oldtownauburnca.com.

Local events/attractions: Both the Western States 100-Mile Endurance Run and the Western States Endurance Ride/Tevis Cup (an equestrian event) are staged in the foothills surrounding Auburn each year. For more information on the run, visit www.wser.org. For information about the ride, go to www.teviscup.org.

Restaurants: Awful Annie's Restaurant, 13460 Lincoln Way, Auburn; (530) 888-9857; www.awfulannies.com. Offering some of the best breakfast scrambles in the region, Awful Annie's is also known for its delicious sandwiches—scrumptious meals between two slices of bread.

19 Empire Mine State Historic Park

Beneath your feet, 367 miles of carefully constructed tunnels wind through the ore beds of the Empire Mine. Aboveground, Empire Mine State Historic Park maintains a much smaller system of trails that, instead of burrowing through rock, wind through a mature mixed evergreen forest and remnants of California's gold rush legacy.

Start: Signed trailhead at the south end of parking lot
Distance: 3.9-mile double loop
Hiking time: 2–3 hours
Difficulty: Moderate due to some hill climbing
Trail surface: Dirt and gravel paths, dirt roadway
Best season: Spring and fall
Other trail users: Mountain bikers, equestrians
Amenities: Picnic facilities, restrooms, visitor center
Canine compatibility: Leashed dogs permitted
Fees and permits: An entrance fee is charged, and additional fees may be levied for living history and other tours.
Schedule: Trails and visitor center are open daily, 10 a.m. to 5 p.m., year-round; closed Christmas, New Year's Day, and Thanksgiving.

The gift shop is operated by Empire Mine Association volunteers; hours vary.
Maps: USGS Grass Valley CA; online at www.parks.ca.gov/?page_id=499 (click on park brochure); available for a small fee at gift shop in visitor center
Trail contact: Empire Mine State Historic Park, 10791 E. Empire St., Grass Valley 95945; (530) 273-8522; www.parks.ca.gov/?page_id=499. Empire Mine Park Association; www.empiremine.org.
Other: The small museum inside the visitor center includes a scale model of the Empire Mine and adjacent mines, as well as collections of mining paraphernalia and precious and semiprecious stones and metals. An interpretive guide and map, which identifies sites along the Hardrock Trail, is available for purchase.

Finding the trailhead: From Sacramento, head east on I-80 for about 24 miles to the exit for CA 49 (Placerville / Grass Valley) in Auburn. Go left (north) on CA 49 for 22 miles to the Empire Street exit. Follow Empire Street right for 1.3 miles (it becomes East Empire Street) to the park entrance and parking lot on the right. **GPS:** N39 12.423' / W121 02.737'

The Hike

To get an idea of the amazing catacomb that exists under your feet when you hike at Empire Mine State Historic Park, the displays in the park's visitor center are a must-see, especially the scale model of the mine's guts, which will blow your mind. The woodland above doesn't hint at the complex man-made maze below, but knowing that a labyrinth weaves through the depths is a provocative enhancement to a walk in this park.

The main attraction in Empire Mine State Historic Park is the estate of the Bourn family, which made its fortune with the Empire. William Bourn Sr. arrived in San Francisco seeking riches, like the rest of the forty-niners, and got lucky (unlike the bulk of his confederates) when he acquired what would turn out to be, literally and figuratively, a gold mine. He also prospered from his interests in the Comstock Lode, which spurred a silver boom on the other side of the Sierra in Nevada.

His son, William Bourn Jr., took charge of the Empire Mine in 1878 and further advanced the family fortune. But the younger Bourn had other business callings, including serving as president of the San Francisco Gas Company (predecessor to today's Pacific Gas & Electric Company, primary provider to much of Northern California). Bourn Jr. was also fond of grand housing. His Empire Cottage is hardly a cottage (a tour is well worth the price of admission); Greystone, his home in St. Helena, is a Wine Country showcase; and his residence outside San Francisco, Filoli (a National Trust for Historic Preservation site available for touring), boasts a ballroom where more than 200 ounces of gold leaf from the Empire Mine was used as decoration.

In addition to the Bourn home and surrounding grounds, Empire Mine State Historic Park encompasses almost 800 acres of prime foothills real estate, with a

Tailings piles slope trailside.

EMPIRE BUILDING (IN BRIEF)

It all started in 1850, when enterprising gold seekers sank "coyote holes"—20 to 40 feet deep—to extract the riches promised by the discovery of gold-bearing quartz in present-day Grass Valley. More than a century later, the deepest point in the Empire Mine complex was 11,000 feet belowground. In this part of gold country, men went as deep as the Sierra Nevada are high.

In the end the underground workings of the Empire and its forty-eight companion mines encompassed 5 square miles and more than 360 miles of shaft. In addition to the maze of shafts and tunnels, a dam was constructed to prevent water from the neighboring Bullion Mine from flowing into the Empire. Instead the water backed up into the Bullion and eventually forced its closure.

Though travel in the mine would later be improved by rail and motor, at first men and muck moved up and down the shaft in buckets. Cornishmen, called "the world's best hard rock miners," were employed at the Empire and its sister operations, starting as young as age seven, according to displays in the Empire Mine State Historic Park museum.

The mine complex encompassed all aspects of ore processing, from blasting it out of the ground to crushing it and running it through the stamp mill, where it was washed with water and quicksilver (mercury). The quicksilver bonded to the gold and made it sink into sand, where it could be more easily extracted. Cyanide was also used in the refining process, hence the toxicity of the mine's waste products. Retort was the last step, where the mercury was removed and the gold "sponge" that remained melted into ingots.

The production record of the Bourn family's Empire Mine is astounding: About 5.6 million ounces of gold were extracted from the earth over the one-hundred-year life of the mine. At the time it closed, when an ounce of gold was worth $35, the value was $196 million; in 2018, with the price of gold at about $1,300 per ounce, the value is more than $7.2 billion.

The mine ceased operation in 1956, and the shafts and tunnels are now filled with water.

trail system exploring the mixed coniferous and oak woodlands. This double loop explores the Hardrock and Osborn Hill areas. If you'd like to see more, check out the trails on Union Hill.

A word about route-finding: Mining is a necessary but toxic business, and some of the terrain covered by this hike bears evidence of this toxicity. If a section of trail is posted for mitigation, please take the recommended detours.

Begin on the east edge of the parking lot adjacent to the mining yard, with its rusting, picturesque equipment protected behind a stone wall. The trail heads south and splits almost immediately. Head right, toward Penn Gate, on the service road, passing the A-frame and following the gravel road down into the woods. The left fork leads to Union Hill.

Enveloped almost immediately in the scent of the surrounding pines, the trail also promptly immerses you in mine remnants. Rusting remains from the Orleans Mine and stamp mill, which competed with the Empire Mine until the Empire absorbed it, litter the forest floor—coils of cable and piles of metal scrap. Signs indicate points of interest and also the route to Wolf Creek and Osborn Hill beyond.

> Wallace Stegner's Pulitzer Prize–winning novel, *Angle of Repose*, describes the lives of several generations of a mining family. A fabulous read, the book takes you to the mines of New Almaden in San Jose, as well as to mines in Leadville, Colorado; Michoacán, Mexico; and rural Idaho. Stegner's protagonist, Lyman Ward, speaks to the reader from the mining town of Grass Valley, site of the Empire.

Wolf Creek is a placid little stream flowing through a deep green woodland. The trees are mixed, with broad-leafed species of oak and maple adding depth and color. This is a great spot to reconnoiter. If you want a really short hike, retrace your steps to the trailhead. A longer loop keeps you on the Hardrock Trail, which heads out toward Penn Gate. The longest option, described here, takes in Osborn Hill before heading out to Penn Gate and then back to the trailhead.

Heading up the Osborn Hill Loop Trail, described traveling clockwise, you pass a couple of intersections with paths to the Prescott Hill Mine Trail, which break off to the left. The Prescott Hill Mine site itself is just off the Osborn trail; its tailings piles are mounded to the left. The legacy of those tailings was in evidence at the junction just beyond the Prescott Hill Mine, where in 2011 signs warned hikers out of an area contaminated with arsenic, lead, and manganese.

Continue the gentle climb to the power line, where trails collide in the clearing. Take the middle track, which continues up into the woods. The trail to the left leads out to Osborn Hill Road; road noise spills into the woods along this stretch. Hiking uphill, a couple of left turns lead to a switchback with a fenced-off mine adit tucked in the crook of its elbow. A bit more climbing leads to the top of the hill; go left to visit the modern remnants of the Conlon Mine, near the park's boundary alongside Osborn Hill Road.

From the Conlon Mine site, head downhill on the Osborn Hill Loop Trail, which begins by running along the highline of Osborn Hill, and passes a scenic overlook framed in manzanita. Drop to the power line, then continue through the woods to close the loop at the junction above Wolf Creek. Back in the hollow, go left on the Hardrock Trail toward Penn Gate, following a broad trail/roadway shaded by overarching stands of bigleaf maple. This is a lovely stretch, with blackberry, broom, and poison oak (negative qualities aside, a handsome shrub or vine) mingling on the verge and the scent of incense cedar strong in the air.

Walking through the peaceful woods above, you'd never suspect the labyrinth of mining tunnels below.

The Hardrock narrows to singletrack at a trail sign that directs you right. Cross a diversion dam and continue alongside a fence that encloses an area protected to preserve its historic significance and artifacts. The Hardrock ends at the Pennsylvania Mine, a large clearing with several concrete structures along the right side. Penn Gate, with a parking area and information sign, is just beyond.

The Empire Street Trail, which takes you back to the trailhead, begins behind the Pennsylvania Mine structures. The narrow singletrack climbs into the woods, skirts a historic mule corral, and passes a junction with the WYOD Loop Trail before paralleling noisy Empire Street.

The last leg of the trail skirts the Magenta Drain settling ponds, which help mitigate damage from mining activities. Cross a park service road: The path, wedged between the stone fence protecting the Bourn estate grounds and the roadway, leads directly back to the trailhead.

Miles and Directions

0.0 Start at the signed trailhead at the east side of the parking area, heading south. At the Y junction just beyond the gate, stay right, following signs for Penn Gate.

0.1 A trail sign directs you left down a paved road that quickly becomes gravel again.

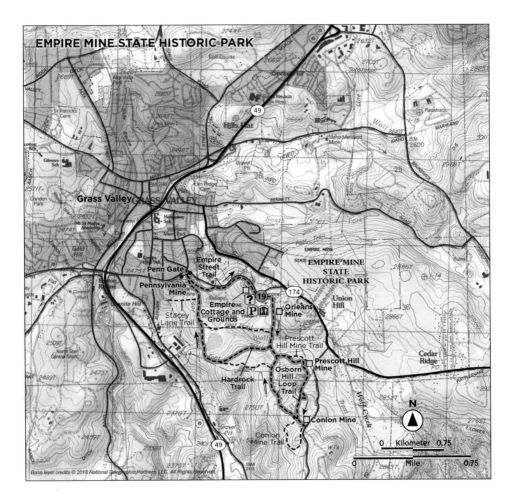

0.3 Pass the Orleans Mine and stamp mill. A series of trail junctions follows. Remain on the signed Hardrock Trail toward Penn Gate, staying left at the first junction, left at the second, and then right to cross Wolf Creek. Once across, head straight (uphill) on the signed Osborn Hill Loop Trail. The start of the Osborn loop is less than 0.1 mile up from the creek; stay left to travel in a clockwise direction.

0.5 Pass the first junction with the Prescott Hill Mine Trail, staying right on the Osborn Hill Loop Trail.

0.7 At the second junction with the Prescott Hill Mine Trail, continue again on the Osborn Hill Loop Trail. The intersection with the Prescott Crosscut Trail is about 30 yards farther; again, remain on the Osborn Hill trail.

0.8 Arrive at the power-line clearing. Continue uphill; the left-hand trail leads out to Osborn Hill Road.

0.9 At the junction, go left onto the dirt roadway. A short distance uphill, stay left again on the gravel path. Switchback around the fenced-off mine adit.

1.0 At the unsigned intersection, stay left.

1.1 Reach the top of Osborn Hill. Go left to visit the Conlon Mine site.

1.2 Arrive at the Conlon Mine site. After exploring, retrace your steps to the previous trail intersection.

1.3 Back at the junction, stay straight and downhill to continue the loop.

1.6 Drop to the second junction with the Prescott Crosscut Trail at the power-line clearing. Continue downhill on the loop trail.

1.8 Where the Osborn Loop Crosscut merges, continue downhill on the Osborn Hill Loop Trail.

1.9 Close the loop and drop to the junction with the Hardrock Trail in the Wolf Creek drainage. Go left on the Hardrock Trail toward Penn Gate.

2.4 Where the Osborn Loop Crosscut merges, remain on the Hardrock Trail. Less than 0.1 mile farther, go right on the signed Hardrock, which narrows to singletrack and crosses a diversion dam.

2.8 The fence surrounding the historic area ends.

2.9 At the junction with the trail to Stacey Lane, stay right on the signed trail to Penn Gate.

3.1 Pass the Pennsylvania Mine buildings and reach Penn Gate. Pick up the Empire Street Trail, a narrow unmarked singletrack that begins behind the mine buildings.

3.3 Pass the mule corral as you climb toward Empire Street. At the junction with the WYOD Loop Trail, stay left, following signs directing you to the visitor center.

3.5 The trail reaches Empire Street and skirts the Magenta Drain reclamation ponds. Cross a park road and continue uphill on the roadside pathway.

3.6 Pass a garden gate; you can peek into the estate from here.

3.8 Pass a second garden gate.

3.9 Arrive back at the trailhead.

Hike Information

Local information: Greater Grass Valley Chamber of Commerce and Visitor Center, 128 East Main St., Grass Valley 95945; (530) 273-4667; www.grassvalley chamber.com. Get information about local communities, area history, and more on the chamber site.

Nevada County Gold; www.nevadacountygold.com. This online guide includes information about sites, events, and visiting Grass Valley and surrounding communities.

Hike tours: Tours of the Bourn cottage and mine yard are offered daily, weather permitting. More tours are scheduled during the summer months, and Cottage Living History is offered between noon and 2 p.m. on weekends. Visit the Empire Mine Park Association website at www.empiremine.org for details.

Organizations: The Empire Mine Park Association provides financial and volunteer support for operations and tours at Empire Mine State Historic Park. Visit www .empiremine.org for more information.

20 Malakoff Diggins State Historic Park

Malakoff Diggins State Historic Park, touted as "Bryce Canyon in miniature," showcases the largest hydraulic mine ever operated in California, as well as the damage wrought by the practice in the Sierra Nevada and the amazing capacity of nature to heal itself.

Start: Trailhead near the general store in historic North Bloomfield

Distance: 4.9-mile lollipop

Hiking time: 2–3 hours

Difficulty: Moderate

Best season: Year-round

Other trail users: Hikers only

Amenities: Museum, restrooms, water, trash cans, and picnic facilities in North Bloomfield; camping at Chute Hill

Canine compatibility: Leashed dogs permitted in developed areas; no dogs allowed on trails

Fees and permits: Entry fee per vehicle

Schedule: Open daily, sunrise to sunset, year-round

Maps: USGS North Bloomfield CA; park map available at the museum/visitor center and online at www.parks.ca.gov/?page_id=494 (click on park brochure)

Trail contact: Malakoff Diggins State Historic Park, 23579 North Bloomfield Rd., Nevada City 95959; (530) 265-2740; www.parks.ca .gov/?page_id=494. Malakoff Diggins Park Association, 23579 North Bloomfield Rd., Nevada City 95959; http://malakoffdiggins statepark.org.

Other: The park museum, where the park fee is collected, is well worth a visit. It houses artifacts from the boom days of North Bloomfield, including mining equipment, a mortician's table, Chinese ginger pots and clothing worn by Chinese laborers, and a replica of a gold bar representing production from the diggings. Be sure to take in the short film, which describes in entertaining detail the rise and fall of hydraulic mining in California. It is open from 10 a.m. to 5:30 p.m. daily.

Finding the trailhead: There are two ways to reach the park from Nevada City. To remain on pavement for the duration, follow CA 49 north from its junction with CA 20, toward Downieville, for 10.5 miles. Turn right onto Tyler-Foote Crossing Road, marked with a Malakoff Diggins State Historic Park sign. Follow the paved road for 15 miles; the name will change to Cruzon Grade, then to Backbone. When the double yellow line ends, turn right onto Derbec Road and proceed about 1 mile to North Bloomfield Road. Turn right onto North Bloomfield Road and drive about 1 mile, past the Chute Hill Campground, to historic North Bloomfield and park headquarters. The Church Trailhead is located at the far end of town by the general store.

Alternatively, you can reach North Bloomfield using graded gravel roads, best done in dry conditions. From the junction of CA 20 and CA 49, head north on CA 49 for 0.3 mile to North Bloomfield Road. Go right onto North Bloomfield Road; at the T junction go right, staying on North Bloomfield Road (following the sign for South Yuba River State Park). Stay on North Bloomfield Road for 8.1 winding miles, driving to the bottom of the river canyon at Edwards Crossing. Proceed across the bridge, and then climb to a junction. Stay right on North Bloomfield Road, and continue on the good gravel road to a second signed junction. Stay right on North Bloomfield Road, signed for Malakoff Diggins State Historic Park. Continue for 2.5 miles to the park boundary; the town and trailhead are about 5 miles from the last junction. This road may be closed in winter due to snow. **GPS:** N39 22.065' / W120 54.048'

The Hike

Malakoff Diggins State Historic Park lies well off the beaten path, but it is well worth the travel time. It preserves a gorgeous swath of the foothills, including a preserved mining town, a secluded waterfall, and the monumental remnants of a remarkable episode in the state's gold rush history.

The main attraction of the park is the Malakoff Diggins. The cliffs of the pit, created by a massive hydraulic mining operation in the late 1800s, are a colorful exclamation point amid the heavy greens of the surrounding pines and firs. Crags and spurs of brilliant orange rock fade to peach, and then to cream, stacked in different configurations in different places. The pit, more than 1 mile long and at least 0.5 mile wide, is slowly being reclaimed by willow on the floor and by evergreens in succession; what was once raw now feels almost natural.

▶ One of the exhibits in the museum in North Bloomfield is a replica of a gold bar representing more than 510 pounds of gold. In 1882 the value of that much gold was a bit more than $114,000. Today it's worth more than $10.6 million.

The diggins were the core operation of the North Bloomfield Mine, a consolidation of prospects that proved fruitful for its operators once they applied what was then a new technology developed by Anthony Chabot. In hydraulic mining, a high-velocity

The cliffs in the pit of the Malakoff Diggins evoke an orange Dreamsicle.

THE LEGACY OF HYDRAULIC MINING

In the mid-1800s, after gold was discovered in the foothills surrounding Nevada City, miners flooded into the hills, some building a camp/town called Humbug (later North Bloomfield). When the placer gold played out, enterprising argonauts turned to more a radical method: hydraulics, a powerful but destructive new mining technique that could carve tons of ore from a mountainside in minutes. Prospectors now were able to train water cannons, called monitors, at the slopes and blast gold out of ancient riverbeds buried over the millennia, making a nice profit in the process.

But hydraulic mining had a huge environmental downside, creating massive tailings piles and washing thousands of cubic feet of debris downstream, first into the Humbug Creek drainage, then down into the South Yuba River, then into the Sacramento River, and on into San Francisco Bay. Accumulations of silt hampered navigation in the bay and surrounding rivers and led to a series of flood in towns in the lowlands.

After Marysville was devastated by flood in 1875, a lawsuit was filed against the North Bloomfield Gravel Mining Company, which operated at Malakoff Diggins. It reportedly took Judge Lorenzo Sawyer 3½ hours to read his findings, but in the end he handed down an injunction against the company that rendered hydraulic mining unprofitable, essentially killing the practice. The Sawyer legislation let to the shuttering of operations at both the mine and mining company.

Willows take root in the pit's sandy soil.

stream of water, shot from a monitor or "little giant," is blasted into a mountainside, washing out gold and other precious metals trapped in the sediments. According to the charming video shown in the park's museum, a single man operating a monitor could move 4,000 cubic yards of gravel in 24 hours, exposing the ore within.

But hydraulic mining was a relatively short-lived practice in the Sierra Nevada, given its dramatic and harmful effects on landscapes and properties downstream. A "tide of mud, sand, and gravel . . . tragic tailings" flowed from the mines into waterways including the Feather, Yuba, and Bear Rivers, clotting them and creating "great glaciers of mud" at their mouths.

▶ **By one account an estimated $12 million in gold remains "unworked" in California's goldfields.**

The flooding that resulted in the Great Valley below led to outrage, and then to an epic battle of miner versus farmer. After a flood left the streets of Marysville under 3 feet of mud, the farmers sued—and eventually won the shutdown of the North Bloomfield Mine. The downside: The mining town became a ghost town. The upside: Marysville (along with other cities downstream) were spared the potential for another mine-driven inundation. The demise of the mine ultimately led to the preservation of the Malakoff Diggins as a state park.

The trail begins in the historic boomtown of North Broomfield, which has been meticulously maintained. Follow the Church Trail across a small bridge and up to the town cemetery, where graves dating back to the late 1800s are mingled with more modern burials. Pick up the Diggins Trail behind the cemetery and then drop—at one point quite steeply—into the diggins.

The loop through the pit is described here circling counterclockwise, taking the north portion of the trail first, but following the south trail out and back is a nice option if you'd like a shorter out-and-back excursion. To complete this route, head right on the North Side Trail. The atmosphere changes within 0.1 mile, as you enter the pit. The vastness of the excavation is striking: A towering wall of pink, orange, and white rock rises across a narrow drainage; its mirror rises nearly a mile distant. But the handiwork of natural reclamation is also front and center, with the reeds and willows flourishing in the sink and pines beginning to thrive on the blasted earth. Curling westward and across the bottom of the pit, rusted pipes are scattered trailside, and the treadway is intermittently paved in river cobbles left behind when the gold-bearing cement was washed away.

Route-finding can be difficult in the washed-out bottom of the pit. Heavy rainfall and snow has washed sediments down onto the floor, mostly burying some of the yellow-topped trail markers. By watching carefully for these markers, following the tracks left by other hikers, and scouting the willows for flags tied on the boughs by rangers, you can pick your way through the maze to the north side of the diggins.

The trail winds along the north face, with the sculpted walls rising hundreds of feet above, for more than 1 mile before it finally bends south and around the overgrown Diggins Lake. The North Side Trail meets the South Side Trail near the West

MALAKOFF DIGGINS STATE HISTORIC PARK

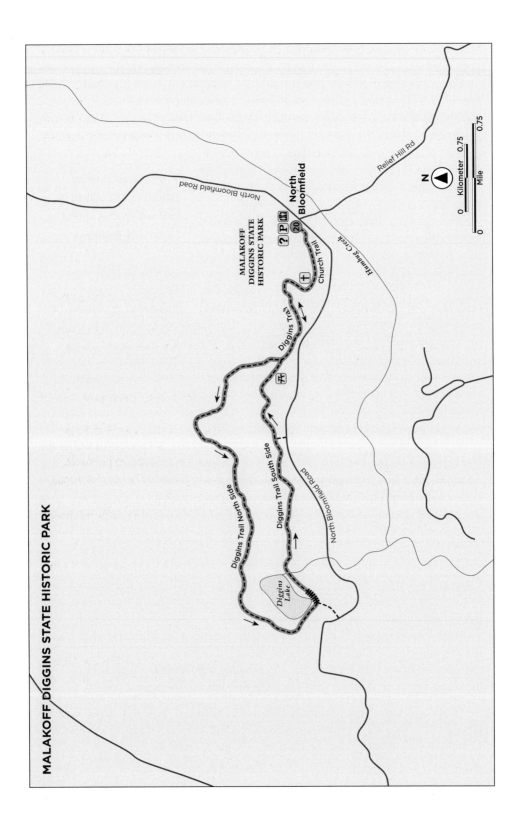

MALAKOFF DIGGINS STATE HISTORIC PARK

North Bloomfield Road

North Bloomfield

Relief Hill Rd

Church Trail

Diggins Trail

Humbug Creek

Diggins Trail North Side

Diggins Trail South Side

North Bloomfield Road

Diggins Lake

20

N

Kilometer   0.75

Mile   0.75

0

0

Point Overlook; look right from the junction to spot the monitor positioned on the high ground, its muzzle pointed past a white cliff face into the diggins.

Follow the South Side Trail across the boardwalk. You may not have noticed that you were headed downhill on the north side, but the South Side Trail presents a modest but steady ascent. Pass several trails leading to overlooks and parking areas as you climb back toward the trail junction where the loop closes. From that junction, retrace your steps back to the trailhead.

Miles and Directions

0.0 Start at the trailhead behind the North Broomfield General Store, at the south end of town. Cross a bridge over a seasonal stream and go left on the Church Trail.

0.25 Reach the cemetery. Walk to the top, turn right, and continue toward the campground on the broad dirt track.

0.4 Turn left onto the Diggins Loop.

0.8 Come out of the woods and cross a gravel roadway, picking up the Diggins Trail on the right. The loop starts about 50 feet beyond. Go right on the North Side Trail.

1.25 Cross the bottom of the pit. Route-finding can be difficult; look for yellow-topped trail posts and flags tied onto brush to stay on track. The trail bends west once it reaches the south-facing cliffs.

2.4 Reach the western side of the pit, where the trail curves to the south around Diggins Lake.

2.8 Diggins Lake comes into view, surrounded by a sea of reeds. Watch for ducks on the murky surface.

2.9 Reach the junction of the North Side and South Side Trails and a spur trail to North Bloomfield Road and the West Point Overlook. A monitor is positioned on the right, about 100 yards from the junction. Go left on the South Side Trail, crossing the boardwalk.

3.1 Climb into the shade and pass the junction with the spur to the Hiller Tunnel. Continue straight on the South Side Trail.

3.7 At the junction with another spur to North Bloomfield Road and an overlook, stay straight on the South Side Trail.

3.9 Pass the spur trail to the monument, again staying straight on the South Side Trail.

4.1 Pass a picnic site, then climb to the junction and close the loop. Retrace your steps from here.

4.9 Arrive back at the trailhead.

Hike Information

Local information: Greater Grass Valley Chamber of Commerce and Visitor Center, 128 East Main St., Grass Valley 95945; (530) 273-4667; www.grassvalleychamber.com. Get information about local communities, area history, and more on the chamber site.

Nevada County Gold; www.nevadacountygold.com. This online guide includes information about sites, events, and visiting Grass Valley and surrounding communities.

21 Independence Trail to Rush Creek Falls

A fabulous, wheelchair-accessible trail winds along the mountainside above the South Yuba River to a wooden flume/bridge overlooking the 100-foot drop of Rush Creek Falls.

Distance: 2.2 miles out and back
Hiking time: About 1.5 hours
Difficulty: Easy
Best season: Year-round
Trail surface: Dirt, wooden flume
Best season: Spring and fall
Other trail users: Hikers only
Amenities: Restrooms, trash cans, information signboard
Canine compatibility: Dogs not permitted
Fees and permits: None

Schedule: Open daily, sunrise to sunset
Special considerations: Take care on the wooden bridges and walkways when conditions are wet or frosty; they can be slippery.
Maps: USGS Nevada City CA; online at www .parks.ca.gov/?page_id=496 (click on park brochure)
Trail contact: South Yuba River State Park, 17660 Pleasant Valley Rd., Penn Valley 95946; (530) 432-2546; www.parks .ca.gov/?page_id=496

Finding the trailhead: From CA 20 in Nevada City, take the CA 49 exit. Go north on CA 49 for 7 miles, dropping into the South Yuba River drainage. The parking area is a pullout alongside the highway, signed for the Independence Trail. If you reach the bridge spanning the river, you've gone too far. **GPS:** N39 17.854' / W121 05.333'

The Hike

Mountainsides in the Sierra Nevada are webbed with hundreds of miles of flume—wooden or earthen channels built in the late 1800s and early 1900s to move water from rivers and streams to mining and logging camps. The slopes of the channels were gentle enough to control water flows, and paths ran alongside so that miners and loggers could maintain the structures and, in the case of those built to transport lumber, clear logjams.

Usually decrepit reminders of gold rush boom times, in the case of the Independence Trail to Rush Creek Falls, a flume has been refurbished as a recreational trail. The route is first-class by any standard but is even more impressive given that it's wheelchair accessible, with ramps, benches, and railings all thoughtfully constructed not only for ease of use but also to blend seamlessly into the surrounding oak woodland.

The trail begins at the uphill end of a stone retaining wall alongside CA 49. It passes under the highway through a tunnel, then winds along the mountainside above the South Yuba River. The route is two-tiered, with a wider path below (in the bed of the flume) and a narrower path on the low berm alongside; the two are connected on occasion by footpaths and short wooden staircases. Footbridges and ramps ease passage when needed, and a number of overlooks with benches have been installed. Views are generally overgrown, though adequate when the leaves are off the deciduous trees in late fall, winter, and early spring.

After crossing a couple of numbered flumes that hint at what's to come, you'll reach the main attraction: a long, arcing structure suspended on the hillside by a string of wooden support beams with Rush Creek's pretty cascades flowing underneath. On the west side of the creek, a switchbacking ramp leads down to picnic sites on the banks at the head of the waterfall. In winter the ramp may be too slick to navigate whether on wheels or on foot. Another trailside picnic site is 0.1 mile down the trail.

The falls are best viewed from the far side of the flume. The water cascades in tiers for more than 100 feet before being lost to sight in the overgrown gorge below. Views open north and west from the flume, finally unobscured by the oak canopy, onto the wooded ridges of the western slope and down toward the South Yuba.

Return as you came.

The final flume on the Independence Trail spans Rush Creek Falls.

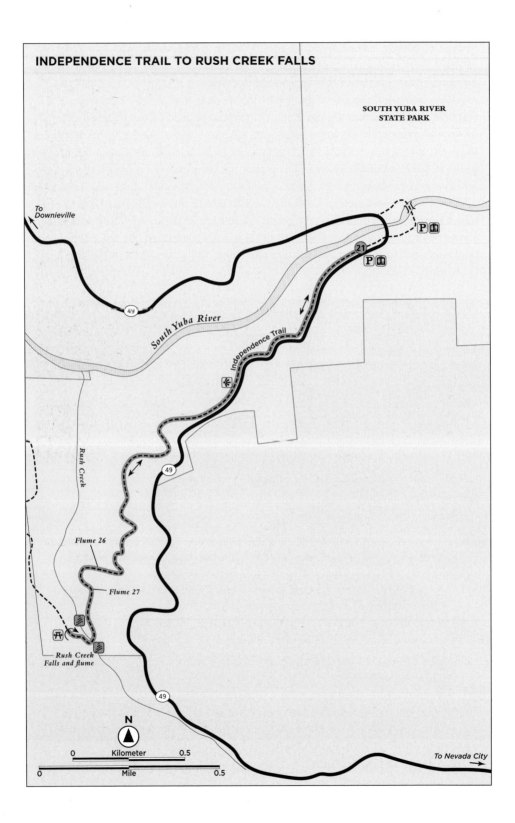

INDEPENDENCE TRAIL TO RUSH CREEK FALLS

SOUTH YUBA RIVER
STATE PARK

To
Downieville

49

South Yuba River

Independence Trail

21

Rush Creek

49

Flume 26

Flume 27

Rush Creek
Falls and flume

N

49

Kilometer
0   0.5
Mile
0   0.5

To Nevada City

Rush Creek Falls drops 100 feet below the Independence Trail flume.

Miles and Directions

0.0 Start by the restroom in the highway-side parking pullout. Go right on the Independence Trail, passing through the tunnel. On the far side, stay left on the obvious, two-tiered track.

0.2 Pass the junction with the Jones Bar Trail, which departs to the right. Stay left on the Independence Trail.

0.4 Pass the covered overlook dedicated to the memory of Thomas Orzalli.

0.5 Pass the Diamond Head outhouse. A picnic site lies just beyond.

0.7 Pass a bench dedicated to Tera, "the best dog ever."

0.9 Cross Flume 26.

1.0 Cross Flume 27.

1.1 Reach the curving flume that overlooks Rush Creek Falls. Cross to the far side for the best views and to descend to the picnic site for a break, if that's an option. This is the turnaround point. Retrace your steps.

2.2 Arrive back at the trailhead.

22 Sutter Buttes

The signature landmark of the Central Valley north of Sacramento, the Sutter Buttes are the eroded remnants of an ancient volcano. Docent-led hikes explore the mysteries of what indigenous Californians considered a sacred place.

Start: Trailhead chosen by the docent
Distance: Variable; anywhere from 3 to 10 miles or more
Hiking time: Variable; plan on a whole day regardless of hike distance
Difficulty: Moderate to strenuous, depending on the hike chosen
Trail surface: Dirt roads and trails; cross-country travel
Best season: Spring, fall, and winter
Other trail users: Hikers only
Amenities: Portable restrooms

Canine compatibility: Dogs not permitted
Fees and permits: Donation requested
Schedule: Docent-led hikes are calendared during the spring, fall, and winter seasons. Weather (excessive heat) and wildlife/grazing considerations preclude hiking in summer.
Maps: USGS Grass Valley CA; none needed, as the docent knows the way.
Trail contact: Middle Mountain Interpretive Hikes; (530) 671-6116; www.middlemountain hikes.org

Finding the trailhead: The buttes are located north of Sacramento and west of Yuba City and Marysville. Roads accessing trailheads are private and gated. Middle Mountain Interpretive Hikes leaders will unlock gates for events. A scenic road tour encircles the range.

The Hike

What once was a nearly perfect conical volcanic peak is now a collection of smaller andesite domes, heavily wooded and resembling the ramparts of a massive castle, protecting swales of grassland pocked with spreading oaks and blooming with wildflowers in season. Known as Middle Mountain, this mysterious circle of summits attracts the eye for miles in the Central Valley north of Sacramento. The magic of the place, experienced by hikers in small groups led by docents schooled in its stories, is transformative. Even if you're not inclined to take guided hikes, consider making an exception to walk within the buttes.

The Sutter Buttes are mostly privately owned and have long been ranchland; prior to that, the southern Maidu (Nisenan) people abided here. The only permanent mark left on the land by its first people are bedrock mortars, where acorns were ground to make bread, porridge, and other staple foods. The ranchers that came after left different marks, including ranch roads, rustic buildings, and fence lines constructed of wood and wire, as well as artfully assembled from fieldstone. While ranching continues in the region, the Sutter Buttes Regional Land Trust, which has worked to protect properties in and surrounding the buttes over the last twenty-five

Sprawling oaks and fields of wildflowers are harbored within the Sutter Buttes.

Fieldstone fences separate pasturelands within the Sutter Buttes.

A bedrock mortar captures rainfall in the Sutter Buttes.

years, has played a significant role in ensuring that the natural values of Middle Mountain are preserved in perpetuity.

Working in conjunction with the land trust and ranchers, the nonprofit Middle Mountain Interpretive Hikes facilitates limited public access to the land. Hikes of varying lengths and difficulties are scheduled in spring, fall, and winter, ranging from long treks linking the summits to shorter, easier, "sacred" walks, where hikers are encouraged to slow down, wander, and just be with the place. On any given hike you might follow a game trail or a ranch road for a portion of the journey, but it's also likely you'll be asked to tread lightly on your own path, meeting up with fellow hikers on a ridge, at a rock outcropping, or in the shade of an ancient oak, its boughs bending to rest on the ground.

No map is provided for hikes in the buttes—only pictures—as the routes vary with the offerings from Middle Mountain Interpretive Hikes and the choice made by the hiker. Hopefully the photos will not only describe the options but also serve as an invitation to both hike and support preservation efforts in the buttes.

◄ *A 700-year-old grandmother oak shows her face, which a Middle Mountain guide notes is furled with the "curl of her thoughts, the curl and swirl of her feelings, her laugh lines and crow's feet." Over the centuries, this tree has witnessed the passage of the Nisenan, explorer John Frémont, ranchers, entrepreneurs, and even the development of Nike missile sites in the Sutter Buttes.*

23 North Table Mountain Waterfall Hike

This showstopper of a hike rambles across the top of a table mountain with endless views to a waterfall that slips down a cliff of broken basalt into a dark pool.

Start: North Table Mountain Ecological Reserve parking area
Distance: 2.5 miles out and back
Hiking time: About 1 hour
Difficulty: Easy
Trail surface: Dirt singletrack, some cross-country over broken basalt and meadow
Best season: Late winter, spring, and early summer for high water and wildflower blooms
Other trail users: Hikers only
Amenities: Information signboard
Canine compatibility: Dogs not permitted
Fees and permits: None

Schedule: Open daily, sunrise to sunset
Maps: USGS Oroville CA
Trail contact: California Department of Fish and Wildlife, (916) 358-2869; www.wildlife.ca.gov/lands/places-to-visit/ north-table-mountain-er. The site is under the purview of the North Table Mountain Ecological Reserve; call (916) 358-2900 for more information.
Other: It's a bit of a drive from Sacramento to reach this preserve—it'll take you more than 90 minutes from downtown—but it is well worth the effort.

Finding the trailhead: From CA 70 in Oroville, take the Nelson Avenue exit (exit 48). Go east on Nelson Avenue for 0.7 mile to Table Mountain Boulevard. Cross Table Mountain Boulevard onto Cherokee Road, and follow Cherokee Road northeast for 6.1 miles to the North Table Mountain Ecological Reserve parking area and trailhead, on the left. **GPS:** N39 35.750' / W121 32.499'

The Hike

The basalt foundation of North Table Mountain Ecological Reserve gives rise to a superlative hiking experience. This place has it all: endless views, renowned wildflower blooms, an abundance of waterfalls, vernal pools supporting unique species, a wonderful formal trail, and the ability to wander cross-country to other sites if you have the knowledge and skills to navigate without a trail.

In winter and spring, a walk atop North Table Mountain is breathtaking. The Central Valley opens below, with the shadowy Coast Ranges defining the western horizon. To the south, the rugged Sutter Buttes punch the sky. If fog or haze has settled onto the valley floor, a carpet of white streaks across the blues and greens and browns of the viewscape. The falls are the destination, but reaching them is sublime.

The formal trail to Hollow Falls, sometimes called Phantom Falls, is relatively new, but the route has been beaten into the rangeland by the thousands of hikers who've gone before. Where the path crosses dark and broken basalt, the rock has been crushed a little flatter by footfall, reducing the potential for ankle twisting. The seasonal stream is the landmark to follow, descending lazily to the west; the footpath runs parallel on the northeast. Hikers share the preserve with cattle. Whether lowing

Hollow Falls spills over a broken basalt cliff.

NORTH TABLE MOUNTAIN WATERFALL HIKE

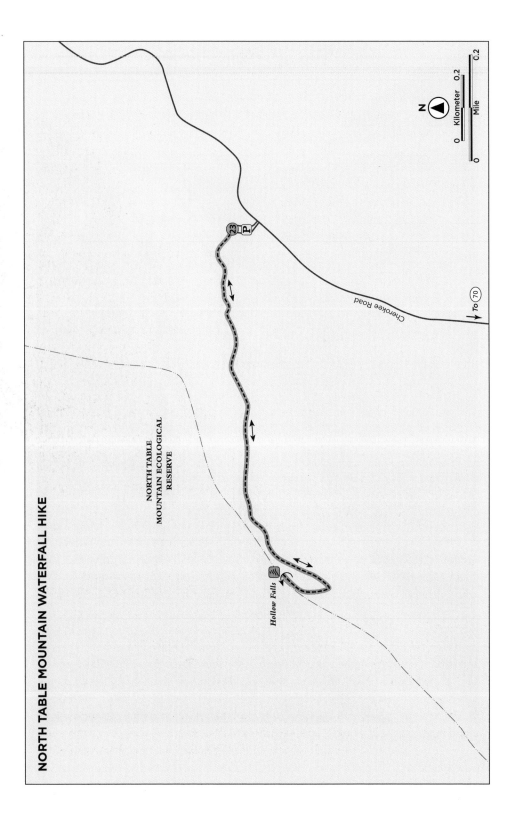

NORTH TABLE
MOUNTAIN ECOLOGICAL
RESERVE

Hollow Falls

Cherokee Road

To 70

N

Kilometer 0.2

Mile

in the distance, grazing trailside, or having left sign of their passage in the form of "pies," they are as much a part of the experience as the vistas.

Cross the stream at a spreading deciduous oak, and continue downhill past a cascade where salamanders and newts congregate to make baby salamanders and newts in late winter. The trail continues down the steepening hillside, skirting the top of the falls and switchbacking down through oak woodlands to the stream below. A trail sign points the way.

Once on flat ground along the creek in Beatson Hollow, travel a short distance upstream to the base of the falls, where a dark pool catches the 100-foot-tall whitewater cascade. Depending on how much water is in the stream—rainfall helps, and the falls in the preserve are also fed by water that pools in the basalt innards of the mountain—Hollow Falls may feather out to wash the east face of the hollow or splinter into two cracks that diverge as they descend.

Once you've taken it all in, and perhaps gone for a dip in the pool at the waterfall's base, return as you came.

A so-called superbloom exploded on the top of North Table Mountain in 2017.

Miles and Directions

0.0 Start by passing through the stile. Pick up the beaten path that follows the stream downhill to the west.

0.5 Cross the seasonal stream at an oak tree.

0.7 From the top of the falls, pick up the trail down into Beatson Hollow.

1.25 Reach the pool at the base of Hollow Falls. Return as you came.

2.5 Arrive back at the trailhead.

Option: Seasonal waterfalls spill into other hollows on the preserve, including Beatson, Crevice, and Western Falls. A long cross-country loop links the falls—depending on rainfall, ten may be visited on this 11+-mile trek. Visit www.chicohiking.org for information.

Honorable Mentions

Little Humbug Falls

Malakoff Diggins State Historic Park is also home to Little Humbug Falls, a hydraulic exclamation point of an entirely different kind. The falls begin with short drops from pool to pool, then the creek is shot as if from a monitor down a relatively low-angled cliff. The sculpted rock face backing the falls features a thin channel that partially hides the flow. A bridge about midway down the steep hillside next to the waterfall offers a safe viewpoint, with cables protecting the steep, rocky path above and below.

The Humbug Creek Trail is 3.3 miles long out and back. It's an upside-down hike, beginning with a long downhill run through shady ravines alongside Humbug Creek, which eventually spills into the South Yuba River. The hike to the South Yuba is 5.4 strenuous miles out and back. For more information contact Malakoff Diggins State Historic Park at (530) 265-2740; www.parks.ca.gov/?page_id=494.

To reach the trailhead, follow CA 49 north from its junction with CA 20, toward Downieville, for 10.5 miles. Turn right onto Tyler-Foote Crossing Road, marked with a Malakoff Diggins State Historic Park sign. Follow the paved road for 15 miles; the name will change to Cruzon Grade, then to Backbone. When the double yellow line ends, turn right onto Derbec Road and proceed about 1 mile to North Bloomfield Road. Turn right onto North Bloomfield Road and drive about 1 mile to historic North Bloomfield and park headquarters. Proceed another 1.5 miles to the trailhead. GPS: N39 21.920' / W120 55.409'

Spring Creek Falls

A rustic, 2.0-mile-long out-and-back path leads along a secluded stretch of the South Yuba River to a sweet little 15-foot waterfall. The path to the confluence of Spring Creek and the Yuba is as rough and tumble as the river that flows next to it, featuring a narrow treadway, uneven footing, and a bit of exposure that demands concentration and nimbleness; it's just plain fun.

The waterfall itself is a short spill from the mouth of the Spring Creek drainage into the South Yuba. At the confluence the formal trail splits into social paths, one leading left to a huge, gnarly old madrone and then splintering into river- and waterfall-bound routes. If the flows are high, it's best to steer clear of the waterways, but if the flows are low, pick a path through the boulders down to the pool at the base of the falls. Scrambling up alongside Spring Creek is also fun, with the creek cascading through boulders, all shaded by oaks and madrones.

The trail to Hollow Falls follows a seasonal stream.

For more information contact South Yuba River State Park, 17660 Pleasant Valley Rd., Penn Valley 95946; (530) 432-2546; www.parks.ca.gov/?page_id=496.

To reach the trailhead from Nevada City, follow CA 20 northeast to the junction with CA 49. Head north on CA 49 for 0.3 mile to North Bloomfield Road. Go right onto North Bloomfield Road; at the T junction go right, staying on North Bloomfield Road (following the sign for South Yuba River State Park). Stay on winding North Bloomfield Road for 7.3 miles, driving to the bottom of the river canyon at Edwards Crossing. Parking is on the south side of the river and bridge. GPS: N39 19.794' / W120 59.052'

South Yuba River State Park

South Yuba River State Park sprawls through in the foothills north and west of Sacramento, with a series of lovely trails branching from different units. A popular spot is about 0.5 mile beyond the Independence Trailhead on CA 49. A large parking area/trailhead is on the south side of the bridge, outfitted with restrooms, trash cans, and information signboards (GPS: N39 17.854' / W121 05.333'). A short walk down to the river leads to the South Yuba's historic rainbow-arch bridge, built in the 1920s. Below the span, the South Yuba crashes through the huge boulders in its bed, green and white and furiously playful. The lovely structure now solely serves pedestrians; the vehicular bridge just downstream, built in 1993, mimics its design. Hoyt's Crossing Trail climbs upstream on the north side of the river, a nice diversion with great views.

Other possibilities in the park include the Buttermilk Bend Trail, which boasts the potential for spectacular wildflower blooms in spring, and the Point Defiance Loop Trail; both originate at the park's Bridgeport headquarters, site of the historic Bridgeport Covered Bridge, located at 17660 Pleasant Valley Rd. The visitor center at Bridgeport, where you can get information on hiking options, is open in summer from 10 a.m. to 4 p.m. daily; in winter from 11 a.m. to 3 p.m. Thu through Sun. For more information on trails in the park, call (530) 432-2546 or visit www.parks .ca.gov/?page_id=496.

West Valley

EXPLORE AN ARBORETUM, WILDLIFE AREAS, AND RANCHLANDS

The cities of Davis, Vacaville, Fairfield, and Winters lie west of Sacramento, clustered close to I-80. While Fairfield and Vacaville could best be described as bedroom communities for Sacramento and cities in the San Francisco Bay Area, Davis is a college town with an agricultural bent. Winters, gateway to Lake Berryessa and the Vaca coastal range, is focused on agriculture, though it has a quaint downtown boasting a pair of fabulous restaurants: the legendary Buckhorn and the Putah Creek Cafe & Bakery, featured on the Food Network.

Winding trails through oak woodlands lead up into the Rockville Hills.

Trails in this region highlight two major geologic features: the Coast Range and the Sacramento–San Joaquin River delta. The Coast Range is a buckling of the earth, where faulting along tectonic plates has heaved up the landscape. The resulting steep-sided, relatively low peaks reach from the western boundary of the Great Valley to the Pacific. The steep loop through Cold Canyon and onto Blue Ridge showcases the rugged beauty of this terrain; Rockville Hills Regional Park offers a gentler exploration of the coastal hills.

The delta, where the Sacramento and San Joaquin Rivers flow into San Francisco Bay, was once a vast maze of wetlands and channels. These days the rivers and their tributaries, as well as the tidal influences of the bay, are contained by levees and development. But pockets of wildlands persist and are being restored, offering refuge for a variety of wildlife and for hikers as well. Premier among the delta explorations are hikes at Rush Ranch and Grizzly Island.

A pair of urban hikes in Davis round out West Valley offerings. The Davis Arboretum offers an educational exploration of flora from around the world, while the Covell Greenbelt epitomizes the potential of a linear park corridor, linking neighborhoods with open spaces.

24 Putah Creek Loop Trail

Tucked along an out-of-the-way stretch of Putah Creek, amid agricultural parcels outside the city of Davis, this loop trail offers seclusion, birding, and a chance to monitor the progress of an effort to restore agricultural land to native habitat.

Start: Main trailhead for the South Fork Preserve on South Putah Creek
Distance: 1.4-mile loop
Hiking time: About 1 hour
Difficulty: Easy
Trail surface: Wide dirt track
Best season: Spring and fall. Summertime heat limits trail use to mornings and evenings. Winter rains may render trails muddy; wait a couple of days for the surface to firm up.
Other trail users: Hikers only

Amenities: Parking, information board with trail map, picnic table, trash cans
Canine compatibility: Leashed dogs permitted
Fees and permits: None
Schedule: Open daily, sunrise to sunset, year-round
Maps: USGS Davis CA; trail map on information board at trailhead
Trail contact: City of Davis Parks and Community Services, 1818 Fifth St., Davis 95616; (530) 757-5626; www.cityofdavis.org, or visit http://arboretum.ucdavis.edu

Finding the trailhead: From downtown Sacramento, head west on I-80 toward Davis. Take the Mace Boulevard exit. Travel 2.3 miles south on Mace Boulevard to the trailhead, which is on the left (east) side of the road. **GPS:** N38 31.038' / W121 41.703'

The Hike

The south fork of Putah Creek drops east out of Lake Berryessa into the Yolo Bypass Wildlife Area, and then into the Sacramento River delta. The flow seems backward, since the Pacific Ocean is to the west, but the creek does eventually reach that goal, providing water for farms and fields in the southern Sacramento Valley along the way.

While Putah Creek is constrained by levees throughout the agricultural bottomlands, in this little preserve it is allowed to flood, as it did before the arrival of Europeans, when Native Americans (possibly Patwin) lived and foraged along its banks. In this way it waters wetlands and riparian zones being restored along its banks.

The man-made forces that have shaped the surrounding landscape for decades still envelop the 84-acre preserve and its trails, with orchards neatly planted at its eastern boundary and an enormous levee bounding the south side. But the creek also supports a complex "riparian ribbon" that includes habitat for chinook salmon, prickly sculpin, California quail, and a variety of raptors. These creatures and the sycamores, willows, and oaks that shelter them find permanent renewal in this preserve.

The riparian corridor along the creek itself, thick with berry brambles, cottonwoods, and willows, rings with birdsong. The meadow between the creek banks and

The first blush of spring green appears on the limbs of an oak shading the trail to Putah Creek.

the levee is exposed, with oaks beginning to gain vigor and size amid the grasses, the majority of which are native perennials.

This pocket of parkland is isolated and little used, a huge bonus for the hiker seeking solitude. Visit in the morning or evening, or on any weekday, and you'll likely be alone with the birds chirping in the brush and the wind humming through the

Abundant winter rainfall swells and quickens Putah Creek.

grasses. But the trail is wide enough to be a walk-and-talk affair, perfect for families or friends seeking a quiet outing to catch up, and perhaps do a little birding.

The route is easy to follow. Begin with a visit to the creek, following a narrow path that leads a short distance down to the broad, quiet waterway. Once you return to the main trail, go left and head east through savanna that blooms in season: wildflowers, sage, wild rose, and chamise. You'll pass the junction with the Inner Loop, which offers an opportunity to shorten the walk if desired. The Outer Loop bends south along the fence line that marks the interface of the shaggy preserve and the orderly rows of a manicured orchard. Continuing the circumnavigation, the route turns west, returning toward the trailhead in the shadow of the levee, a sloping grassy wall that rises to the left (south). Make a final turn, now headed north again, and you are back at the trailhead.

Miles and Directions

0.0 Start by heading left on the gravel trail, taking the loop in a clockwise direction.

0.1 At the trail intersection go left, toward the creek. After you take in the streamside scene, return to the trail junction and continue on the broad main trail.

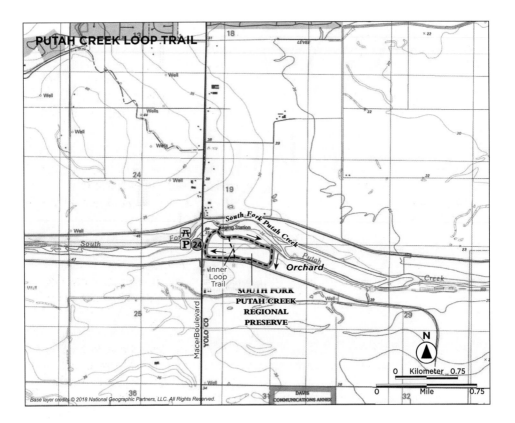

0.3 Reach a junction with a road/trail at a fence line. Stay left (eastbound). At a second trail intersection (with the Inner Loop), stay straight (east), remaining on the Outer Loop.

0.6 At the junction stay straight on the Outer Loop Trail.

0.7 Circle south toward the levee. The property boundary is fenced on the left.

0.8 Head westward along the foot of the levee.

1.0 Pass the junction with the Inner Loop and a gated roadway that leads up onto the levee. Stay straight (west) on the Outer Loop Trail.

1.3 Round the last curve of the loop, heading north parallel to Mace Boulevard toward the trailhead.

1.4 Arrive back at the trailhead and parking area.

Hike Information

Local information: Davis Chamber of Commerce, 604 Third St., Davis 05616; (530) 756-5160; www.davischamber.com. Community events and other information can be found on the Davis chamber website.

25 UC Davis Arboretum Trail

Travel from an environment you might find in Australia to an oak grove that includes exotic species from Spain and the Middle East, all while following the UC Davis Arboretum Trail. This winding interpretive path follows Putah Creek through downtown Davis and the adjacent university campus.

Start: Signed trailhead behind Davis Commons shopping center
Distance: 4.25-mile lollipop
Hiking time: 2-3 hours
Difficulty: Easy
Trail surface: Pavement, crushed gravel
Best season: Year-round
Other trail users: Cyclists, dog walkers, joggers

Amenities: Parking at the trailhead; anything you need in nearby shopping centers
Canine compatibility: Leashed dogs permitted
Fees and permits: None
Schedule: Open daily, year-round
Maps: USGS Davis CA and Merritt CA; online at http://arboretum.ucdavis.edu
Trail contact: UC Davis Arboretum, 1 Shields Ave., Davis 95616; (530) 752-4880; http://arboretum.ucdavis.edu

Finding the trailhead: Head west from Sacramento on I-80 for about 14 miles to Davis. Take the Richards Boulevard exit and turn right (north) onto Richards. Drive 0.1 mile to the junction with First Street. Turn left on First, at the Davis Commons shopping center. Go 1 block and turn left again onto D Street. Park in the shopping center lot. The signed Davis Arboretum trail begins across the road from the lot's southwest corner. **GPS:** N38 32.489' / W121 44.413'

The Hike

Take a botanical tour of the world without ever leaving California's Great Valley by exploring the trail through the Davis Arboretum. Interpretive signs along the winding urban path, which borders a stretch of Putah Creek, identify the stunning variety of plants that have been nurtured here. It's a chance to get educated while you exercise.

The arboretum, a scenic greenbelt that transects the UC Davis campus, serves a variety of purposes. Recreation is premier among them, with cyclists, joggers, and walkers using the path at all hours. The 100 acres of gardens are also integral to university research and are the site of guided tours led by university experts for school groups and families. The arboretum also hosts horticultural sales, during which locals and savvy visitors can pick up plants best suited for sustainable gardens in the region.

The trail is accessed from the Davis Commons parking lot, but take the time to visit the arboretum's Terrace Garden, located on the east side of the shopping center, before you set off on your hike. In the garden you'll find a fountain, plantings identified with discreet signage, and tables and chairs from which to enjoy it all. A brief exploration of the garden is a nice prelude to what you'll find along the trail proper.

Arboretum trails run on either side of Putah Creek, with footbridges spanning the waterway to link them. The described route alternates sides. A number of linkages break away from the main path to access Arboretum Drive and campus service roads, but as long as you remain creekside, you won't get lost. Sounds from the nearby freeway are muffled but present for much of the walk. Those sounds, coupled with a variety of other trail users—cyclists, dog walkers, researchers, and students—are a constant reminder that this is an urban trail, albeit one of the finest in the area.

The paved path begins by dropping into the Australian Collection. Well signed and maintained, the collection includes a wide variety of eucalyptuses and other species native to the continent. It is the perfect introduction to the caliber of exhibits you'll walk through along the route.

Follow signs toward the Redwood Grove and the Wyatt Deck. The Redwood Grove is a popular destination, offering benches in perpetual shade, cool temperatures even in the heat of summer, and interpretive signs. Just in case you've forgotten that you are in a college town, students gathered in clusters socializing or sitting singly with textbook or computer in hand are clear reminders.

The path continues through the East Asian Collection and skims the shores of Lake Spafford, where green lawns and benches offer more room for study and reflection. Campus halls are visible on either side of the creek corridor.

Cross a bridge to the Mary Wattis Brown Garden of California Native Plants and continue west, now on a crushed-gravel path still suitable for wheelchairs and strollers. The trail proceeds through several garden rooms focused on California natives, including foothills botanicals and valley oaks. The Acacia Grove and Mediterranean Collection follow before the trail enters the manicured environs of the Putah Creek Lodge. Verdant lawns, an amphitheater, a boathouse and launch, and the Early California Garden are on the grounds. The path winds along the south shore of a small lake, then climbs a hill and bends right, passing an equestrian center.

Pass the Carolee Shields White Flower Garden and the Moon Garden gazebo, then turn left onto the gravel Oak Discovery Trail. Oaks from around the world grow here—Persian oak, cork oak, oak of Tabor, cozahuatl, and English oak, as well as California natives—and are identified with mosaic tile signs. The Latin name for oak, *Quercus*, translates to "fine tree," and the specimens along the winding path more than live up to the moniker. After you've looped through the grove, check out the Valley Wise Garden, where plants that thrive in the local area are showcased, before following the paved path back down to the lake and the Putah Creek Lodge.

After crossing the bridge back to the lodge, retrace your steps to the bridge at the Valley Oak Collection. Cross to the north side of the creek, exploring garden rooms including the conifer and redbud collections. The UC Davis water tower rises above. The Native American Contemplative Garden is just before Mrak Hall Road; in this garden you'll find native plantings mingled with standing stones that invite you to reflect on the legacy of the native Patwin people who once thrived on the shores of Putah Creek.

The Valley Wise Garden highlights plants that will thrive in the local ecosystem.

After passing under Mrak Hall Road, follow the north-side path back to Lake Spafford. Cross the bridge to the south side of the creek to explore the sages, ceanothus, and buckeyes of the California Natives Garden. You'll arrive back at the Wyatt Deck; from there retrace your steps to the trailhead at Davis Commons.

Miles and Directions

0.0   Start at the trailhead behind Davis Commons, descending into the Australian Collection.

0.3   Cross the footbridge, following signs for the Redwood Grove and Wyatt Deck. Pass a side trail that offers street access, staying right and dropping through an underpass. Enter the Redwood Grove.

0.5   Arrive at the Wyatt Deck. Cross the bridge back to the north side of the creek and turn left, following signs for Lake Spafford and the East Asian Collection.

0.75 Cross the bridge to the left, entering the California Natives Garden. Turn right on the garden path, which becomes crushed gravel. Cross Mrak Hall Road and pick up the obvious paved path, marked with a California Foothill Collection sign.

0.9   Pass a bridge, staying left on the paved path.

1.0   Stay right on the obvious main trail where two paved walkways access a service road to the left. Walk through another underpass and enter the Valley Oak Collection.

1.1   Pass another bridge, staying left on the paved path and entering the Acacia Grove. Stay right where a side path to the parallel roadway intersects.

1.25 Proceed into the Mediterranean Collection, passing yet another access path. Cross a campus service road.

1.4   Arrive at the Putah Creek Lodge. Continue on the obvious paved path around the south shoreline of the adjacent lake, passing the amphitheater and boat launch.

1.7   Pass another access road, staying right.

1.8   Climb a short hill to the east end of the loop. The trail curls right.

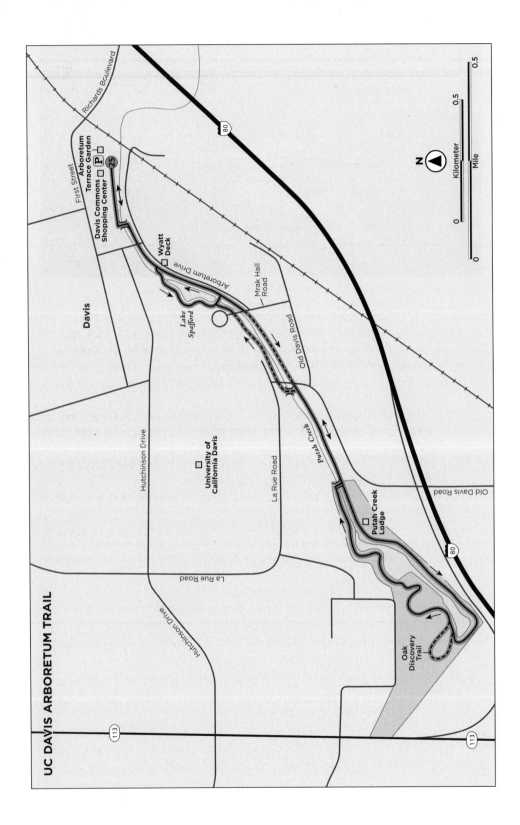

UC DAVIS ARBORETUM TRAIL

Red hot poker blooms along the UC Davis Arboretum Trail.

2.0 Reach the junction with the Oak Discovery Trail and head into the oak grove. Circle through the oaks in a counterclockwise direction, exiting at the gazebo. Turn left, pass the restroom, and visit the Valley Wise Garden. Turn left when you leave the Valley Wise Garden and follow the path down toward the lake.

2.6 Go left on the asphalt path above the lake. Enter the Mediterranean Collection. Stay left where paths merge.

2.9 Cross the bridge at the South American Collection to return to the Putah Creek Lodge. Turn left to retrace your steps back to the bridge spanning Putah Creek at the Valley Oak Collection.

3.25 Cross the bridge at the Valley Oak Collection to the north side of the creek, then turn right, passing through the Conifer and Redbud Collections.

3.5 After exploring the Native American Contemplative Garden, cross Mrak Hall Road, rejoining the trail on the other side.

3.6 Cross the bridge back to the California Natives Garden on the south side of Lake Spafford, crisscrossing the path you took earlier.

3.8 Return to the Wyatt Deck. Retrace your steps from here.

4.25 Arrive back at the trailhead.

Hike Information

Local information: Davis Chamber of Commerce, 604 Third St., Davis 05616; (530) 756-5160; www.davischamber.com.

Hike tours: UC Davis experts lead guided tours of the arboretum as well as host workshops, classes, and family programs. To access the calendar of events, visit http://arboretum.ucdavis.edu or call (530) 752-4880.

Restaurants: Mikuni Sushi, 500 First St., Ste. 11, Davis; (530) 756-2111; https://mikunisushi.com. Located in Davis Commons, adjacent to the arboretum trailhead, this urban sushi bar offers delicious, refreshing bites that will satisfy before or after a hike.

26 Covell Greenbelt

Stroll along pleasant paved paths in a leisurely loop that encompasses ponds, wildlife viewing platforms, and greenspaces.

Start: Davis Community Park on Covell Boulevard, at the pedestrian bridge
Distance: 2.75-mile lollipop
Hiking time: About 1 hour
Difficulty: Easy
Trail surface: Pavement
Best season: Year-round
Other trail users: Cyclists, joggers, in-line skaters
Amenities: Parking, restrooms, playing green, tot lot
Canine compatibility: Leashed dogs permitted

Fees and permits: None
Schedule: Open daily year-round
Maps: USGS Davis CA and Merritt CA; online (along with other greenbelt trails in Davis) at http://cityofdavis.org/home/showdocument?id=5842
Trail contact: City of Davis Community Services Department, 23 Russell Blvd., Davis 95616; (530) 757-5610; http://cityofdavis.org/city-hall/community-development-and-sustainability

Finding the trailhead: From Sacramento, head west on I-80 for about 14 miles to the Richards Boulevard exit. Head north for 0.1 mile on Richards to First Street. Turn right on First Street and go 1 block to F Street. Turn left on F Street and drive 1.2 miles to East Covell Boulevard. Turn left on Covell and drive 1 long block to the Davis Community Park parking lot on the left (south) side of the road. **GPS:** N38 33.628' / W121 44.816'

The Hike

This looping tour along paved paths links Davis Community Park, next door to Davis Senior High School, with the quieter Covell and Northstar neighborhood parks. The paths run through greenspaces that back up to suburban homes, with links to residential streets and cul-de-sacs. Ideal for a Sunday outing with the family or easy-access exercise after a long day at work, the paths are local favorites.

Though you can jump on the trails at several access points, and can extend the hike by linking to other bike and walking routes in the area (check out the City of Davis's online bike map for options), this loop begins and ends at Community Park. Start by crossing the pedestrian bridge that spans Covell Boulevard, which deposits you immediately into 5.2-acre Covell Park. The linear park encompasses benches, broad green lawns, playground areas, restrooms, and tennis courts. The first major trail intersection, located just inside Covell Park, marks the start of the loop. Stay right (heading north) to travel in a counterclockwise direction.

The next major junction is near the tennis courts; again, stay right. Parallel paths continue north, one dirt and one paved, alongside an open field. Cross Grande Avenue and travel through quiet neighborhoods, passing several signed access paths.

Next up is 13.5-acre Northstar Park, which encompasses soccer fields and Julie Partansky Pond. Named for a former Davis city council member and mayor, the pond functions both as the centerpiece of a wildlife viewing area and as a stormwater retention basin. Thickets provide cover for songbirds such as warblers, swallows, and sparrows; larger birds, including great egrets, great blue herons, and a variety of ducks, can be seen at water's edge and on the pond. A pair of observation decks border the pond, offering opportunities to break from walking and just watch instead.

▶ **Keep your dog on leash on public walkways and trails. Tying a waste bag around the leash is a sure way to guarantee you can clean up after your pet no matter where you walk.**

The path circles a second, more developed pond in the center of a huge green, then links with a gravel path that leads through the Northstar Nature Garden. A series of arbors arc over the path, which is planted with drought-resistant species. The path is very short and ends back on the paved greenbelt trail near a tot lot and soccer fields. The greenbelt trail bends southward, toward downtown Davis, skirting backyards.

The greenspace around the trail widens, and at the 1.6-mile mark you'll pass the first of the Art in Public Places installations along the trail. Titled *Three Frolicking Dogs*, the bronze statues depict lifelike canines doing the ordinary (sniffing a sprinkler) and extraordinary (riding a tricycle). The sculptures were created by Jean van Keuren and installed in 2005. You could call the statues whimsical, evocative, or playful, but a quote from the Davis Wiki website offers another point of view: "They are, as are most works of dogs behaving like humans, thoroughly creepy."

Public art installations along the Covell Greenbelt trail include this exhausted mutt on a trike.

The Covell Greenbelt trail winds through shade and sun.

The greenbelt trail eventually bends east and reenters Covell Park, where the loop closes at the trail sign and tot lot. Turn right and retrace your steps to the trailhead.

Miles and Directions

0.0 Start by crossing the pedestrian bridge that leads into Covell Park.

0.25 At the Y junction near the Baja Avenue tot lot, stay right to begin the loop, traveling in a counterclockwise direction.

0.4 The trail splits; you can walk either way, picking up the path heading north on the other side of the tennis courts.

0.7 Cross Grande Avenue. Enter Northstar Park and pass the wildlife area.

0.9 At the junction with the trail leading out to Anderson Road, stay left, circling the pond in the center of the green and passing the Northstar parking lot and restroom.

1.25 At the intersection with the signed Northstar Nature Garden Trail, turn right onto the gravel path (the paved path runs parallel).

1.6 Pass the first of the *Three Frolicking Dogs* sculptures.

1.8 Pass the second dog sculpture. At the third dog sculpture, the trail splits. Take the left-hand fork, remaining in the greenbelt. At the tot lot stay left again, avoiding the path that leads to the tunnel.

2.3 Cross Catalina Drive and reenter Covell Park. Close the loop at the trail that leads south toward Davis Community Park, turning right to retrace your steps.

2.75 Arrive back at the trailhead.

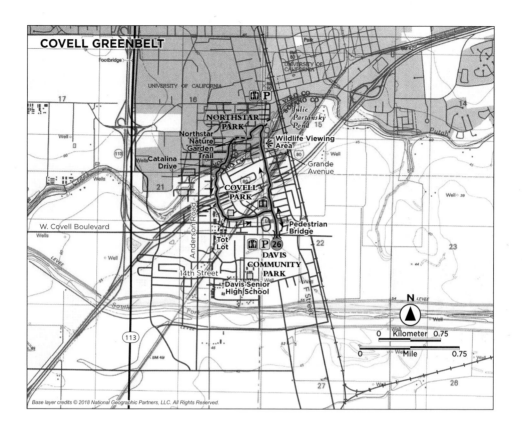

Hike Information

Local information: Davis Chamber of Commerce, 604 Third St., Davis 05616; (530) 756-5160; www.davis chamber.com.

Restaurants: The Hotdogger, 129 E St., A-1, Davis; (530) 753-6291; www .thehotdogger.com. Where better to satisfy your hunger after visiting the Covell Greenbelt, with its canine statuary, than at a hot dog joint? Kraut dogs, chili dogs, Chicago dogs—even tofu dogs—are served up at this local favorite.

A viewing platform overlooks the small wildlife area in Northstar Park along the Covell Greenbelt loop.

27 Rush Ranch

Two trail loops showcase very different ecosystems on Rush Ranch. The first loop takes you through delta salt marsh and freshwater marsh, thick with rushes, reeds, and birdcall. The second loop crosses pasturelands with views extending west to Mount Diablo.

Start: Signed Marsh Trailhead behind the museum and visitor center
Distance: 4.1-mile double loop
Hiking time: 2-3 hours
Difficulty: Easy
Trail surface: Dirt ranch roads
Best season: Spring for wildflowers; late fall and winter for migrating birds
Other trail users: Hikers only
Amenities: Picnic tables, restrooms, signboard with information and maps. Restrooms and information are available in the visitor center and exhibit room.
Canine compatibility: Dogs not permitted

Fees and permits: None
Schedule: Open daily, sunrise to sunset, year-round
Maps: USGS Fairfield South CA; online at http://rushranch.net; map in interpretive trail brochures available at visitor center
Trail contact: Solano County Land Trust, 1001 Texas St., Fairfield 94533; (707) 432-0150; http://rushranch.net; www.solanolandtrust.org/RushRanch.aspx
Special considerations: Insects, including wasps, can be pesky at Rush Ranch. Wear repellent.

Finding the trailhead: From Sacramento, head west on I-80 for about 38 miles to the CA 12/Abernathy Road exit. Turn left on the Suisun Highway and cross over the freeway; the name changes to Chadbourne Road. After about 0.5 mile, turn left onto CA 12, heading toward Rio Vista. Go 3.5 miles on CA 12 to Grizzly Island Road and turn right (a left turn at this arterial will put you on Sunset Avenue). Follow Grizzly Island Road for 2.4 miles to Rush Ranch, on your left.
GPS: N38 12.530' / W122 01.537'

The Hike

At Rush Ranch—where salt marsh meets freshwater marsh, coastal plain meets Central Valley prairie, shady eucalyptus groves meet open ranchland—the emphasis is on the ecotone. A quote from Richard Louv's *Last Child in the Woods*, displayed on the wall in the exhibit hall of the ranch's visitor center, explains why:

> *Look for the edges between habitats;*
> *Where the trees stop and a field begins;*
> *Where rocks and earth meet water.*
> *Life is always at the edges.*

The edges along the ranch's two loop trails are very different. Follow the Marsh Trail over a hilltop covered in annual grasses typical of the uplands of the coastal ranges, then slide down to the salt marsh, then through brackish marsh into the managed freshwater marsh. On the South Pasture Trail, trace a finger of marshland where Native Americans (possibly Patwin) used a large stone as a bedrock mortar, then into the uplands, where grazing cattle crop the grasses before they crisp in the summer sun.

From grassland to marshland the flora varies widely—bunchgrass is just a stone's throw from pickleweed, which in turn is a few paces from cattail, which backs up to hedges of nonnative blackberry. The fauna, which includes a variety of songbirds, shorebirds, waterfowl, and raptors, as well as river otters, coyotes, and raccoons, transition from habitat to habitat as instinct or opportunity dictates. The creatures of Rush Ranch often find what they need—and can be most easily observed—at the edges. Among

▶ A fixture on many ranch properties, eucalyptus, an Australian native, was originally imported to California to serve as a timber crop. When the wood proved unsatisfactory as lumber, furniture, or floorboards, the trees were employed as windbreaks.

Historic farming gear rusts in the "boneyard" at Rush Ranch.

the unique (and sometimes endangered) species found on the 2,000+-acre ranch are the Suisun shrew and the Suisun song sparrow; rare plants include the Suisun aster and Jepson's tule pea. The delta smelt, a species of some controversy because protection of its freshwater-saltwater habitat has reportedly resulted in job losses within California's agricultural community, is also present in the waterways of the ranch.

HISTORY OF RUSH RANCH

Before it was a ranch, the Suisun Marsh area served as winter hunting and gathering grounds for natives known as the Suisunes (which translates as "people of the west wind"), a subgroup within the Patwin tribe. These indigenous people left one lasting mark in what is now a park: the grinding stone overlooking the marsh. The depth of the holes attests to the many meals prepared there before the arrival of settlers from Mexico and the United States. All other signs of the Suisunes—their tule canoes, shelters, and granaries—have been reclaimed by time.

European settlers left a much more lasting mark on the land. Ranch founder Hiram Rush came to California in 1849—not to seek gold, like so many others, but to run cattle. He arrived with a seed herd and started out with a holding of about 5,000 acres, which he eventually parlayed into more than 50,000 acres on properties in the Suisun Valley and Monterey County. At Rush Ranch he ran thousands of head of cattle and sheep. After amassing both wealth and influence, Hiram Rush met a tragic and unexpected end when he was killed in a buggy accident on his Suisun property. He was sixty years old.

Hiram's son, Benjamin Franklin Rush (1852–1940), took over ranch operations, which continued to flourish under his watch. He ran as many as 5,000 head of cattle and sheep on the land. He and his wife, Anna, raised seven children; he also became a publisher and a bank director and was active in valley agricultural societies.

Significantly, neither the junior nor the senior Rush did much to alter the natural tidal ebb and flow in the Suisun Marsh, leaving the basic underpinnings of the landscape and its rich habitats untouched. The relative lack of development, coupled with the ranch's niche in the shrinking San Francisco Bay delta region, attracted preservation efforts. The signboard in the parking area says it best: The ranch may be "40 miles from the Golden Gate . . . but it's still the edge of the bay."

Rush Ranch was acquired by the Solano Land Trust in 1988 with a grant from the California Coastal Conservancy. Its remarkable attributes, including its status as part of one of the largest estuarine marshes in the western United States, have also resulted in its inclusion in the San Francisco Bay National Estuarine Research Reserve.

The Suisun Marsh, one of the largest contiguous estuarine marshes in the western United States, is a fragment of what was once a sprawling wetland delta system that reached well into the Central Valley. About 90 percent of that vast marshland has been eroded by the activities of humankind in the 250 years or so since European contact. The water has been corralled by levees and channeled into sloughs; vast tracts have been drained for farmland, and other areas have been filled to provide a foundation for residential and commercial development. At Rush Ranch you will walk on levees that restrict tidal action on all but 5,000 of the marsh's 85,000 acres.

Both the Marsh and the South Pasture Trails are described, but one can be taken without the other. At about 2 miles each, and given their different emphases, it's a nice combination. Be sure to pick up interpretive guides for the trails at the visitor center; return them for the next user when you're done.

Begin on the Marsh Trail, which starts directly behind the visitor center in a grove of eucalyptus. The first highlight on the Marsh Trail is the top of Overlook Hill. Take a seat on a bench and survey the marsh, which stretches north toward the Vaca range and west toward the steep flanks of Mount Diablo. To the south and east are the treeless Potrero Hills, emerald green in the wet season and hot gold in summer and fall.

At the base of the hill are re-creations of a Patwin tule house, shade shelter, and granary, used as part of the ranch's educational program. The trail then leads into

A sun-bleached bedrock mortar once used by Native Americans overlooks the marsh at Rush Ranch.

the wetland, following a mown path that threads through reeds and tules, hedges of blackberry, and wild fennel that can tower overhead. The dense foliage provides shelter and sustenance for ducks, red-winged blackbirds (which chatter incessantly in the reeds), and other resident and migrating birds. Cross a tidal gate, which helps regulate the inflow and outflow of salt water, carefully managed to provide optimum habitat for wildlife. Typically, the marsh is drained in summer and allowed to refill in winter.

As you swing east, Suisun Slough, looking much like a lazy river, comes into view. Beyond the water you can see some of the development around Fairfield (likely you've already been buzzed by a plane taking off or landing at nearby Travis Air Force Base). The Vaca Mountains rise behind. An interpretive marker identifies Goat Island and Japanese Point, but you won't know you're on an island unless the

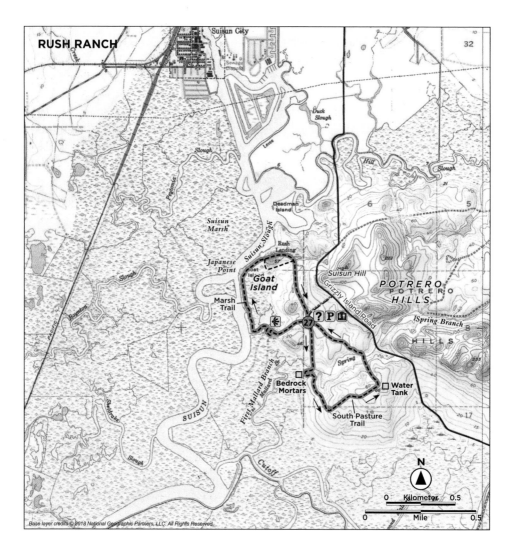

marsh has water in it. Pass the tidal gate and go left on the ranch road, circling the hill to a ranch gate. If you visit in winter or early spring, you'll see the wildlife pond off to your left; this dries up later in the year. Climb the two-track trail and cross the grassland back to the main ranch, where you'll pick up the South Pasture Trail at the signed trailhead under the water tower.

The South Pasture Trail begins in the "boneyard," where ranch implements have been left to do what a rancher would let them do when they were no longer of use: rust and decay. The trail follows a ranch road east toward Mount Diablo, passing through the summer homes of thousands of solitary native bees that burrow into the ground, creating distinctive "chimneys." Look right to the Notch, a cleft in the rise where dirt was excavated for use in levee building.

At Spring Branch Creek, the marsh extends across the trail up into the swale on the left. Trail signs indicate the crossing with the Spring Branch Creek Cutoff, which is an option for a shorter loop. Stay right instead, heading out a short distance to the Indian grinding rock, where Native Americans processed the foodstuffs they harvested from the marsh, leaving holes in the soft pale rock. An arrow directs you up to an overlook, then the route launches into pastureland.

The views across the tidal plain to the ridges of the coastal ranges are spectacular and unimpeded. The peaceful, remote-feeling trail curls to the east and then south. You might see cattle grazing or a horse at the water tank; keep your distance and the livestock will do the same. Off in the distance, through a gap in the Potrero Hills, you can see wind turbines spinning in the nearly constant breeze.

Follow the low trail markers as they direct you across the uplands, then down into the swale and across Spring Branch Creek again. Beyond the boardwalk that spans the marsh, the trail rolls back to the boneyard and trailhead.

Miles and Directions

Marsh Trail

- **0.0** Start at the signed trailhead behind the visitor center.
- **0.1** Trails merge; proceed toward the Overlook Hill on the broad dirt ranch road. Pass through a fence, go left, then quickly right, to pick up the trail that climbs onto the hill.
- **0.3** Reach the top of Overlook Hill. Take in the views, then descend left (to the west), following signs to the trail at the base. Go right on the Marsh Trail, passing the mock native structures.
- **0.4** At the trail junction, go left into the marsh.
- **0.5** Cross the tidal gate.
- **1.0** The trail arcs east over a rise, then south toward the Potrero Hills.
- **1.25** Pass through a gate and go left, circling the hill on the ranch road.
- **1.5** At the gate, continue straight up the hill on the two-track road toward the ranch.
- **2.0** Arrive back at the ranch and trailhead.

South Pasture Trail

0.0 Start at the signed trailhead under the water tower in the boneyard. The trail splits immediately; stay right to complete the loop in a counterclockwise direction.

0.3 Reach the junction with the Spring Branch Creek Cutoff and the trail to the Indian grinding rock. Visit the grinding rock, then continue up to the overlook. The South Pasture Trail continues to the right.

0.8 A bench affords great views of Mount Diablo.

1.0 Reach the water tank. Stay right on the ranch road that leads to another viewing bench. Go sharply left at the bench, heading downhill on the mown track.

1.5 Cross the swale and pass through a stile at a break in the fence line. At the junction with the Spring Branch Creek Cutoff, stay right, following the path across the boardwalk.

1.7 Pass a second fence line via a stile. Follow the ranch road up and over the small hill.

2.0 Reach the boneyard.

2.1 Arrive back at the trailhead.

Hike Information

Local information: Fairfield-Suisun Chamber of Commerce, 1111 Webster St., Fairfield 94533; (707) 425-4625; https://fairfieldsuisunchamber.com. The chamber provides resources for visitors and residents alike. You can also find information about parks and trails at www.fairfield.ca.gov/visitors.

Organizations: The Rush Ranch Educational Council, an all-volunteer nonprofit organization, develops and administers educational programs at Rush Ranch for both schoolchildren and adults. The programs focus on local native history and culture, native wildlife, marsh biology, and Rush Ranch history, among other themes. Write to the council at PO Box 2088, Fairfield 94533; call (707) 422-4491; or visit http://rushranch.net.

28 Howard Slough at Grizzly Island Wildlife Area

A circuit through this wildlife refuge in San Francisco Bay's delta region offers views of Mount Diablo, excellent birding, and an opportunity to see one of California's rare tule elk herds.

Start: Across Grizzly Island Road from parking lot 4

Distance: 4.75-mile lollipop

Hiking time: About 3 hours

Difficulty: Moderate due to distance

Trail surface: Gravel and dirt levee roads

Best season: Spring, during bird migrations; late Sept, during the tule elk rut

Other trail users: Hikers only

Amenities: Information and restrooms at the wildlife area's headquarters

Canine compatibility: Dogs not permitted Mar through June; permitted on-leash rest of year

Fees and permits: Fee charged. You must get a permit and sign in and out at the self-registration booth at the California Department of Fish and Game entry station. Carry the permit with you on the trail.

Schedule: Open for hiking Feb through July and the last 1 to 2 weeks of Sept. The area is closed for general public use, including hiking,

during special tule elk hunts in Aug and early Sept, and Oct through Jan during waterfowl hunting season. Contact the wildlife area for precise dates of hunting seasons, which vary. When open for hiking, hours are from sunrise to sunset.

Maps: USGS Honker Bay CA; online at www .wildlife.ca.gov/Lands/Places-to-Visit/Grizzly -Island-WA#45872427-recreation; also available at the entrance kiosk

Trail contact: California Department of Fish and Game, Grizzly Island Wildlife Area, 2548 Grizzly Island Rd., Suisun 94585; (707) 425-3828; www.wildlife.ca.gov/Lands/ Places-to-Visit/Grizzly-Island-WA

Other: Grizzly Island may close in winter due to flooding. Contact the wildlife area before your visit to check on conditions and access.

Special considerations: Insects, including wasps, can be prolific in season. Use repellent.

Finding the trailhead: From Sacramento, head west on I-80 for about 38 miles to the CA 12/Abernathy Road exit. Turn left on the Suisun Highway and cross over the freeway; the name changes to Chadbourne Road. After about 0.5 mile, turn left onto CA 12, heading toward Rio Vista. Go 3.5 miles on CA 12 to Grizzly Island Road and turn right. Follow Grizzly Island Road for 5.3 miles to Belden's Landing, a Solano County park and boat launch. Turn right, staying on Grizzly Island Road, and cross the Montezuma Slough Bridge. Stay left on the other side of the bridge, following Grizzly Island Road for another 3.5 miles to the Grizzly Island Wildlife Area entry station. Check in at the station, then continue another 5.8 miles to parking lot 4. The trailhead is across the road from parking lot 4. **GPS:** N38 06.461' / W121 55.634'

The Hike

When the Spaniards arrived in California in the late eighteenth century, herds of tule elk roamed the region's grasslands. But the arrival of the Europeans nearly spelled extinction for the smallest members of the elk family, which were driven to the brink by market hunters and loss of habitat to ranching and agriculture.

The story goes that the population dwindled to a single breeding pair, but fortunately there were others (though not many). Protected by conservation-minded landowners, the sparse population was allowed to propagate unmolested, and now several herds roam public properties within the state, including on Grizzly Island.

Other critters don't need such intensive management to survive—just a place to live and breed unhindered. Grizzly Island is also that place. Songbirds find shelter in the cattails and brush that thrive on the borders of ponds and sloughs. Crickets scatter crazily from underfoot along the trails in late summer. Dragonflies scour the shorelines for mosquitoes and other prey. Fish jump in the slow waters of Howard Slough, a soft plop followed by rings that spread to the brushy banks. The wings of ducks thrum the surfaces of ponds as the birds take flight en masse.

The area is managed by the California Department of Fish and Game for the benefit of the tule elk, as well as for river otters and a bonanza of resident and migrating birds. Ponds between the area's many levees are filled and drained to suit

The quiet waters in the Roaring River Slough ebb and flow with the tides.

Hulking Mount Diablo looms on the western skyline above the ponds at Grizzly Island Wildlife Area. The ponds are managed via sloughs and gates to meet the needs of resident and migratory birds.

the needs of its wildlife, providing forage for resident species and enabling hikers to experience different seasons in different ways.

Paying attention to the seasons is critical if you want to see the tule elk. They rut in the fall, making September a prime time to see males with full racks in velvet. February is another prime time, as the males still have their antlers. This hike is scenic and a good leg stretcher in any season, but it doesn't border prime tule elk viewing territory; stop by the Grizzly Island office and check with officials to obtain information about the best routes to view elk, if that's your chief goal. For birders, species change with the time of year. The wildlife area is on the Pacific Flyway, so both migrating species and year-round residents can be seen, depending on the season.

Begin this hike by crossing Grizzly Slough. The distinctive dark silhouette of Mount Diablo rises above the folds of Coast Range hills. Follow the levee road straight west toward the hills, ignoring other roads that border ponds and ditches on either side. After a stretch the levee road bends southward, with Mount Diablo on the right and the white-winged towers of a wind farm on the left. The gray towers to the south are part of a refinery near Benicia. A lazy S curve swings the trail westward again, between ponds

▶ **An estimated 500,000 tule elk roamed the grasslands of California prior to the gold rush. As of 2014, one report placed the tule elk population at about 4,200, in twenty-two herds located in protected wildlife areas.**

and the slough that fills them, with noxious star thistle and sweet-smelling wild fennel crowding the road's edge in late season. Birdcall rings from the brush, and white egrets and pelicans take wing when startled. Look for the hairy scat of the area's carnivores—coyotes, in particular—on the treadway.

HOWARD SLOUGH AT GRIZZLY ISLAND WILDLIFE AREA

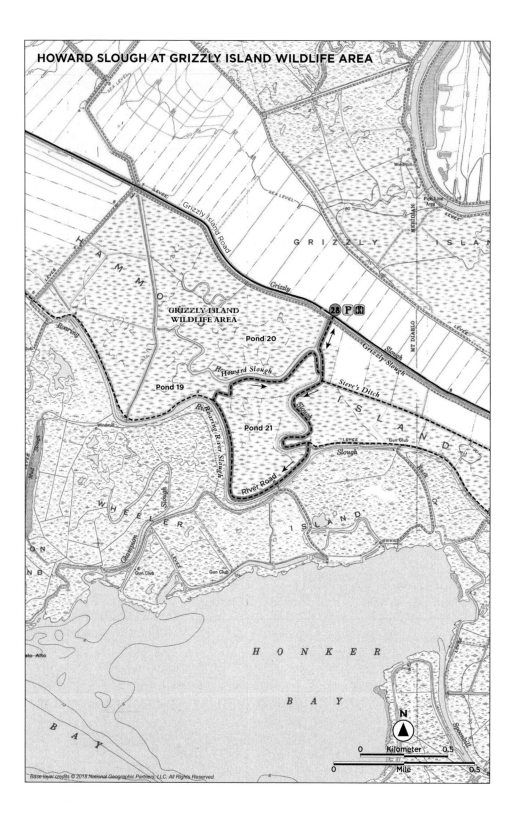

GRIZZLY ISLAND ROAD

SEA LEVEL

SEA LEVEL

LEVEE

HAMMO

Roaring

G R I Z Z L Y   I S L A N

GRIZZLY ISLAND
WILDLIFE AREA

Grizzly

28 P

Pond 20

Howard Slough

Grizzly Slough

MT DIABLO

LEVEE

Pond 19

Steve's Ditch

Slough

Roaring River Slough

Windmill

I S L A N D

Pond 21

Slough

Gun Club

LEVEE

Slough

River Road

Gun Club

W   H   E   E   L   E   R

I S L A N D

Champion Slough

Mud Slough

ON

Windmill

Slough

LEVEE

N D

Gun Club

Gun Club

lo   Alto

H   O   N   K   E   R

Stonehill

B   A   Y

N

B   A   Y

0   Kilometer   0.5

0   Mile   0.5

After the levee road curves to the east, it spills onto River Road, which runs alongside the Roaring River Slough. Turn right and follow the broad roadway southwest and then north, toward the Vaca range (you may encounter a vehicle or two on this stretch). The Roaring River is hardly that: Placid and wide, it is bordered by cattails, reeds, and ceanothus, which provide perfect cover for even the largest shorebirds, including great blue herons (so well camouflaged you may only spot one when it takes flight). The roadway is perfect for walking and talking with friends, scanning the waterways for otters, and searching the reeds and brush for songbirds and shorebirds.

Just beyond the 3-mile mark, take the levee road that branches right (east). It points toward the wind farm, the great white blades spinning or still, depending on the wind and the whim of the energy grid. The road is slightly overgrown, bending right where it meets water. A bit farther you'll meet the roadway along Howard Slough, which you follow back to the levee road you came in on. A left turn on the original levee path, and it's an easy walk back to the trailhead.

Miles and Directions

0.0 Start by crossing Grizzly Slough and heading west down the levee road.

0.25 The trail reaches Howard Slough, with water on either side (depending on whether ponds are full).

0.4 At the junction stay straight (west) on the obvious primary levee road.

0.5 At Steve's Ditch, with trails on either side of the waterway, again stay straight (west) on the levee road.

1.5 The trail empties onto the gravel River Road, alongside Roaring River Slough. Go right on the broad, well-maintained River Road.

2.3 River Road curves northward, skirting Pond 21 on the right.

3.1 Take the levee road that branches right off River Road.

3.2 The levee road bends right where it meets the water.

3.4 Meet the Howard Slough road. Go right, keeping the slough on the left.

4.3 The levee road hitches southward, then intersects a connector path that leads over the slough and onto the levee road linking to the trailhead. Turn left on the levee road and retrace your steps.

4.75 Arrive back at the trailhead.

Hike Information

Local information: Fairfield–Suisun Chamber of Commerce, 1111 Webster St., Fairfield 94533; (707) 425-4625; https://fairfieldsuisunchamber.com. The chamber provides resources for visitors and residents alike. You can also find information about parks and trails at www.fairfield.ca.gov/visitors.

Restaurants: Quick, easy, and delicious, Yo Sushi is a great pre- or post-hike stop. Located at 1430 North Texas St., Fairfield; (707) 425-1100.

29 Rockville Hills Regional Park

This exploration of Rockville Hills, a regional park on the western fringe of Fairfield, leads to a lake and cave, and then through part of a natural rock garden.

Start: Rockville Hills park trailhead on Rockville Road

Distance: 3.1-mile lollipop

Hiking time: About 2 hours

Difficulty: Moderate due to elevation changes

Trail surface: Dirt road, dirt singletrack

Best season: Spring for wildflowers

Other trail users: Mountain bikers

Amenities: Trash cans, information signboard with map

Canine compatibility: Leashed dogs permitted

Fees and permits: Entrance fee

Schedule: Open daily, dawn to dusk, year-round

Maps: USGS Cordelia CA and Mount George CA; online at www.fairfield.ca.gov/gov/depts/pw/open_space/rockville_hills_regional_park/rockville_trail_map.asp

Trail contact: City of Fairfield Public Works, 1000 Webster St., Fairfield 94533; (707) 428-7614 (park ranger); www.fairfield.ca.gov/gov/depts/pw/open_Space/rockville_hills_regional_park/default.asp

Finding the trailhead: From Sacramento, head west on I-80 for about 40 miles to the Suisun Valley Road / Green Valley Road exit. Head north on Suisun Valley Road for 1.4 miles to Rockville Road. Turn left on Rockville Road and go 0.7 mile to the signed trailhead parking area, on the left. **GPS:** N38 14.907' / W122 07.959'

The Hike

Sometimes the best trails are the backyard trails, the ones locals turn to when they need an afternoon escape. Having a destination like a waterfall or a historic site might be the best reason to seek out a trail, but sometimes the point is simply the pleasure of walking.

That's what Rockville Hills offers. Yes, there's a lake, there's a cave, there's a hilltop rock garden, and there are wonderful views. But much of this 633-acre park's appeal lies in the good condition and easy pitch of its trails, its calming oak woodlands and open meadows, and its unpretentious friendliness.

The route begins by climbing the wide, dirt Rockville Trail. Part of the Bay Area Ridge Trail, the path winds through a woodland of broadly spaced oaks, buckeyes, and bay laurels. As you gain altitude via the gentle grade, views open out across the Suisun delta region, reaching south all the way to Mount Diablo on a clear day.

The trail tops out at the junction with Oakridge Road. Pass the gate and the information signboard, and then skirt the pond, which may go dry in late season. Even when there is no water visible in the shallow basin, herons and other waterbirds find sanctuary in the reeds and rushes of its marshy edges.

The trail proceeds through an oak-studded swale to the dam of the small lake at Rockville's heart. The lake is a congregation point for visitors; a place to picnic and relax. The power lines that run through the park are most visible in the open lake basin, but in spring wildflowers draw the eye and the wetlands clamor with birdlife—red-winged blackbirds singing in the reeds, ducks plying the shallows, and the occasional hawk using the dam as a roost.

Proceed around the lake on the Lake Front Trail, following signs for the overlook. A boardwalk spans the wetlands surrounding the lake's inlet stream. Pass through the fence via a stile, then follow the single-track trail along the fence line. Singletracks pour off the hillside to the left, indicative of the park's popularity with mountain bikers. The trails are numbered and graded much like ski slopes, with green trails being easy, blue trails moderate, and black trails difficult.

▶ In a park with lots of mountain biking traffic, such as Rockville Hills, staying on the broader trails (fire roads and service roads), where it is easier to pass, helps minimize potential user conflicts.

A second little boardwalk marks the end of the fence-line trail. A moderate climb leads up to Paradise Pass—more of a saddle—then a rather steep descent through burgundy-trunked manzanita takes you down and around a high point to where you can check out the

Annual grasses blush green in winter along trails in Rockville Hills.

cave. Keep an eye out on the uphill side of the slope once you reach the open stretch of trail overlooking Rockville Road. The cave is not easily explored. It sits above the trail, with rugged use trails leading up the rock slope, and its narrow, dark mouth is not inviting. Check it out, then retrace your steps to the pass and go right, up onto the rock garden ridge.

HIKING THE RIDGETOP

A portion of the Bay Area Ridge Trail, a regional path that, as the name implies, follows ridgelines around San Francisco Bay, passes through Rockville Hills Regional Park. The segment is part of 370 miles of trail that have been cobbled together since the idea was first discussed back in 1987. The goal is to create a path upon which hikers and other users can circumnavigate the bay. Once complete, more than 550 miles of trail will be incorporated.

Thus far the route primarily consists of trails running through existing parklands. The gaps cross private land, and efforts to secure passage are ongoing. Spearheading the effort is the Bay Area Ridge Trail Council, a nonprofit organization formed in 1992 specifically to promote the trail.

A wonderful interactive map of the trail is available at https://ridgetrail .outerspatial.com/applications/12/ embed#9/37.8171/-122.1416. It shows existing trail segments and designates whether sections are multiuse or limited to foot traffic or other specific uses.

For more information on the effort, as well as to find out how you can help, and for specifics of the existing and proposed route, contact the Bay Area Ridge Trail Council by calling (415) 561-2595, or visit http://ridgetrail.org.

A trail sign directs hikers in Rockville Hills Regional Park, and indicates that a portion of the route is part of the much longer Bay Area Ridge Trail.

A maze of paths explores the rock garden, jumbles of lichen-stained boulders crowding a long ridgetop. Pick your way through the garden, staying to the left (lake) side and enjoying views down over the reservoir and out across the hills to the south and west. All trails merge with a dirt fire road. Once on the broad track, go left and downhill toward the lake.

At the bottom of the hill, you'll encounter an intersection where nine trails converge. Fortunately, a trail sign explains which path goes where. Better still, there is the lake; simply take the trail leading left, along the shoreline and back to the dam. Pick up the Pond Pass Trail, which will lead you around the south side of the pond and back to the junction with the Rockville Trail at Oakridge Road. From there, retrace your steps to the trailhead.

Miles and Directions

0.0 Start by climbing away from the parking area on the Rockville Trail. The trail splits almost immediately; stay left and uphill.

0.1 At the second trail split, above the ranch buildings, stay straight on the main path.

0.25 Where singletrack trails intersect, stay on the broad main path.

0.5 Reach the junction with paved Oakridge Road (aka the Bay Area Ridge Trail) at the top of the hill. An entrance station with a restroom is down the road to the left. Cross the road to the information signboard, passing through the gate toward the lake. At the trail intersection just beyond the gate, stay right on the broad dirt track signed Lake Trail.

0.6 Where the dirt roadways/trails merge, stay left on the obvious path toward the lake.

0.8 Arrive at the lake. Go right on the wide trail. Where side trails intersect over the next 0.1 mile, stay left, circling the shoreline. Cross the boardwalk through the marsh at the trail's inlet.

1.0 Pass through a stile at a break in a low fence. Singletracks collide on the other side of the fence. Take the singletrack to the right, along the fence.

1.2 At the junction for Paradise Pass, go left and up on the dirt roadway. A series of paths intersect the main route: Stay left at the trail leading to paved Oakridge Road, left again at the junction with the Lake Front Trail, and right at the junction with the Charmise Loop, climbing straight for the pass, an obvious break in the ridgeline ahead.

1.4 Drop over the pass to see the cave, above the trail to the right. After you've checked it out, return to the pass.

1.6 Go right into the rock garden. A maze of trails explores the area. Stay right at the trail post, then left on the lake side of the ridgetop. Where the rock garden path meets the broad dirt road/trail, go left and downhill. Pass junctions with the Rock Garden and Tower Trails as you begin to descend.

1.8 Pass the May-December Trail, staying on the broad dirt track.

2.0 Reach a mousetrap of trail junctions, with nine paths converging at a trail sign. Take the broad trail leading left to the lakeside. After about 100 yards go left, over a stile at a break in the fence, and onto a shoreline trail leading to the dam.

2.25 Pick up the Pond Pass Trail, which leads down and around the lower pond via singletrack and boardwalks.

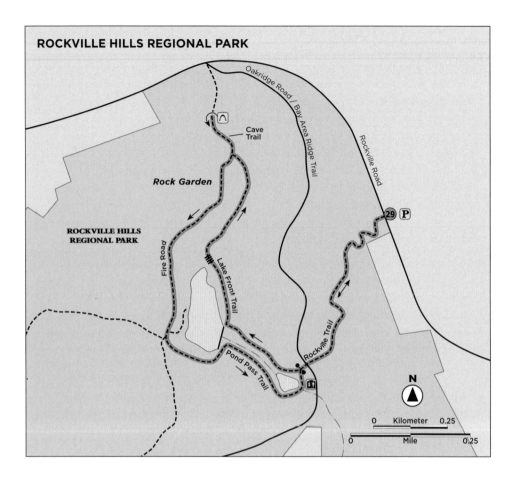

ROCKVILLE HILLS REGIONAL PARK

Oakridge Road / Bay Area Ridge Trail

Cave Trail

Rock Garden

Rockville Road

ROCKVILLE HILLS
REGIONAL PARK

Fire Road

Lake Front Trail

Pond Pass Trail

Rockville Trail

29

P

N

| 0 | Kilometer | 0.25 |
| 0 | Mile | 0.25 |

2.4 Stay left where trails diverge at the pond's dam, crossing back toward the junction at Oakridge Road.

2.5 Back at the start of the loop, go right to retrace your steps down the Rockville Trail.

3.1 Arrive back at the trailhead.

Hike Information

Local information: Fairfield-Suisun Chamber of Commerce, 1111 Webster St., Fairfield 94533; (707) 425-4625; https://fairfieldsuisunchamber.com. The chamber provides resources for visitors and residents alike. You can also find information about parks and trails at www.fairfield.ca.gov/visitors.

Hike tours: Interpretive hikes led by park rangers are offered. Call (707) 428-7614 for more information.

30 Homestead and Blue Ridge Loop (Stebbins Cold Canyon Reserve)

Steep-walled Cold Creek canyon, near Lake Berryessa, harbors wildness, history, and adventure. The Homestead Trail leads up alongside seasonal Cold Creek to the remains of an old goat ranch. From there stairs and switchbacks climb to the multiple summits of the Blue Ridge, with views down over Berryessa and out across the surrounding ridges of the coastal ranges.

Start: Gate on CA 128 above the parking area, near Lake Berryessa's Monticello Dam
Distance: 4.6-mile loop
Hiking time: 3–4 hours
Difficulty: Challenging due to steep and/or rocky stretches and numerous ups and downs. You will gain and lose more than 1,300 feet in elevation.
Trail surface: Dirt singletrack, unmaintained dirt roadway
Best season: Spring and fall, when temperatures are moderate
Other trail users: Hikers only
Amenities: Portable toilet
Canine compatibility: Dogs not permitted
Fees and permits: None; small donation suggested to help maintain the preserve
Schedule: Open daily, sunrise to sunset, year-round. Trail may be closed during heavy rains, for wind events, and in the event of high fire danger. Consult the preserve website for current conditions.
Maps: USGS Monticello Dam CA and Mount Vaca CA; online at https://stebbinsreserve.com/nrs/hiking/; posted on trail signs at the trailhead
Trail contacts: Reserve Director, UC Davis Natural Reserve System, The Barn, 1 Shields Ave., Davis, CA 95616; (530) 752-9178; https://naturalreserves.ucdavis.edu/stebbins-cold-canyon
Special considerations: The steep, rocky terrain requires good hiking skills and strong legs and lungs. The Cold Creek crossing on the Homestead Trail may be impassible during high water (after significant rains). Other potential hazards, all of which are native to the coastal hills and thrive in this reserve, include poison oak, rattlesnakes, and ticks.

Finding the trailhead: From Sacramento, head west for about 11 miles on I-80 to the exit for CA 113 in Davis. Go north on CA 113 for about 2 miles to the Russell Boulevard exit (CR 32) and head west toward Winters. Follow Russell Boulevard / CA 32 for about 11 miles; the road will cross I-505 and enter Winters as Grant Avenue / CA 128. Continue on CA 128 for another 10 miles. Cross the bridge over Putah Creek; the trailhead parking area is on the right side of the road before it makes a sharp curve up toward the Monticello Dam. A short access path leads under the highway to the trailhead proper. **GPS:** N38 30.700' / W122 05.803'

The Hike

The Homestead and Blue Ridge Trails, which traverse the Stebbins Cold Canyon Reserve, present a rewarding challenge in the steep staircase climbing from Cold Creek to the ridgetop. Rebuilt following the Wragg Fire in 2016, which destroyed

► **The 2016 Wragg Fire burned through the chaparral and oak woodlands east and south of Lake Berryessa, scorching more than 8,000 acres (including portions of the Stebbins Cold Canyon Reserve) and destroying several structures before it was contained. Fires burn hot and move quickly in this region, as in other areas of the state, which is why hikers are advised to avoid these trails when temperatures rise and fire danger is extreme.**

the preserve's man-made infrastructure and cleared the mountainsides of thick brush, the route still presents one of the best fitness challenges in the area. You have been warned.

This hike also offers the opportunity to step into one of the newest additions to America's national parks system, Berryessa Snow Mountain National Monument, designated in 2015 by President Barack Obama. Though a patchwork of public lands administered by different agencies underlies the trail, and you won't know when you cross the boundaries as you hike, the Stebbins preserve serves as a gateway to the monument, which encompasses more than 330,000 acres from sea level to 7,000 feet on Snow Mountain.

The trail has a rocky start. To reach the creek canyon proper from the carpark, follow trails studded with cobbles of various sizes. The potential for ankle twisting exists, so tread carefully. You'll also have to pay attention to the weather, as passing through the twin tunnels (culverts) under the highway requires low water or no water.

Once at the trailhead proper, where there is a gate and an informational signboard, take the Homestead Trail into the riparian corridor along Cold Creek. Evidence of the Wragg Fire was still evident in late 2017, the hillsides clear of brush and scorched brush and trees alongside the path (plus parking spots in the carpark are delineated with fire hose). Side trails break to the right toward the creek, which is dry in late season and a spirited companion when fed by rainfall in winter and spring. The trail gently ascends for the most part, with a few sets of stairs hinting at the more arduous climb to come. The thick brush and bay laurel that shaded the path before the fire has been cleared, opening the canyon to the sky and surrounding hillsides. Scat on the path is wrapped with hair, indicating a carnivorous depositor—you'll need a guidebook (or a poop expert) to determine if it is the spoor of a cat or a coyote.

The trail crosses the creek about a half mile in. Most of the time this is not a difficult proposition. Rock-hop or wade if the water is low and slow moving; when the creek is dry, it's a walk-across. When the water is high, however, this might be the turnaround point. Use your good judgment.

Beyond the crossing the trail continues up the narrowing canyon. You'll find the charred remnants of the Vlahos homestead at the 1-mile mark. A stone wall is the first visible remnant, built on the creek side of the trail at the junction with the path leading left and up onto the Blue Ridge. The trail that continues straight explores the homestead site, where John Vlahos raised goats in the early twentieth century, using

A winter's sun spills over the steep walls of Cold Creek canyon.

the milk for cheese making. If you don't want to tackle the climb up to and along the ridge, this is a nice turnaround point for a pleasant 2-mile out-and-back trek.

To continue the loop, climb the short flight of steps leading away from the homestead site. The trail steadily but easily ascends into the canyon. Reach the base of the steep flight of steps at the 1.5-mile mark, and the climb begins. One guidebook writer calls these "monster" stairs, and he's got a point: The steps assist in an ascent of more than 500 feet in about 0.2 mile, a rather frightening statistic. Before reconstruction some of the steps, where erosion had eaten away the dirt below the thick wooden risers, were thigh burners. While the new construction conforms to trail-building standards, you still may wonder about (or curse) the superhuman (or masochist) who conceived the route. Fortunately, short traverses between flights and switchbacks allow you to catch your breath, and mercifully it's over swiftly. Once on the ridge there are no more stairs, but there's plenty more climbing.

The Blue Ridge Trail rolls over five summits, each seemingly higher than the last. But that's not true, according to the US Geological Survey. You'll have reached the apex on the first peak, at more than 1,500 feet above sea level. Vistas unfurl across row after row of coastal hills breaking away to the north and west, blue and purple in the distance. The Vaca range surrounds you, cloaked in grassland and dark oak woodlands, its steep folds dropping into dark drainages. Westward rise the Mayacamas—like the Vacas, pleated by the fault lines that have crumpled California through the millennia. Beyond the Mayacamas the long bulk of Sonoma Mountain hunkers, a former volcano worn to roundness by time and the elements.

Short saddles separate the individual summits. Climbing through these saddles involves negotiating steep, sometimes rocky terrain. Pay particular attention on the third summit, where the hiking involves hands-on concentration as you negotiate steep drops, lever yourself down around boulders, and pick your way across ankle-twisting rocky stretches.

A fire-altered start: To reach the beginning of the Homestead Trail in Stebbins Cold Canyon Reserve, hikers must pass through a large culvert. If the water is high following winter rains, return to hike another day.

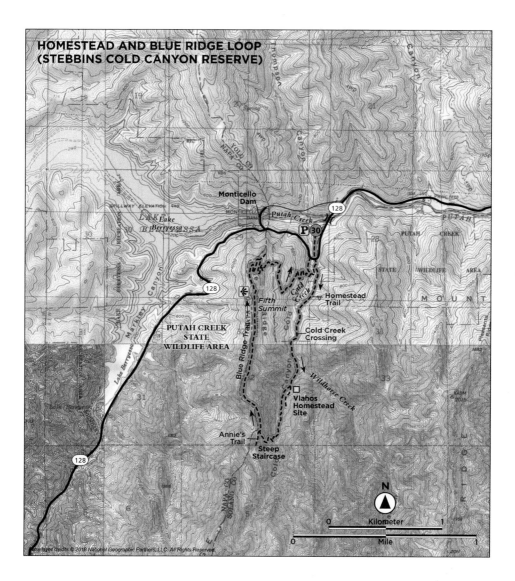

Lake Berryessa comes into view by the summit of the third peaklet, smooth and jewel blue as viewed from on high. Lake views become more prominent as you continue, and rock outcrops offer great vantage points, as well as opportunities to rest and take on fuel and water. Arguably the best views come as you begin the final descent from the last summit, where a pair of outcrops overlook the reservoir.

The descent is aided by more wooden steps, again with switchbacks and long traverses through the chaparral. As you near trail's end, the route expands to roadway width. Drop to the gate and information signboard just above CA 128, then cross under the highway to return to the trailhead parking lot.

Miles and Directions

0.0 Start by taking the short access path out of the parking area and crossing under CA 128 to the trailhead. Pick up the Homestead Trail and head upstream along Cold Creek.

0.6 Cross Cold Creek.

1.0 Arrive at the Vlahos homestead. Go right, up the short flight of stairs, to continue the loop.

1.5 Take a deep breath. The stair climb begins.

1.7 Arrive at the crest of the ridge and the signed junction of Annie's, Homestead, and Blue Ridge Trails. Go right on the Blue Ridge Trail. Annie's Trail offers a 2-mile additional loop for those interested in extending their hike.

1.8 Attain the first summit.

2.0 Arrive on the second summit. A short saddle separates the two.

2.1 Atop the third summit, a rock outcrop affords the first views of Lake Berryessa.

2.8 Arrive at the top of the fourth peaklet.

2.9 A quick up and down leads to the top of the final summit. Begin the descent.

3.1 The trail splits at an unsigned junction with a short overlook trail. Stay right, descending toward the Putah Creek drainage.

4.0 The trail widens into roadway.

4.4 The connector trail breaks off to the right. Stay straight on the wide Blue Ridge Trail.

4.5 Reach the end of the trail at the gate.

4.6 Arrive back at the trailhead.

Hike Information

Local information: Winters Chamber of Commerce, 201 First St., Winters 95694; (530) 795-2329; www.winterschamber.com. The chamber provides information on local businesses, events, and activities.

Local events/attractions: Lake Berryessa, a US Bureau of Reclamation property, hosts a variety of recreational activities including boating and other water sports, fishing, and camping. For more information on recreational opportunities at the lake, visit the bureau's field office and visitor center at 5520 Knoxville Rd. in Napa; call (707) 966-2111; or visit www.usbr.gov/mp/ccao/berryessa.

Camping: A number of campgrounds circle Lake Berryessa. Visit www.usbr.gov/mp/ccao/berryessa for information.

Restaurants: Putah Creek Cafe & Bakery, 1 Main St., Winters; (530) 795-2682; www.putahcreekcafe.com. This downtown eatery uses an outdoor pizza oven to bake delicious pies and offers a variety of other entrees, as well as a breakfast and lunch menu.

Buckhorn Steak & Roadhouse, 2 Main St., Winters; (530) 795-4503; http://buckhornsteakhouse.com. This award-winning bar and restaurant is located on the ground floor of the historic De Vilbiss Hotel in downtown Winters. The steaks are the main attraction, but the sides (especially the fries) are delicious as well.

South Valley

SPRAWLING VISTAS, RESERVOIR WALKS, AND THE REGION'S ONLY FREE-FLOWING RIVER

Much like the region north of the Sacramento metropolitan area, the valley to the south is composed of flatlands dedicated to farming and ranching. The south valley is also influenced by the second major river emptying into the San Francisco Bay delta: the San Joaquin. Like the Sacramento, the San Joaquin is contained by levees and dams, which allow it to flow tamely through Central Valley towns like Stockton and Lodi. Its headwaters are in the southern Sierra Nevada, and its tributaries include the Merced River, flowing out of Yosemite National Park; the Kings River, spilling out of Sequoia–Kings Canyon National Parks; and the Cosumnes, the largest free-flowing river coursing out of the mountains.

A railroad bridge and fall foliage along the Cosumnes River catch the light of the setting sun.

Old ranch roads and cattle paths make up the North Pond loop trail through Deer Creek Hills Preserve.

Water is the focus of many of the trails in this region, whether rivers like the Cosumnes, featured on the Cosumnes River Walk, sloughs like those found in Delta Meadows River Park, or lakes like Camanche Reservoir, focal point of the China Gulch Trail. In Deer Creek Hills Preserve, you'll wander through the foothills on old ranch roads and trails blazed by cattle. Howard Ranch is notable for its skyline, which includes distant views of the Sierra front as well as the cooling towers of the decommissioned Rancho Seco nuclear power plant. Up in the foothills, a state park surrounds one of the most remarkable artifacts left by California's native peoples: a grinding rock supporting more than a thousand bedrock mortars.

The major highways heading south from Sacramento are I-5 and CA 99. In the foothills you'll follow scenic two-lane roads such as CA 88 to access trailheads.

31 Stone Lakes National Wildlife Refuge

Once threatened by urban growth sprawling south from metropolitan Sacramento, a short paved loop through restored wetlands at Stone Lakes National Wildlife Refuge focuses on education and expanding awareness of what came before shopping malls and freeways.

Start: Trailhead on the east side of the parking lot
Distance: 0.5-mile loop
Hiking time: About 30 minutes
Difficulty: Easy
Trail surface: Pavement; wheelchair and stroller accessible
Best season: Year-round
Other trail users: Hikers only
Amenities: Restrooms, information signboards
Canine compatibility: Dogs not permitted

Fees and permits: None
Schedule: Open daily, sunrise to sunset, year-round
Maps: USGS Bruceville CA; online at www .fws.gov/refuge/Stone_Lakes/map.html. The trail is straightforward enough that no map is needed.
Trail contact: US Fish & Wildlife Service, Stone Lakes National Wildlife Refuge, 1624 Hood-Franklin Rd., Elk Grove 95757; (916) 775-4421; www.fws.gov/refuge/stone_lakes/

Finding the trailhead: From Sacramento, head south on I-5 to the Hood-Franklin Road exit. Go right (west) on Hood-Franklin Road for about 0.8 mile to the refuge entrance, on the left. **GPS:** N38 22.198' / W121 29.728'

The Hike

This one is for the kids.

Though the Stone Lakes National Wildlife Refuge has been around since 1994, and guided hikes have been taking place on a small parcel of the 6,500-acre refuge near North Stone Lake for years, the Blue Heron Trails are a relatively new addition, opened to the public in November 2011. The paved paths wind through a restored wetland and circle three small ponds that attract a variety of birdlife, including the stately sandhill crane.

But it's the educational emphasis that makes these little trails sing. Interpretive panels focus on the various attributes and inhabitants of the refuge. A number of educational programs take place within the boundaries of the refuge, and when the Little Green Heron Playscape is complete, kids will be able to explore a child-friendly garden, a "messy materials" area, and other environmentally educational amenities. For youngsters growing up in metropolitan Sacramento, who might be limited by time or money in their opportunities to explore the natural environment that surrounds them, Stone Lakes is the perfect introduction.

This trail definitely qualifies as an urban hike: It's paved; it has a number of nonnatural amenities (including an amphitheater); power-line towers interrupt the viewscape; and noise from I-5 wafts across its flat fields. But this portion of the Stone Lakes refuge has undergone significant transformation; the property was planted in grape vines before the restoration began in 2001. The vineyard has been removed, the ponds dredged, and the wetlands restored. When native shrubs and trees planted by schoolchildren from nearby Elk Grove mature, insulating the small park from its agricultural surroundings, a dollop of wildland will have been revived.

GREEN TIP
Pass it down. The best way to instill good green habits in your children is to set a good example.

An easy counterclockwise loop around the outermost paved path, decorated with the footprints of birds and imprints of cattails, is described. The path winds past the playscape, then between a pair of ponds, with bridges spanning ditches between the water bodies. Interpretive signs enrich the route. Curl around a power tower to an interpretive kiosk, then head back toward the wildlife refuge headquarters, located in the two-story house next to the parking area. Search the reeds around the pond

The reeds that crowd trails and bridges in the Stone Lakes National Wildlife Refuge ring with birdsong.

A play area at the Stone Lakes refuge allows young ones to experience nature hands-on.

for birds or other critters, check out a last interpretive sign, and arrive back at the trailhead after an easy, informative 0.5-mile stroll.

Docent-led interpretive hikes are regularly scheduled and take place on a 2-mile-long trail that begins at the Elk Grove gate (located off I-5 at the Elk Grove Boulevard exit). The hike leads through seasonal wetlands managed for the benefit of resident and migratory birds, including hawks, shorebirds, and songbirds. Visit the national wildlife refuge website for a schedule of guided hikes. The refuge also hosts docent-led wildlife observation paddle tours, allowing visitors to learn more about refuge residents from a kayak or canoe. An annual waterfowl hunt is conducted on the South Stone Lake Unit. In addition, visitors can participate in a citizen science project on the site in conjunction with Project Budburst, which is documenting the effects of long-term climate change on selected plants within the refuge.

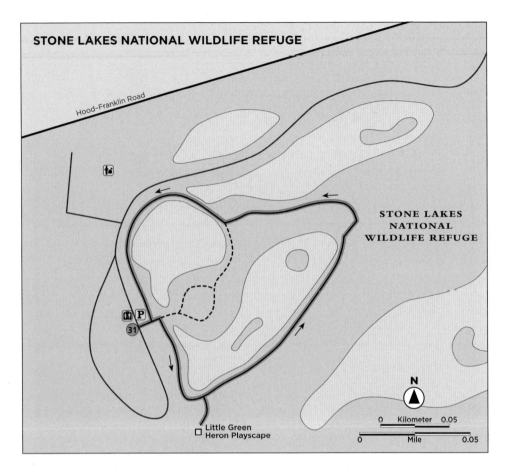

STONE LAKES NATIONAL WILDLIFE REFUGE

Hood-Franklin Road

STONE LAKES
NATIONAL
WILDLIFE REFUGE

31

N

0   Kilometer   0.05

0   Mile   0.05

Little Green
Heron Playscape

Miles and Directions

0.0 Start at the information kiosk, heading right on the paved path toward the playscape.

0.1 Pass a bridge that leads left to the amphitheater, staying right on the outer path.

0.4 At the trail junction between ponds, stay right, on the outside path.

0.5 Arrive back at the trailhead.

Hike Information

Local information: City of Elk Grove, 8401 Laguna Palms Way, Elk Grove 95758; (916) 691-2489; www.elkgrovecity.org. The Elk Grove website provides business, visitor, and community information.

Organizations: Friends of Stone Lakes NWR is a volunteer organization that provides support for the refuge. In addition to funding educational programs, members lead guided hikes on the property. Visit www.friendsofstonelakes.org or call (916) 775-4418 for more information.

32 Delta Meadows River Park

This straight-ahead walk follows an old railroad grade through the dense riparian habitat—blackberry, wild grape, and fig twined with willow and cottonwood—flourishing along sleepy Railroad Slough.

Start: White gate behind Chuck Tison Memorial Park in Locke

Distance: 3.4 miles out and back, including a short detour along a second levee road

Hiking time: About 2 hours

Difficulty: Easy

Trail surface: Dirt and gravel roadway

Best season: Spring through fall; trail may be muddy in winter

Other trail users: The occasional mountain biker

Amenities: None

Canine compatibility: Leashed dogs permitted

Fees and permits: None

Schedule: Open daily, sunrise to sunset, year-round

Maps: USGS Isleton CA, Courtland CA, and Bruceville CA; no map necessary, essentially only one trail

Trail contact: California Department of Parks and Recreation, Delta Sector, 17645 CA 160, Rio Vista 94571; (916) 777-7701; www.parks.ca.gov/?page_id=492

Other: The Delta Meadows park property is unimproved; there are no services. The property is patrolled by California Department of Fish and Game wardens. Foot traffic is permitted on the trail.

Finding the trailhead: From Sacramento, follow I-5 south about 20 miles to the Twin Cities Road exit. Take Twin Cities Road west about 4 miles to River Road, which is perched on the levee. Turn left on River Road and drive through the historic town of Locke. Look for the sign for Chuck Tison Memorial Park on the left, just outside town, before River Road makes a sweeping turn into Walnut Grove. Turn left on the unsigned paved road at Tison, then quickly left again toward a white gate, where there is parking for about five cars. **GPS:** N38 14.832' / W121 30.528'

The Hike

This obscure little park has been "closed" since 2010—the result of budget constraints like those that resulted in the threat of closure for many California state parks in 2012—but the single trail, built on a former railroad grade, is still open to foot traffic.

Obscurity lends Delta Meadows a unique feel. Even the most minimal amenities are missing, and toward trail's end lush, untamed riparian plants and grasses encroach on the treadway. It could be viewed as a neglected child, a bit sad and a little shabby, but instead it feels content and grandmotherly. Perhaps those qualities—a sense of calm and of hidden depths—drew park planners to acquire the property in the first place.

Obscurity also means the trail is little used. You may find yourself alone on the track, perhaps accompanied by only another party or two. Locke and Walnut Grove, with their historical sites, quaint shops, and cozy eateries, are nearby, but crowds are typically not an issue.

The trail has a decidedly undistinguished start, with the trailhead and dirt parking area surrounded by rusting shipping containers and other industrial flotsam and jetsam. The former railroad grade shoots straight ahead, and the cottonwoods and willows are far enough removed so the sun bakes the trail surface. The sound of cars driving on nearby River Road wafts into the park, cell towers rise from open meadows, and you can look down on the backyards of trailer park homes through openings in the brush.

But within 0.25 mile, all that is left behind. Grand old oaks reach over the track, and blackberries, poison oak, wild grape, and other scrubby plants thicken the understory. At your first glimpse of Railroad Slough, take the short path that breaks right. This out-and-back spur dead-ends at a gate and a service road that leads back to the cell tower, but not before passing figs that, instead of growing into majestic trees, have adopted a bush-and-vine form, their giant leaves unmistakable amid the less-flashy oak and grape. After you reach the turnaround, retrace your steps to the junction

Dense foliage screens views of Railroad Slough in Delta Meadows River Park.

BUDGETS AND PARKS

More than seventy sites in the California State Parks system were targeted for closure in 2012 due to a budget crisis brought about by economic recession and accounting irregularities within the park department itself. At the time, the closures represented a savings of $22 million to the state, which then owned more than 270 park properties encompassing more than 1.4 million acres.

The Sacramento area wasn't as hard hit as other California communities, but in parks like Malakoff Diggins, as well as others, local community organizations were forced to step into the breach. Fearing potential adverse effects, including increased fire danger and vandalism, and the loss of public access to significant natural and historic resources, a number of "Friends of" organizations were born. While the obvious solution would have been to increase revenues for the parks system—not likely in tax-phobic California—these private and nonprofit organizations now successfully operate parks from the Pacific coastline to the foothills of the Sierra Nevada, and from the redwood forests in the north to the deserts of the southland.

Still, the financial health of the park system is not robust. As of 2016, the state owns 280 properties encompassing 1.6 million acres, with more than 4,700 miles of trail on the ground and more than 67.8 million visitors annually, according to the *California State Park System Statistical Report* for the 2015–16 fiscal year. Revenues totaled more than $130 million, but operating expenses were more than $267 million, a deficit of about 48 percent. The upshot: Revenues continuing to fall short may translate into further cutbacks despite the popularity of park properties.

The tenuous financial footing of the state parks system makes it all the more important that users pay entrance fees, even when free access might be available by hopping a fence or accessing through a community. Hikers, cyclists, equestrians, and sightseers should also support the nonprofits that bolster the financial underpinnings of their favorite parks with monetary donations, by volunteering as docents, or by helping maintain trails and facilities.

with the rail trail and go right, passing a gate and a fenced-off utility station, the last man-made items you'll encounter for a nice, long stretch.

The trail becomes more remote feeling the farther you walk. Meditative if you are on your own, and an easy walk-and-talk if you have a companion, the setting is quieting. The slough running parallel to the trail, and others nearby, are popular with boaters; the park has been dubbed by the state a "labyrinth of sloughs, channels, and islands crowded with stands of oaks, walnuts, willows and cottonwoods [that] is

An old rowboat lies beached amid the reeds alongside the slough in Delta Meadows River Park.

unique in the modern delta." But the curtain of trees and brush is so dense that it's hard to get a clear view of the water or anyone in a kayak or canoe.

As you approach trail's end, a meadow opens on the left and a gate blocks passage onto an intersecting roadway that leads into private property. Farther on, ponds can be glimpsed, their surfaces obscured by water plants with vibrant purple blooms. Now distinctly overgrown, with noxious star thistle erupting along the centerline and thick on the verge, the path ends not far beyond the ponds. A berm and sign mark the endpoint; beyond the berm the path is overwhelmed by a bank of blackberry. Retrace your steps to the trailhead.

Miles and Directions

0.0 Start by passing the gate and heading down the obvious but unsigned former railroad grade.

0.25 At the junction—the only one in the park—leave the main trail and drop past a gate on a short side spur.

0.4 Arrive at the end of the spur. Retrace your steps to the junction with the railroad grade.

0.6 Back at the junction, turn right onto the rail trail.

0.7 Pass the gate and utility installation.

1.25 A meadow opens to the left. Pass a gated dirt roadway, continuing straight on the obvious track.

1.7 Reach the end of the line at a berm and a state park boundary sign. Retrace your steps to the trailhead.

3.4 Arrive back at the trailhead.

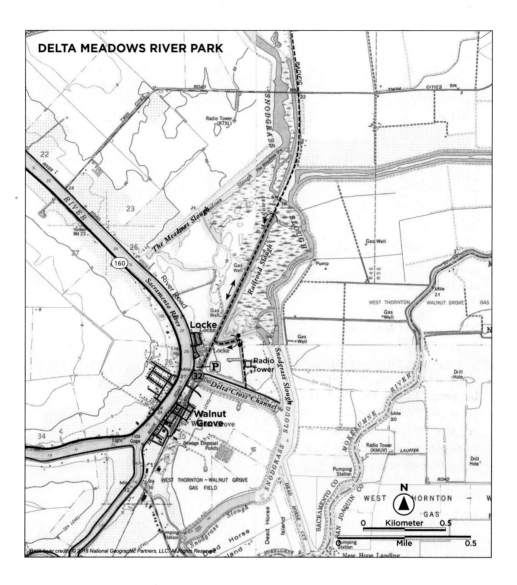

Hike Information

Local events/attractions: Visit www.locketown.com for information about attractions in historic Locke.

33 Deer Creek Hills Preserve

Follow the North Pond loop trail, which rambles along ranch roads and cattle paths through blue oak woodlands and open meadowlands to a small man-made pond, then traces segments of Crevis Creek to a natural seasonal pond.

Start: Preserve's dirt parking area off Latrobe Road

Distance: 3.1-mile lollipop

Hiking time: 2-3 hours

Difficulty: Moderate due to the rolling nature of the terrain

Trail surface: Dirt ranch roads and cattle trails

Best season: Spring for wildflowers and vernal pools; late autumn for cooler temperatures

Other trail users: Guided horseback and mountain bike rides permitted on the property

Amenities: Gravel parking lot, picnic shelter, restroom

Canine compatibility: Dogs not permitted

Fees and permits: None

Schedule: The self-guided North Pond loop is open Sat from 9 a.m. to 1 p.m.; Sacramento Valley Conservancy docents are on hand. Guided hikes are held at other times on weekends; sign up on the Sacramento Valley Conservancy website.

Maps: USGS Folsom SE CA; online at www .sacramentovalleyconservancy.org/admin/ upload/DCHTrailGuide_web.pdf

Trail contact: Sacramento Valley Conservancy, PO Box 163351, Sacramento 95816; (916) 731-8798; www.sacramentovalley conservancy.org

Special considerations: Though Latrobe Road can be navigated by an ordinary passenger vehicle, there is a substantial creek crossing that some drivers may not wish to negotiate. If available, use a high-clearance vehicle to access the trailhead, or carpool.

Finding the trailhead: From downtown Sacramento, head east on US 50 to the Sunrise Boulevard exit in Rancho Cordova. Head south on Sunrise Boulevard, traveling about 7.3 miles to the junction with CA 16 (Jackson Road). Go left (southeast) on CA 16 for 7.7 miles, toward Rancho Murieta, to the junction with Stone House Road. Turn left on Stone House Road and go 1.4 miles to the junction with Latrobe Road. Latrobe Road is gravel; follow it for 0.9 mile to the Deer Creek Hills Preserve gate and parking area, on the left. **GPS: N38 31.611' / W121 05.218'**

The Hike

Deer Creek Hills Preserve is remarkable for several reasons. First there is the setting: Straddling the ecotone between the ranchland/grassland of the southern Sacramento Valley and the mixed woodlands of the Sierra foothills, the property is composed of rolling hills cloaked in annual grasses and wildflowers, and shaded by widely spaced blue oaks.

Then there is the preserve's environmental significance. Within its boundaries flow watershed streams for Deer Creek, which flows into the Cosumnes River, which flows into the San Joaquin River, which flows into San Francisco Bay. Little Crevis Creek may not seem all that impressive (though it has carved out a nice miniature canyon), but it plays a part in a larger scheme, with widespread implications for environmental health.

▷ **Deer Creek Hills Preserve contains 170 species of birds, 105 mammal species, 58 species of amphibians and reptiles, and an estimated 5,000 kinds of insects.**

And then there is the story of the ranchland's unlikely preservation, spearheaded by a fledgling conservancy that, before Deer Creek Hills presented itself, had only protected much smaller properties that required much less funding.

To hear Aimee Rutledge of the Sacramento Valley Conservancy tell the story, you can't help but be inspired. The script reads like this: A small group of like-minded citizens with a love of wildlands, a preservation bent, and not a whole lot of money encounter a developer whose ambitious residential and commercial project has been rejected by the County of Sacramento and local voters. Seizing the opportunity, the citizens meet to discuss the possibilities.

An old ranch road fades to doubletrack trail at Deer Creek Hills Preserve.

▶ Carry your cell phone with you, but set it on vibrate or airplane mode so that you don't annoy others in the park. Deer Creek Hills, like many other parks and preserves in the Sacramento area, has full cellular coverage.

They are upping the conservancy's ante by thousands of acres and millions of dollars. But they take on the challenge. They contact the investors behind the beleaguered developer to see if they can purchase the land; they partner with public agencies to augment their effort; and they secure a prime property as open space.

That was back in 2002–2003. These days the conservancy is a veteran manager of the 4,060-acre Deer Creek Hills property (co-owned with Sacramento County and the California Departments of Fish and Game and Parks and Recreation), and conducts youth programs, stewardship programs, and restoration projects on the former sheep ranch.

The trail through Deer Creek Hills Preserve borders sections of Crevis Creek, part of the watershed for Deer Creek and, ultimately, the San Joaquin River.

For most of its history, Deer Creek Hills Preserve was accessible only on guided hikes led by docents. As of 2012, however, the lollipop loop to the North Pond has been open on Saturday mornings in spring (February through May) and fall (October and November) as a self-guided trail. The route follows old ranch roads and cattle trails. It is well signed, but the cattle sometimes use the trail markers as rubbing posts, knocking them flat. If by chance a preserve volunteer hasn't been out to replace/restore the markers, no worries. The route is relatively easy to navigate with a trail map.

Begin by following the ranch road, which leads to the North Pond. The old roadway, gently climbing and wide enough to walk side by side, leads into rolling hills dotted with blue oak (and the occasional live oak). Reach the junction at the start of the loop; you can travel in either direction, but the route is described here traveling clockwise.

While you're hiking, scan the skies, treetops, and wetlands for some of the more spectacular birds that frequent the preserve, including golden eagles, tricolored blackbirds, and kestrels. Interesting geologic formations include low vertical rocks that jut from the grasses, looking almost like stone fences. These standing stones can be found all along the edge of the foothills uplift. In late fall, watch where you put your feet or your trekking poles: Tarantulas—big, hairy, and harmless—reside on the preserve.

North Pond sits in a small basin ringed in cattails and reeds. Amenities are minimal—there's a salt lick for the cattle that run on the property in winter—but it makes a great place for a snack or a picnic.

From the pond, hike up onto a wooded hill, then down through a gentle swale to Crevis Creek, which has carved a mini-canyon into the soft soils of its bed. Dry in late season, the creek can be wet in winter.

Climb up and around a low, oak-shaded ridge, then along the well-defined trail next to the creek. The trail continues around a shallow basin—a natural pond or vernal pool that holds water into July and is dry until the rain returns in late October or November. From the pond the trail climbs gently through grasslands to hitch up with the ranch road. Turn left on the road, and retrace your steps back to the trailhead.

Miles and Directions

0.0 Start by hiking up the ranch road to the north.

0.4 Reach the trail junction at the start of the loop portion of the hike. Stay on the ranch road, heading toward the North Pond. The ranch road eventually splits, with the trail heading right (east) to the pond.

1.3 Reach the North Pond. Cross the dam, then climb the singletrack path up into an oak-lined swale.

1.5 At the trail marker go right.

2.0 Cross Crevis Creek.

2.2 At the trail marker go right, then right again, passing along the edge of a natural pond.

2.7 Close the loop on the ranch road. Turn left and retrace your steps to the trailhead.

3.1 Arrive back at the trailhead.

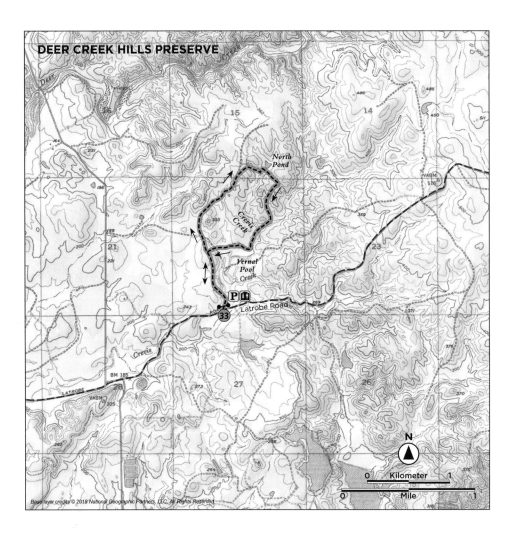

Hike Information

Hike tours: To participate in docent-led hikes on the eastern portion of the property, which resembles the Scottish Highlands when it greens up in winter, visit the Sacramento Valley Conservancy website at www.sacramentovalleyconservancy.org.

Other resources: Sacramento County's regional parks page, www.regionalparks .saccounty.net/Parks/OpenSpaces/Pages/DeerCreekHills.aspx, also includes information on Deer Creek Hills Preserve.

34 Cosumnes River Walk

Meander through riparian thickets bordering the Cosumnes River, the largest dam-free river in Northern California, which nourishes habitat for resident and migratory birds.

Start: Adjacent to the visitor center at the signed River Walk Trailhead
Distance: 3.3 miles of interlocking loops
Hiking time: About 2 hours
Difficulty: Easy
Trail surface: Boardwalk, dirt singletrack, dirt road
Best season: Spring for wildflowers; spring and fall for color and bird migrations
Other trail users: Hikers only
Amenities: Restrooms, water, information kiosks
Canine compatibility: Dogs not permitted
Fees and permits: None, but donations welcome
Schedule: Open daily, sunrise to sunset, year-round

Maps: USGS Bruceville CA; trail maps available at Cosumnes River Preserve Visitor Center and online at www.cosumnes.org/wp-content/uploads/2015/03/Nature-Trail-Guide.pdf
Trail contact: Cosumnes River Preserve, 13501 Franklin Blvd., Galt 95632; (916) 684-2816; www.cosumnes.org
Other: The visitor center is open weekends from 9 a.m. to 5 p.m. year-round; in July and Aug it is also open weekdays from 8 a.m. to noon (call to confirm the schedule). Inside you'll find interpretive displays describing the Cosumnes River ecosystem and the resident and migratory birds you might spot in the preserve. Interpretive publications and trail maps are also available.

Finding the trailhead: Travel south from Sacramento to the preserve via either I-5 or CA 99. If traveling down I-5, take the Twin Cities Road exit and head east. Follow Twin Cities Road for 1 mile to Franklin Boulevard. Turn right (south) on Franklin Boulevard and continue for 2 miles to the visitor center parking area on the left (east).

Alternatively, take CA 99 south to the Twin Cities Road / CA 104 exit. Go west on Twin Cities Road for 7.4 miles to the stop sign at Franklin Boulevard and turn left (south). Follow Franklin Boulevard south to the preserve. **GPS:** N38 15.933' / W121 26.430'

The Hike

The Cosumnes River, unobstructed from its headwaters in the Sierra Nevada to where it empties into the Mokelumne River (which in turn empties into the Sacramento–San Joaquin River delta), is the only river in the state that looks and acts much as it has for millennia. No dams obstruct its flow and, at least within the Cosumnes River Preserve, no levees corral its floods.

This remarkable waterway supports a wide variety of wildlife, including both resident and migratory birds; like many of the wetland sanctuaries in the Central Valley, the preserve lies on the Pacific Flyway. Seasonal visitors include sandhill cranes, ancient birds with 7-foot wingspans that stop here in winter, along with tundra swans

A bridge spans Willow Slough at the outset of the Cosumnes River Walk.

and Canada geese. Resident birds range from Swainson's hawks to black-crowned night-herons and kites. The riparian thickets and stands of valley oaks that crowd the riverbanks provide cover for an abundance of songbirds. As you might expect, this avian richness also attracts flocks of bird-watchers.

Aside from the river itself, the Cosumnes River Preserve, established by The Nature Conservancy in 1987, protects its surrounding floodplain. This natural area includes freshwater wetlands; riparian zones crowded with cottonwoods, willows, and oaks; and meadowlands that bloom with wildflowers in season. The Cosumnes River Walk leads you through each of these ecosystems. The birds are a major attraction, but the trails also afford the opportunity to spy other creatures, such as raccoons, mule deer, and mink, as well as river otters and beavers.

Like all rivers, the 80-mile-long Cosumnes rises and subsides with the seasons, occasionally spilling out of its channel when swollen with snowmelt and rainfall. The flooding, typical of all Central Valley rivers before dams and levees contained them, deposited rich, fertile soil in the valley bottom. Outside the preserve the bottomlands support the productive farms and ranches that comprise central California's agricultural powerhouse.

The Cosumnes may not harbor a dam, but it is not untouched by development. The railroad tracks and scenic railroad bridge at the south end of the trail are one example; the hum of traffic on the nearby interstate, pervasive background noise to the birdcall, is another.

The Cosumnes River Walk begins on a boardwalk and bridge that leads across the birdsong-filled Willow Slough, which, despite being more than 100 miles from the Golden Gate, is subject to tidal ebb and flow. Beyond the bridge the trail splits, with the Wetlands Walk (a nice addition if the Cosumnes walk is not enough) headed left (north) and the River Walk headed right (south).

Lined with interpretive markers keyed to a guide available at the visitor center and online, the dirt River Walk travels through a bower of tangled willow, cottonwood, wild rose, and berry brambles, tracing the little levee containing Middle

High water fills the flatlands alongside the Cosumnes River Walk.

Slough. Circling around the south end of the route, side trails drop right to the riverside, where views open of the railroad bridge that spans the wide, calm river.

Pass under the elevated Western Pacific railroad tracks, and follow the trail through savanna and past the marsh to the signed nature trail. Circle through the trees, following blue trail markers. A series of benches overlook the river on this gentle path. As you head back toward the savanna, birdcall from the tule marsh to the right (north) may drown out any car noise.

Beyond the riverside loop, the trail leads back into the savanna, where wildflowers flourish and the occasional valley oak provides shade. Walk north through the meadow to yet another marsh, then head back under the railroad tracks to hitch back up with the levee-top path next to Middle Slough. Turn right and retrace your steps back to the trailhead and visitor center.

Though the Cosumnes River Walk is adequately signed and lined with interpretive posts, a number of options may shorten or lengthen your tour. These options may be confusing, but with the river as one landmark and the railroad tracks as another, you won't lose your way.

Miles and Directions

0.0 Start on the boardwalk north of the visitor center, which leads down and across the bridge over Willow Slough.

0.1 The River and Wetlands Walks split. Go right (south) on the signed River Walk.

0.3 Reach a trail intersection. Continue straight (south) at this junction.

0.7 Reach a three-way trail intersection. Stay straight (south), ignoring the trail that leads left (east) into the savanna and toward the elevated railroad tracks (you'll visit these later). Continue alongside Middle Slough.

1.0 The trail curves east along the riverbank, passing interpretive markers and smaller tracks leading waterside. Pass the railroad bridge.

1.2 The trail breaks out of the woodlands at a trail sign. Head north on the broad roadway that parallels the elevated tracks, passing the first trail that leads right (east) into the savanna. You will return to this junction via this trail after completing a short loop.

1.3 Go right (east), passing under the tracks.

1.5 Pass an interpretive marker and a bench overlooking the marsh, then swing southeast through a meadow.

1.6 Cross a roadway and continue straight on the nature trail. At the next intersection go right (south) on the nature trail.

1.8 At the four-way trail junction, go straight (south) toward the river.

1.9 A nature trail sign points you right on the riverside path.

2.0 Pass an interpretive marker as the loop swings back to the west, passing a marsh.

2.2 The trail hops onto a levee and skims northwest through brambles toward the savanna.

2.3 Arrive at a four-way trail junction. Go straight (west) toward the railroad tracks, passing an interpretive marker.

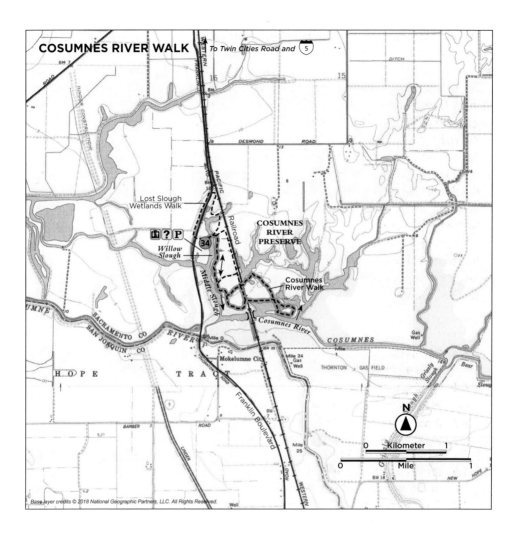

2.5 Cross a road and pass under the tracks to the junction with the first trail loop. Turn right (north), and walk the path parallel to the railroad tracks.

2.7 At the junction turn left (west), crossing the meadow to link up with the trail alongside Middle Slough. Go right (north), back toward the visitor center.

3.3 Arrive back at the trailhead and parking area.

Hike Information

Hike tours: The paved Lost Slough Wetlands Walk is a 1-mile trek through the wetlands on the west side of Franklin Boulevard, offering the opportunity for further exploration of this lovely sanctuary. Occasional guided tours are offered; for more information visit www.cosumnes.org.

35 Howard Ranch Trail

This tour of the Rancho Seco Lake shoreline and a working cattle ranch offers a sampling of big-sky country in the Central Valley, with views stretching across the prairie to the Sierra Nevada. Vernal pools fill along the route, followed by wildflower blooms in season.

Start: Signed Howard Ranch Trailhead in Rancho Seco Recreation Area
Distance: 6.9-mile lollipop
Hiking time: 4–5 hours
Difficulty: Moderate
Trail surface: Dirt singletrack, dirt ranch roads
Best season: Spring for vernal pools; late fall for moderate temperatures and color along the lakeshore
Other trail users: Hikers only
Amenities: Restroom, trash cans, information board with trail map
Canine compatibility: Dogs not permitted
Fees and permits: Day-use fee
Schedule: Open daily at 7 a.m., year-round. Closing hours change seasonally, but generally correspond with sunset.

Maps: USGS Goose Creek CA; map and fact sheet at www.cosumnes.org/retro/recreation/Howard%20Trail.pdf. Trail maps also available at the Cosumnes River Preserve Visitor Center, located about 17 miles east of Rancho Seco at 13501 Franklin Blvd., near Galt.
Trail contact: Sacramento Municipal Utility District, 6301 S St., Sacramento 95817 (mailing address: PO Box 15830, Sacramento 95852-1830); (888) 742-SMUD (7683); www.smud.org. The recreation area phone number is (209) 748-2318.
Special considerations: You'll travel through a working cattle ranch on this hike. The cows most likely will scatter as you approach. Please don't chase them. Be sure to stay on trails and close all gates behind you.

Finding the trailhead: From Sacramento, head south on CA 99. Take the Twin Cities Road / CA 104 exit and head east toward Jackson and Ione. Drive 13.9 miles, through Herald and into Clay, staying left when the road splits at Clay East Road (which leads to the decommissioned Rancho Seco nuclear facility). The signed park entrance is on the right (south). Follow the access road for 0.3 mile to a left (east) turn into the park proper. Pass the entry kiosk and continue for 0.6 mile to a gravel road on the left, signed for the Howard Ranch Trail. Follow the gravel road for 0.3 mile to the dirt parking lot. The trailhead is in the northeast corner of the lot at the information board. **GPS:** N38 20.425' / W121 05.800'

The Hike

Canyon walls, levees, and thickets of trees and shrubs hem in many trails in the Sacramento region, but at Howard Ranch those boundaries fall away. Open range rolls in all directions, spotted with cattle and the occasional lonely oak or sycamore, seasonally abloom with wildflowers reflected in the still waters of vernal pools, with the distant rampart of the Sierra Nevada hovering on the eastern skyline.

But if you seek cottonwoods, willows, and water, never fear: This hike is not all big sky and big prairie. The trail begins as a sinuous meander along the tree-shrouded shoreline of Rancho Seco Lake. Gently curving boardwalks span seasonal streams feeding into the lake. In summer the lake and its campgrounds bustle with visitors, creating an engaging, active scene. When the weather cools and the days shorten, the lake grows as quiet and calm as the grasslands that surround it.

The Howard Ranch once belonged to Charles Howard, owner of legendary racehorse Seabiscuit. Still a working ranch, it operates under a conservation easement that protects its rare ecosystems, including vernal pools. The vernal pools are a huge attraction, the subject of guided hikes and solitary explorations when they fill in winter and when they bloom in spring. Rare and threatened species associated with the ephemeral ponds include fairy shrimp and the California tiger salamander; wildflowers include vibrant spreads of goldfields and meadowfoam.

Boardwalks have been artfully placed along the shore of Rancho Seco Lake. In addition to helping hikers keep their feet dry, the walkways protect fragile wetland plants and habitat.

A significant, provocative tableau looms over the ranch and lake, the highlight of the western viewscape. Rancho Seco's neighbor is a decommissioned nuclear power plant, its two huge cooling towers rising from the flats adjacent to the park. For the most part the towers are out of sight, behind you as you walk east across the ranch and hidden by grassy rises as you curve south and west—which is pretty amazing given their height and bulk. The towers do not detract from the attractiveness of this long hike—they add depth and complexity to the journey. No matter how you feel about nuclear power as a political or environmental issue, the towers spark the imagination and present the opportunity to consider the issues posed by any interface of wildland and human development.

▶ **Many species of shrimp occupy Sacramento's vernal pools, thriving only in this ephemeral environment. They include the fairy shrimp (a threatened species), seed shrimp, vernal pool tadpole shrimp, and clam shrimp.**

The route is well marked and easy to follow, even if trail markers have toppled out of their rock cairn bases, likely pushed over by cattle rubbing up against them. It begins as a singletrack along the lakeshore, linked with boardwalks and small bridges spanning seasonal inlet streams. Pass through a gate, and the views grow Montana-big across the grasslands, stretching eastward to the distant Sierra. As you approach the 1.5-mile mark, you enter vernal pool territory, where depressions in the landscape hold water as the rains diminish in late winter, blooming brilliantly when the water evaporates. When dry, rocks litter the pockets in the fields.

The trail widens to ranch road beyond the second gate, where odd, orderly hummocks pop from the otherwise rolling landscape. You can't see what's on the other side, but the presence of trees indicates the existence of a pond. Where the trail splits at the start of the loop, go left, heading toward the mountains.

The trail narrows to singletrack again as it weaves through the grasslands at the southeastern reach of the loop. More rugged now, the track and the landscape show little sign of human handiwork.

Swing westward, and what you forgot about as you headed east—the nuclear plant's cooling towers—now pop in and out of view. You are on high ground: The prairie drops to the southeast, dotted with cattle, fences, and ponds. The track swoops through several broad swales overlooking the pastoral scene as it proceeds south and west.

The final stretch of the loop follows a ranch road along a ruler-straight fence line to the start of the loop. From there, retrace your steps to the trailhead.

Miles and Directions

0.0 Start in the northeast corner of the trailhead parking lot by the information signboard.

0.2 The trail winds along the lakeshore, crossing the second of many boardwalks that curve over seasonal streams.

0.7 Cross a wooden bridge.

1.0 Cross a set of twin bridges.

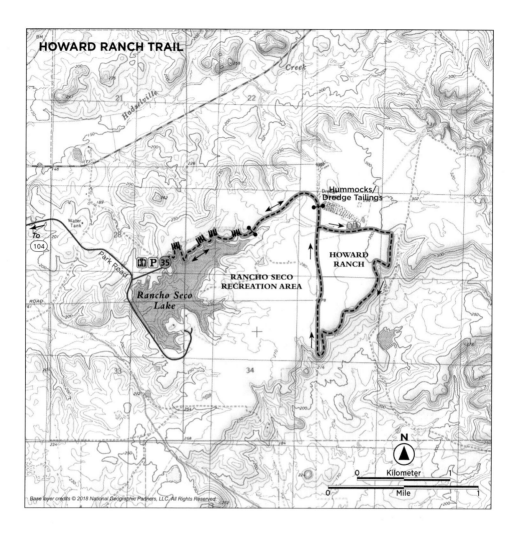

HOWARD RANCH TRAIL

1.1 Reach a ranch road and gate. Pass through the gate (be sure to close it behind you) and continue on the singletrack trail.

1.4 Cross a bridge over a gentle depression in the range, an area where vernal pools form.

1.8 Pass through the second gate, closing it behind you, and turn right (south) on the ranch road. Hummocks rise on your left (east).

2.0 Arrive at the start of the loop. You can go in either direction, but it is described clockwise. Turn left (east) on the singletrack trail.

2.1 Cross the first of a series of small bridges spanning seasonal streams that feed man-made ponds on the left (north).

2.5 The trail swings south at a fence line.

2.8 The trail curves west through a huge swale.

3.9 Reach a fence line at a ranch road; turn right (north).

4.3 Veer away from the fence on the roadway, still headed north, and pass a trail marker.

4.5 Pass through an area that may be mucky when wet; the road returns to the fence line.

4.9 Reach the trail junction at the start of the loop. Stay straight (north) on the ranch road, retracing your steps to the trailhead.

6.9 Arrive back at the trailhead and parking area.

Hike Information

Local information: Information about Galt, located just west of the Rancho Seco Recreation Area, is available from the city of Galt, 380 Civic Dr., Galt 95632; (209) 366-7130; www.ci.galt.ca.us.

Local events/attractions: Rancho Seco Recreation Area offers a bounty of outdoor activities, including boating, camping, fishing, swimming, and picnicking. For more information contact SMUD by calling (916) 732-4913, or visit https://www.smud.org/en/about-smud/community/recreational-areas/rancho-seco-lake.htm.

The Amanda Blake Memorial Wildlife Area, named for the actress who played Miss Kitty on TV's *Gunsmoke* (1955–1975), is part of SMUD's Rancho Seco complex. The preserve is a refuge for exotic animals born in captivity, including emus, ostriches, and African antelope. The refuge is open from 9 a.m. to 3 p.m. Mon through Thurs. Call (800) 416-6992 or (209) 748-2318 for more information.

Hike tours: Tours of the vernal pools at Howard Ranch are offered through the Cosumnes River Preserve. For more information and a schedule, call (916) 684-2816 or visit www.cosumnes.org.

Camping: Tent, RV, and group camping is available at Rancho Seco Recreation Area. To make a reservation, call (800) 416-6992 or visit https://www.smud.org/en/about-smud/community/recreational-areas/rancho-seco-lake.htm.

36 Indian Grinding Rock State Historic Park

Travel through a mixed evergreen forest containing stands of fragrant incense cedar and maroon-barked manzanita to a reconstructed Sierra Miwok village where the focal point is the largest *chaw'se*, or grinding rock, in North America.

Start: Signed trailhead in front of the Chaw'se Regional Indian Museum
Distance: 1.6-mile loop
Hiking time: About 1 hour
Difficulty: Easy
Trail surface: Dirt singletrack, pavement
Best season: Spring through fall
Other trail users: Hikers only
Amenities: Restrooms, information, water, and other amenities in the museum
Canine compatibility: Dogs not permitted on trails; may be on leash in the parking area

Fees and permits: Day-use fee
Schedule: Open daily, sunrise to sunset, year-round
Maps: USGS Pine Grove CA; online at www.parks.ca.gov/igr
Trail contact: California State Parks, Indian Grinding Rock State Historic Park, Chaw'se Regional Indian Museum, 14881 Pine Grove-Volcano Rd., Pine Grove 96556; (209) 296-7488; www.parks.ca.gov/igr
Other: Portions of the North Trail and the Loop Trail are accessible.

Finding the trailhead: From Sacramento take CA 99 south to the Twin Cities Road / CA 104 exit. Go east on Twin Cities Road for about 23 miles to Ione, then another 2.2 miles beyond Ione to the junction with CA 88. Turn left onto CA 88 and go 17.9 miles, through the foothills town of Jackson, to Pine Grove. Turn left on Pine Grove–Volcano Road (with a sign for Volcano) and drive 1.6 miles to the park entrance, on the left. **GPS: N38 25.505' / W120 38.465'**

The Hike

For generations the Sierra Miwok gathered to prepare meals in the lovely foothills meadow that is now part of Indian Grinding Rock State Historic Park. A huge flat rock lies at the heart of the meadow—and there the women worked, in one of the most glorious kitchens nature could provide, surrounded by a woodland scented with incense cedar and thick with the oaks from which the Miwok harvested their staple crop: acorns.

Native American women throughout California prepared acorns for meals in pretty much the same fashion. Once gathered, the nuts were cracked and the kernels removed, then winnowed in baskets to remove any chaff. The nutmeats then were taken to the creek to soak so that tannins causing bitterness could be leached away. The washed kernels were ground into meal or flour using a pestle (a handheld stone) and what, over time and with repeated use, became mortars—circular depressions in the bedrock itself. Once processed, the acorn meal could be cooked in a basket with hot stones into a soup, or baked into cakes or bread and served with whatever game or fish the hunters brought to the table, as well as with berries or greens gathered from the woods and meadows.

▶ Don't collect souvenirs along the trail. This includes natural materials, such as plants, rocks, shells, and driftwood, and historic artifacts, such as fossils and arrowheads.

Native Californians left bedrock mortars all over the state—two other examples lie along hikes in this guide, at Miners Ravine and Rush Ranch—but this chaw'se trumps the rest. It's massive, with more than 1,100 individual mortars worked into the limestone. More than 360 petroglyphs were carved into the stone as well, though these are harder to discern from the chaw'se overlook. This was no simple kitchen—it was a place where feasts were created, where meals to celebrate births and deaths and harvests were created, where women labored in unison to feed their families and tribe.

The park has done a wonderful job of showcasing the chaw'se and the lost way of life it represents. Surrounding the bedrock mortar are re creations of native struc tures destined to return to the earth over time, including bark houses typical of those found in Sierra Miwok villages and a roundhouse still used for ceremonial and social

More than a thousand bedrock mortars have been counted in the chaw'se at Indian Grinding Rock State Historic Park.

events. Finely crafted interpretive signs describe native beliefs and practices. Native plants with medicinal uses are nurtured in a small garden.

The Chaw'se Regional Indian Museum is a must-see. Its exhibits encompass the gamut of the native Californian experience, from life before the arrival of the Spaniards to the present day.

Begin exploring the park in the woods, following the North Trail away from the village and museum. The path is wedged between the park road and Volcano Road for a stretch, then crosses the park drive near a historic farmhouse that, in the late nineteenth century, was part of the ranching and farming operation of Serafino Scapuccino. Interpretive materials suggest that Scapuccino allowed the Sierra Miwok to use the chaw'se even after he laid claim to the land.

The trail switchbacks up into a more secluded section of the park, where thick stands of manzanita, with its distinctive burgundy-colored bark and bell-shaped flowers in season, crowd the edge of the trail. Baby incense cedars also buck up against the route, their distinctive featherlike needles vibrantly green. Oaks are also present, dropping leaves thickly in fall, which is when the acorns can be gathered as well.

Climb over a low ridge, then quick switchbacks deposit you in a drainage that holds water in the rainy season and dries out come summertime. Cross the creeklet a couple of times before reaching the edge of the meadow.

After a quick jog across the gravel park road, then across the creek, then past the reconstructed bark huts, the North Trail meets up with the interpretive South Nature Trail. A bridge spans the stream just above its confluence with Else Creek, then the trail climbs to the property line. Interpretive signs mark your passage; pick up a guide near the trailhead at the museum.

The steepest climb on the route follows the property line, then dips into and out of a drainage to a bench near a big dead-standing (fire-blackened) madrone. Ignore the social trails, staying left on the main track. Off in the woods to your right is another massive madrone, a virtual twin of the first.

The trail leads down past the campground into the interpretive area, ending on the broad path near the sloping bark roof of the roundhouse. Go right on the trail, which leads past the roundhouse entrance and the game field. (Park literature explains that ball games were played girl versus boy. To even things out, boys could only kick the ball, but girls could kick, throw, and run with it. However, if a girl with

▶ **More than sixty different tribes, speaking sixty different languages, occupied California before the arrival of the Spanish in 1769. Four of the tribes are generally considered to be Miwok, related through linguistics. They include the Sierra Miwok (living on the western slope of the Sierra Nevada in the foothills); the Coast Miwok (living north of San Francisco Bay); the Plains Miwok (living in the northern delta area around the confluence of the Cosumnes, Mokelumne, and Sacramento Rivers); and the Lake Miwok (living near Clear Lake).**

Reconstructed bark houses are clustered near a section of the South Nature Trail at Indian Grinding Rock State Historic Park.

the ball didn't unload it quickly enough, a boy could pick her up and carry her to the goal.) The platform overlooking the chaw'se is on the left, along with a cluster of bark houses. Interpretive signs notable for their colorful art and insightful stories line the path leading back to the museum and trailhead.

Miles and Directions

0.0 Start on the signed North Trail next to the Chaw'se Regional Indian Museum. The trail climbs a flight of steps into the woods.

0.1 Cross a little stream via a small bridge, then cross the park road. Pick up the trail on the other side, walking past the historic farmhouse.

0.3 At the junction with the Loop Trail, stay right and uphill on the North Trail.

0.4 At the second junction with the Loop Trail, again go right on the North Trail.

0.6 Go sharply left on the North Trail at the signpost.

0.7 Reach the meadow. Go right on the service road, then quickly left onto the trail leading to the South Nature Trailhead and the interpretive area.

0.8 Cross a bridge over the stream, then stay right where the path splits at the bark houses on the South Nature Trail.

1.1 Climb to a bench near a huge dead madrone. Stay left on the South Nature Trail.

1.25 Skirt the campground by staying left on the gravel path.

1.3 Enter the interpretive area near the roundhouse and go right.

1.4 Check out the platform overlooking the chaw'se, then return to the main path and continue toward the museum.

1.6 Arrive back at the trailhead.

Hike Information

Local information: The Amador Council of Tourism website (www.touramador .com) is a clearinghouse of things to see and do in the historic mining town of

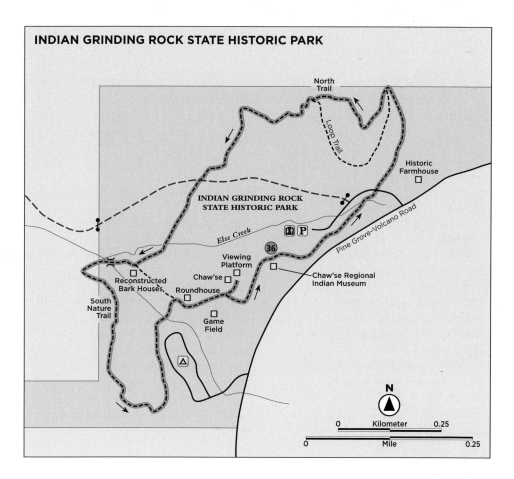

INDIAN GRINDING ROCK STATE HISTORIC PARK

Pine Grove and other communities in gold country. Call (209) 267-9249 for more information.

Local events/attractions: The Big Time, an annual Native American ceremony celebrating the acorn harvest, is held in late September. Spectators are invited. Contact the park for more information.

The Chaw'se Regional Indian Museum—well worth a visit before or after your hike—is open Fri through Mon from 11 a.m. to 4 p.m. daily; closed on Christmas, Thanksgiving, and New Year's Day.

Black Chasm Cavern National Natural Landmark, 15701 Pioneer Volcano Rd., Volcano; (866) 762-2837; www.caverntours.com/BlackRt.htm. Guided tours of the cavern are conducted year-round.

Camping: A 22-site campground in the park operates on a first-come, first-served basis. See the park website for more information.

Organizations: The nonprofit Chaw'se Indian Grinding Rock Association provides support for the park. Contact the park for more information, or visit https://chawse.org.

37 China Gulch Trail

The wide, gentle trail leading to China Gulch and beyond is popular with equestrians and hikers alike. It follows old ranch roads through rolling meadows still grazed by big-eyed bovines. The loop winds through a pastoral setting, open to sun and wind with only scattered stands of oaks providing shade, but with expansive views extending out across Camanche Reservoir.

Start: China Gulch staging area
Distance: 3.2-mile lollipop
Hiking time: About 2 hours
Difficulty: Easy
Trail surface: Dirt ranch road, dirt path
Best season: Spring for wildflowers; late fall for cool weather
Other trail users: Equestrians
Amenities: Restrooms and trash cans at the trailhead; camping, fishing, picnicking, and boating elsewhere in the park
Canine compatibility: Leashed dogs permitted
Fees and permits: A trail permit is required and may be purchased at the entry station or online at www.ebmud.com/recreation/trail-use-permits.

Schedule: Open daily, sunrise to sunset, year-round
Maps: USGS Wallace CA; online at www.lakecamancheresort.com/wp-content/uploads/2014/11/Mokelumne_Area_Trails.pdf; available at the Camanche Reservoir entrance station
Trail contact: East Bay Municipal Utility District, PO Box 24055, Oakland 94623; (866) 40-EBMUD (403-2683); www.ebmud.com/recreation/sierra-foothills/camanche-reservoir/
Special considerations: This trail bakes in the summer sun, with little shade and no access to water. Bring plenty of drinking water, use sunscreen, and wear a hat if you decide to hike on a hot day.

Finding the trailhead: From Sacramento, head south on CA 99 for 24.7 miles to the Liberty Road exit. Go left on Liberty Road for 19.9 miles (crossing CA 88 at the stop sign) to Camanche Road. Turn right on Camanche Road and go 0.8 mile to the entrance station. Follow the park road for 0.1 mile; at the junction, stay left toward China Gulch. Continue 0.4 mile to the China Gulch staging area parking lot and trailhead. **GPS:** N38 14.218' / W120 56.512'

The Hike

Consider hiking Camanche Reservoir in the off-season, when the lake is quiet and still, glinting under a winter sun hanging low in the sky. The houseboats are moored, and only the occasional sound of a motor may drift up onto the China Gulch Trail. The grasses start greening up after the first rain (though the setting is still lovely, if a little crunchier, when the sun has dried them gold). Wildflowers begin to bloom by January, though they may be tiny and hard to find, and increase in abundance, size, and color into and through the spring—showy California poppies and bright blue lupine among the most vibrant. Camanche's trails are also hikable in summer, but it can be screaming hot; it's much better to be on the water then, not on the sunbaked trail.

Camanche Reservoir, its adjacent recreation area, and the trails are operated by the East Bay Municipal Utility District (EBMUD), which provides water and other utility services to communities in San Francisco's East Bay. The lake covers more than 12 square miles, and recreational activities—other than hiking on extensive trail systems on both the north and south shores of the lake—include boating, camping, and fishing. Trails on the south shore link with EBMUD's Mokelumne-area trails and include the lengthy Mokelumne Coast to Crest Trail, which climbs along the shoreline of neighboring Pardee Reservoir and up the Mokelumne River into the Sierra foothills.

The China Gulch Trail is on the north shore and follows fire roads for 5.1 miles, passing the sites of former gold rush–era mining towns at China Gulch and Lancha Plana. The Loop Trail leaves the China Gulch route a little over 1 mile in, circling back toward the trailhead in a traverse above the reservoir and incorporating the path of an old water canal along the way.

Camanche Reservoir shimmers in the winter sunlight.

Be prepared to share the trail with two large ungulates. In addition to providing themselves with sustenance, cattle grazing along the route help control the spread of noxious weeds, and reduce fire danger by consuming some of the fuel load. Bovines are timid and will likely move away when you approach. In the event they don't, slow your pace and say a quiet hello; they will passively watch you walk by. The other hoofed trail users are horses; their riders generally ensure that encounters are friendly and risk-free. Again, quiet hellos are encouraged.

To begin, pass through the cattle gate and sign in at the register. Low signposts identify the trail; you'll pass these periodically. A broad gravel ranch road, the China Gulch route climbs gently at first, then drops through a grassy swale. The reservoir is shielded from view by widely spaced stands of oaks.

Top another small crest then drop into another swale, with a strip of riprap in the bed of the seasonal stream that runs through it. Pass a faded signpost, then a junction with the Loop Trail, which is where you'll close the loop on the return. Like a long, lazy roller coaster, the trail/road rises out of the swale into a mixed oak woodland, with a few buckeye trees thrown in. First to leaf out in spring and first to lose their leaves as autumn approaches, buckeyes are distinctive for their fruits: orbs with fuzzy coats that hang like Christmas ornaments from the bare branches. Shuck the fruit to expose the smooth, rusty-orange nut. These trees also produces fragrant flowers in late spring.

A trail crossing in the oaks along the China Gulch route.

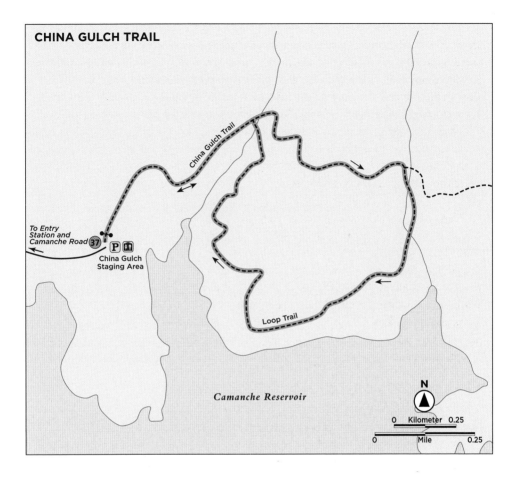

When the deciduous oaks have lost their leaves, usually by early December, check the bare branches for balls of mistletoe, which look like big messy birds' nests. It's also easy to spot woodpeckers in the winter months: The acorn woodpecker, black with white wing patches and a flashy red patch on the top of its head, can sometimes be seen flitting from tree to tree. Though you may think the bird is stockpiling the nuts, in fact each woodpecker family typically has only one storehouse, called a granary tree; acorns are stored in various cavities in this single tree.

Round a switchback, and the trail winds through another fold in the hills. Pass another trail marker, then head downhill past a cattle trail that branches right, leading across the broad swale. Stay straight on the China Gulch route, which drops into the bottom of the swale to the second junction with the Loop Trail.

Turning right onto the Loop Trail, hike through the base of the drainage, which can be boggy (and may even boast a vernal pool) in spring. The stream, dry in late season, runs to the trail's left. Cross the rocky streambed twice before the trail narrows to singletrack and climbs onto a hillside overlooking Camanche Reservoir.

The long traverse across open slopes overlooking the lake can be hot in summer, but it affords beautiful views year-round. The springtime wildflower bloom is lovely, and lone trailside oaks lend drama to the vista. The trail bends into an arm of the reservoir and loops through a triad of gullies, wet in winter and bone dry in late season, and offering the only shade you'll experience along this leg of the loop. Look for a stand of digger pines on the hillside to the right of the third gully.

Cross the riprap swale to close the loop on the China Gulch road. Turn left and retrace your steps to the trailhead.

Miles and Directions

0.0 Start by walking down the gravel road and through the gate. Sign in, then proceed up the ranch road.

0.6 The Loop Trail takes off to the right (this is the return route). Stay straight (left) on the China Gulch Trail.

0.8 Pass a trail post.

1.0 Pass another trail post at a cattle trail that breaks right. Stay left on the China Gulch Trail.

1.2 Reach the second junction with the Loop Trail. Turn right on the Loop Trail, dropping down toward the lake.

1.3 Cross a rocky streamlet and pass a trail post; about 0.1 mile farther, cross another rocky creek bed and pass another trail post. The route narrows to singletrack and climbs onto a hillside overlooking the lake.

2.0 Curve north, away from the lake proper, and traverse above an inlet.

2.1 Bend through the first gully.

2.3 Round the second gully. Ignore the horse trail that takes off to the right (uphill).

2.6 Switchback through the third gully. Close the loop on the China Gulch trail/road less than 0.1 mile beyond. Turn left to retrace your steps.

3.2 Arrive back at the trailhead.

Hike Information

Local information: Lake Camanche Recreation; (209) 763-5121; www.lakecamanche resort.com. Recreation area concessions, including boating, camping, fishing, and cabins, are offered by the Camanche Recreation Company.

Camping: Camping is available on the north and south shores of the reservoir. Camps with complete amenities, as well as a primitive campsite, are available on the north shore. For information and reservations contact Lake Camanche Recreation; (209) 763-5121; www.lakecamancheresort.com; e-mail: camping@camancherecreation.com.

Foothills South of I-80

AN ABANDONED RAILROAD GRADE, A DAM, GOLD RUSH SITES, AND VIEWS OF SNOWCAPPED PEAKS . . .

Though Sacramento sprawls across the Central Valley floor, flat as the proverbial pancake, it serves as gateway to the lofty Sierra Nevada. The main foothills attraction within an hour's drive east of the metro area is the Auburn State Recreation Area (SRA), a vast tract of public land encompassing the spectacular landscapes that surround the confluence of the North and Middle Forks of the American River. Given the scenic values of the recreation area, as well as its proximity to the capital city, the bulk of trails in this section lie within its boundaries.

Routes in the Auburn SRA include a trail that follows an abandoned railroad grade, a trail that climbs to the dam at Lake Clementine, a trail following a tributary of the

Fence lizards like this one, warming up on a fieldstone, are common throughout the foothills.

An old foothills oak catches the sun.

American River to a secluded waterfall, and a long route circling through the upper reaches of the recreation area. These selections are just a few of the options available in the region; feel free to explore above and beyond.

Trail gems in the foothills aren't limited to the recreation area, however. Regional parks offer great opportunities, such as the route through Cronan Ranch. Venture back to gold rush days at the Marshall Gold Discovery State Historic Park outside Placerville. And the long tour around Jenkinson Lake provides a taste of what you'll enjoy if you venture higher into the Sierra Nevada, with dense forest crowding the path and views of snowcapped peaks.

Trails in the foothills are accessed via I-80 and US 50, both of which connect Sacramento with the Lake Tahoe basin. Scenic CA 49 runs north–south between the interstate and US 50, linking two mountain towns with mining heritages, Auburn and Placerville, as well as Grass Valley and other gold country hamlets north of I-80.

38 Stevens Trail Falls

A walk into the canyon of the North Fork American River offers views of a cascade, a great overlook, and insights into what it took to carve a railroad through the Sierra Nevada.

Start: Trailhead at the end of North Canyon Road in Colfax
Distance: 3.0 miles out and back
Hiking time: About 2 hours
Difficulty: Moderate
Trail surface: Dirt singletrack
Best season: Spring and early summer
Other trail users: Mountain bikers; equestrians
Amenities: Restrooms, trash cans, information signboards

Canine compatibility: Leashed dogs permitted
Fees and permits: None
Schedule: Open daily, year-round
Maps: USGS Colfax, CA
Trail contact: Bureau of Land Management, Mother Lode Field Office, 5152 Hillsdale Circle, El Dorado Hills, CA 95762; (916) 941-3101; www.blm.gov/visit/american-river-north-middle-south-forks

Finding the trailhead: From I-80 westbound in Colfax, take exit 135 for Colfax/Grass Valley. Go left at the stop sign onto North Canyon Road. Follow North Canyon Road, which parallels the interstate, for 0.5 mile to the signed trailhead and parking area on the left. If the lot is full, park carefully along North Canyon Road. **GPS:** N39 06.330' / W120 56.824'

The Hike

The Stevens Trail dates back to the California gold rush, built and managed as a toll road by an enterprising miner named Truman Allen Stevens and a partner. The trail linked Colfax with the boomtown of Iowa Hill and was well traveled in the late 1800s. When the boom went bust, the trail fell out of service—and essentially out of sight. It began its renaissance in the late 1960s when a Boy Scout from Sacramento rediscovered and revived it.

Now on the National Register of Historic Places, the trail sees a lot of traffic as hikers, mountain bikers, and equestrians head out to take in expansive vistas and moderately challenging terrain. The track ultimately leads to the North Fork American River, but this upside-down trek will take you as far as the 300-foot waterfall that spills under the route and a stony overlook of the steep river canyon.

The trailhead is adjacent to busy I-80, so the start features highway noise. This fades fairly quickly as the path heads downhill across a slope forested in oaks and weaves across several seasonal streams feeding a more substantial creeklet.

At the base of the first descent, rock-hop the ephemeral waterway in the bed of the ravine and bear right on a dirt road, which leads up into a saddle where several

An overlook on the Stevens Trail offers views down into the canyon of the North Fork American River.

unsigned dirt roadways meet. Head down and left on the singletrack that heads back into the oaks; an inconspicuous trail sign points the way.

It's a relatively short drop from the saddle to the waterfall, which flows in tiers down the brushy cleft of Robbers Ravine. You can walk to its base or beat a path through brush and poison oak up alongside, but arguably the best place to experience the falls in all (or most) of its glory is from the substantial rock outcropping passed on the descent. A use trail leads out onto the fractured rock of the outcropping's summit. Look north to check out the entire waterfall, which begins hundreds of feet above what can be seen from the approach.

Keep looking up toward the arc of Cape Horn, where a great sweep of railroad bed was carved into the mountainside in the mid-1860s. Cape Horn is one of many storied locales along the Central Pacific Railroad as it punched through the Sierra Nevada and on to Promontory, Utah, where it

The tiered cascade on the Stevens Trail tumbles about 300 feet down Robbers Ravine.

met the Union Pacific and the transcontinental railroad was completed. Legend had it that "Chinese basket drillers" etched the railbed into the mountainside, suspended off precipices in handwoven buckets, several hundred perishing in the effort. At least one author has debunked this tale—he notes the story of the baskets was born long after construction took place.

But that doesn't take away from the dangers of the work or the fact that men died on the Horn. Workers secured on the steep slopes by ropes still had to carve the platform into the mountainside and then drill and set charges for the dynamite that blasted the route clear. Ropes are safer than baskets, right? Either way, this treacherous work could only have been undertaken by brave, hungry men who were, perhaps, also a little crazy.

Look away from the mountainside, and vistas open down into the wooded American River canyon, where the silver thread of North Fork winds through shadowy, folded walls. This spectacular view was enjoyed by travelers on the railroad once it was completed; the Central Pacific stopped the train on Cape Horn so that patrons could disembark and gain a fuller appreciation of the beauty and challenge of the mighty Sierra and its foothills.

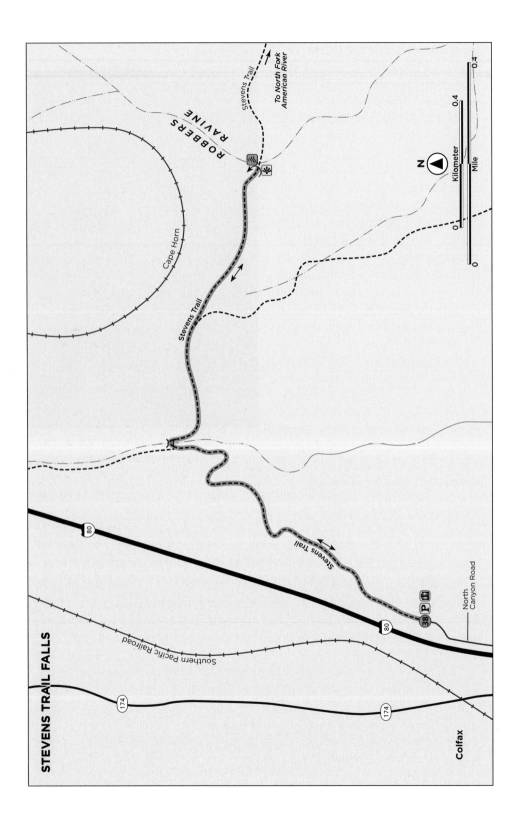

STEVENS TRAIL FALLS

If time and leg power permit, you can continue downhill from the rock outcrop to the confluence of the North Fork and Steep Ravine, where the Stevens Trail comes to an end. Keep in mind that it's all uphill on the return trip. The round-trip distance is 9.0 miles, and the elevation change is about 1,200 feet. Highlights include better views of Cape Horn and the remnants of gold rush–era mines, as well as the river itself.

Return as you came.

Miles and Directions

0.0 Start by heading down along the trail through an open area. The path soon passes into oak woodland, the trees and a hillside screening the sounds of the nearby freeway.

0.8 Reach a substantial creek crossing in the bed of a ravine. If the water is high, cross either on rocks or on a narrow plank. On the far side a trail sign with an arrow points to the right, down a wide dirt road.

1.0 At the saddle stay left for a short distance on the roadway; then go left again on the trail.

1.3 At the Y junction stay left on the signed hikers' trail. The route to the right is for cyclists.

1.5 Round a bend, and the falls come into view. Descend to the base, and then retrace your steps to a substantial rock outcropping, which offers waterfall views as well as views down into the North Fork American River canyon. Retrace your steps.

3.0 Arrive back at the trailhead.

Hike Information

Local information: Colfax offers a variety of services, restaurants, and community events. The municipal website (www.colfax-ca.gov) includes links to visitor information and recreational and historical resources. The Colfax Area Chamber of Commerce is another source for information about the area; visit www.colfaxchamber .com/colfax-area-1.html or call (530) 346-8888.

Organizations: Protect American River Canyons (PARC) is an organization "dedicated to the protection and conservation of the recreational, cultural, and historical resources" of the North and Middle Fork American River canyons. Visit www .parc-auburn.org for more information; you'll also find links to area guides and maps on the website.

39 Mountain Quarry Railroad Trail

The trail that rides on the abandoned bed of the Mountain Quarry Railroad rolls across the historic No Hands Bridge below the confluence of the Middle Fork and North Fork American River, then follows the river downstream through a lovely stretch of canyon.

Start: Gate #150, on the east side of the CA 49 bridge that spans the confluence
Distance: 4.2 miles out and back
Hiking time: About 2 hours
Difficulty: Moderate
Trail surface: Dirt and ballast on a former railroad bed
Best season: Spring and fall. Summer may be very hot, but you can cool off in the water. Winter rains or snow may render the track muddy, but it generally dries out within a couple of days.
Other trail users: Trail runners and equestrians. Mountain bikers are not permitted on the trail, but tracks in the dirt indicate they sometimes poach the route.
Amenities: Restrooms at the Stagecoach Trailhead on the west side of the Old Foresthill

Bridge, about 0.5 mile north of the CA 49 trailhead for the Mountain Quarry Railroad Trail. No water is available; bring all that you need.
Canine compatibility: Leashed dogs permitted
Fees and permits: None
Schedule: Open for day use from 7 a.m. to sunset year-round
Maps: USGS Auburn CA; Auburn State Recreation Area brochure available at recreation headquarters on CA 49 and online at www .parks.ca.gov/?page_id=502. *Note:* In some resources the trail is known as the Railroad Bed Section of the Western States Trail.
Trail contact: Auburn State Recreation Area, 501 El Dorado St., Auburn 95603-4949; (530) 885-4527; www.parks.ca.gov/ ?page_id=502

Finding the trailhead: From Sacramento, head east on I-80 to the CA 49 exit in Auburn. Take CA 49 south through Auburn (toward Placerville), following the signs for 0.5 mile through the downtown area to where the highway plunges into the American River canyon. CA 49 meets Old Foresthill Road at the base of the hill at 2.5 miles. Turn right (southeast), cross the bridge, and park alongside the road. The trailhead is at the gate (#150) immediately on the southeast side of the bridge. **GPS:** N38 54.894' / W121 2.404'

The Hike

The modern riches typical of California's gold country surround this easy route. They can't be mined from mountainsides or sifted from river bottoms, but consist instead of self-propelled travel through rugged canyon country awash in sunshine and watered by a rushing river.

The Mountain Quarry Railroad Trail lies on the bed of a historic rail line that linked a limestone quarry on the Middle Fork American River with the town of Auburn and the Southern Pacific rail line that continued from the foothills town down into Sacramento. The rail trail includes passage over the No Hands Bridge, so named, according to local trail guides, because for many years it didn't have guardrails (now it does). Once the longest bridge of its kind in the world, the scenic span survived the collapse of the Hell Hole dam in 1964 as well as subsequent floods; it now affords hikers a tangible encounter with history.

Enjoyably straightforward, the trail deviates from the original rail line only where trestles have been removed. Their concrete abutments, overgrown with shrubs and inscribed with the dates they were poured—1915, 1921—border the gullies they spanned. Because trains were unable to negotiate the sharp natural curves of the river canyon, trestles were built to straighten the line. Hikers don't need straight lines; swinging through folds in the terrain poses no hardship to those on foot.

Along the track you'll encounter numerous signs of the defunct rail line, including sections where cut-and-fill construction techniques left grass-covered berms on

Begin your hike down this former railbed by passing over the American River via the historic No Hands Bridge.

BRIDGES OF THE CONFLUENCE

You can link a hike on the Mountain Quarry rail trail with the first 0.5 mile of the Lake Clementine Trail in an interpretive loop that focuses on historic bridges in the American River canyons. The Confluence Interpretive Trail is marked with numbered posts along both stretches of the trails keyed to an interpretive guide in the Auburn SRA Canyon Keepers' *American River Canyon Hikes* booklet. A short stretch of roadside walking separates the Mountain Quarry Railroad Trail from the Lake Clementine Trailhead. The route takes you along CA 49 and back across the bridge, then up Old Foresthill Road on the right (north), across the Old Foresthill Road Bridge to the Lake Clementine Trailhead, and upstream toward the towering Foresthill Bridge.

either side. The gentle grade is also typical of a rail line; steep inclines and declines aren't easily negotiated by trains, and the Mountain Quarry line was built to accommodate that limitation. You'll encounter only one steep set of pitches along the route, where the trail dips into a gully washed by a small waterfall dubbed the "Black Hole of Calcutta." The year-round cascade offers a dark, cooling respite along the track.

The rest of the route is flat, sunny, and pleasant, offering great views down to the river. The exposed section at the base of Eagle Rock—a steep, flaking monolith with debris spilling downslope—is particularly striking. Side trails lead both uphill and down to the riverside, but the route is obvious; you'll never lose your way. If there's a downside to this hike, it's only that road noise from nearby CA 49 echoes in the canyon.

The Mountain Quarry Railroad Trail is part of the Western States Trail, 100 miles long and the venue for endurance races for runners and equestrians. No need for endurance on this trek, however. A water bottle, a granola bar, and a camera are all you'll need. The interpretive guide put together by the Auburn State Recreation Area Canyon Keepers is also a helpful resource. Keyed to posts along the trail, it provides information about the natural and human history of the route.

Miles and Directions

0.0 Start by passing the gate at the trailhead.

0.2 Pass the junction with the Pointed Rocks Trail (which leads up toward Cool) on the left (south). Go right (west) across the No Hands Bridge.

0.3 Reach the west side of the No Hands Bridge and continue on the obvious rail trail. An interpretive sign at the end of the bridge offers information about its historic significance.

0.8 Reach the first trestle abutment. The trail departs from the railroad grade, narrows to singletrack, and scoops through a gully.

1.0 Pass a trestle foundation dated 1915.

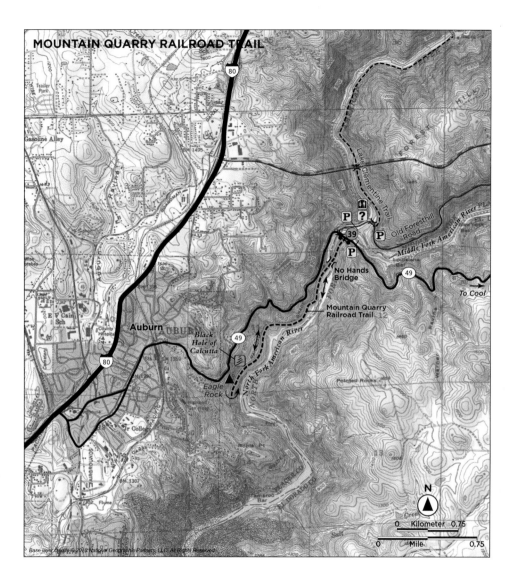

1.1 Reach the only steep drop and climb of the route, through the "Black Hole of Calcutta." Once back on the railroad grade, pass a Western States Pioneer Express Trail marker.

1.3 Pass another trestle abutment.

1.4 At the trail intersection, stay left (straight/west) on the obvious railroad grade.

1.7 Skirt Eagle Rock.

2.1 Pass a mile marker and another Western States Pioneer Express Trail marker at the end of the railroad grade. This is the turnaround point. Retrace your steps to the trailhead.

4.2 Arrive back at the trailhead.

Hike Information

Local information: The City of Auburn, 1225 Lincoln Way, Auburn 95603; (530) 823-4211; www.auburn.ca.gov. The city site offers information for residents as well as visitors. Information about Auburn and its environs can also be found at the Auburn Visitor Center and through the Old Town Auburn Business Association. Call (530) 451-6822 or visit https://oldtownauburnca.com.

Local events/attractions: Both the annual Western States 100-Mile Endurance Run and the Western States Endurance Ride / Tevis Cup, an equestrian event, pass through Auburn. For more information on the run, visit www.wser.org. For information about the ride, go to www.teviscup.org.

Hike tours: Docent-led interpretive hikes are conducted throughout the Auburn SRA. Contact the Auburn State Recreation Area Canyon Keepers (www.canyon keepers.org) for more information.

Restaurants: Ikeda's California Country Market, 13500 Lincoln Way, Auburn; (530) 885-4243; www.ikedas.com. The diner serves up delicious burgers and a BLT to die for; the pies are out of this world, and the market is stocked with fresh local produce and munchies for the trail.

Organizations: Volunteers with the Auburn State Recreation Area Canyon Keepers help with a variety of programs in the recreation area, from leading hikes to supporting the ranger staff. Visit www.canyonkeepers.org for more information, or contact the Auburn SRA ranger station.

Other resources: *American River Canyon Hikes*, a guide to trails along the Middle Fork and North Fork American River, is a wonderful compendium of hiking options in the Auburn State Recreation Area. Compiled by members of the Auburn SRA Canyon Keepers, it is available locally and from online retailers.

40 Lake Clementine Trail

This scenic stretch of gravel trailway traces the North Fork American River, passes beneath the towering, newer Foresthill Bridge, offers access to a swimming hole, and culminates at an overlook of Lake Clementine's spillway waterfall.

Start: Gate #139, on the east side of Old Foresthill Bridge

Distance: 4.6 miles out and back

Hiking time: 2–3 hours

Difficulty: Moderate due to trail length

Trail surface: Dirt roadway, short stretches of paved road, dirt singletrack

Best season: Spring and fall

Other trail users: Mountain bikers, trail runners

Amenities: Restrooms, information boards, and additional parking at the Stagecoach Trailhead on the west side of the Old Foresthill Bridge. Bring plenty of drinking water.

Canine compatibility: Leashed dogs permitted

Fees and permits: None

Schedule: Open for day use from 7 a.m. to sunset year-round

Maps: USGS Auburn CA; Auburn State Recreation Area brochure available at recreation headquarters on CA 49 and online at www.parks.ca.gov/?page_id=502

Trail contact: Auburn State Recreation Area, 501 El Dorado St., Auburn 95603-4949; (530) 885-4527; www.parks.ca.gov/?page_id=502

Finding the trailhead: From I-80 in Auburn, take the CA 49/Placerville exit. Follow CA 49 through downtown Auburn (signs point the way) for about 0.5 mile to where the highway dives into the American River canyon. Proceed another 2.5 miles to the floor of the canyon and the junction of CA 49 and Old Foresthill Road. Continue straight for about 0.5 mile on Old Foresthill Road to the trailhead, on the left, on the east side of the Old Foresthill Bridge. Parking is alongside the roadway just beyond the bridge. The trail begins behind gate #139 (signed for Lake Clementine). **GPS:** N38 54.978' / W121 2.129'

The Hike

The confluence of the North and Middle Forks of the American River, in the bottom of a steep, spectacular canyon, draws thousands of visitors to the Auburn State Recreation Area each year. But many of those visitors don't know that the river valleys—and the historic sites within them—have long been slated for submersion beneath a huge and controversial reservoir. Fortunately for recreationalists, the proposed Auburn Dam, besieged by seismic, environmental, and economic concerns since construction began in the mid-1960s, was brought to an apparently permanent halt in late 2008 when water rights held by the US Bureau of Reclamation were revoked. If it were ever completed, the dam would drown the confluence behind a 690-foot arcing wall of concrete, and the popular trails exploring the forks would drown along with it.

The newer Foresthill Bridge, built to accommodate a reservoir that has yet to materialize, towers over the trail to Lake Clementine.

The trail to Lake Clementine showcases the lovely natural setting of the canyon, but man-made structures along the route also demand attention. The green lattice arches and massive concrete support columns of the new Foresthill Bridge frame the trail's outset, the boom and clank of cars passing high overhead echoing down into the canyon. The span, reportedly the tallest bridge in California, was built to proportions intended to accommodate a reservoir that has never materialized; the water would have reached as high as 22 feet below the deck if the lake was full. More

The overlook of Lake Clementine's dam and spillway highlight the turnaround point for this relaxing out-and-back trek.

information on this bridge, and others along the route, is provided in an interpretive guide produced by the Auburn SRA Canyon Keepers.

Below the structure, the wide dirt road to Lake Clementine follows the river's curves, with anglers' trails dropping left to the rocky riverbanks. Foundations of historic bridges jut from forested hillsides, which are also scarred by minor slides and small fires. In low water, islands and rocky shoals in the middle of the river harbor stands of willow that blush yellow in fall.

A little less than a mile upstream from the confluence, the river widens and deepens into Clarks Hole, a popular swimming spot formed by an "underwater dam" built by placer miners more than one hundred years ago. This popular destination makes a great turn-around spot for those seeking a shorter hike.

Beyond Clarks Hole, the trail begins an easy, steady climb through a mixed evergreen forest, heavy on the oaks and light on the pines. It eventually reaches the paved Lake Clementine Road; a short trek on the pavement and along a singletrack trail leads to

▶ Back in the day, according to the Auburn SRA Canyon Keepers, folks were charged tolls to cross the Foresthill Covered Bridge, built in 1875 and located upstream from Clarks Hole on the North Fork American River: 6 cents per cow, 50 cents for a horseman, and $1 for a wagon pulled by two horses.

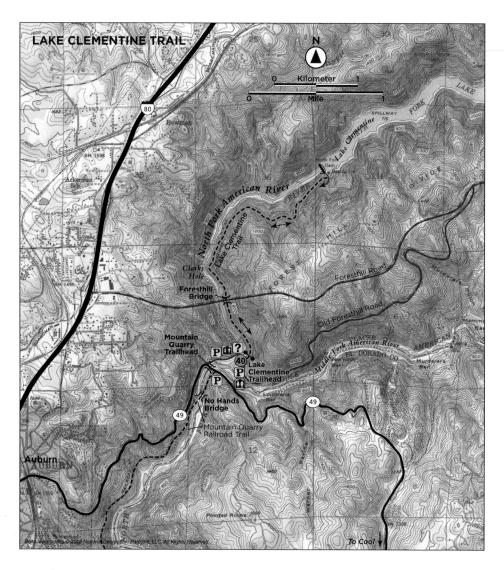

an up-close and personal view of the spillway waterfall over the North Fork Dam, with Lake Clementine pooling behind. The dam overlook is a perfect place to snack, rest, and watch boats ply the smooth waters of a reservoir that filled behind a dam built to capture mining debris.

From the dam, retrace your steps to the trailhead.

Miles and Directions

0.0 Start by passing gate #139 at the signed trailhead.

0.1 Stay left (riverside) at the trail fork; 0.1 mile farther, pass an interpretive marker at a concrete bridge abutment.

0.5 The trail narrows to singletrack as it passes beneath the massive support tower of the Foresthill Bridge.

0.8 Reach Clarks Hole. Social trails drop left to the riverside for the length of the pond-smooth pool. This is a good turnaround point for those seeking a shorter hike.

1.0 The abutment for a historic (now defunct) covered bridge juts from the opposite bank. The trail begins to climb.

1.2 Pass a social trail leading down to the riverside. The trail continues to climb through oaks and scrub, with limited views opening of the North Fork Dam and Lake Clementine.

1.8 Arrive at the end of the dirt road/trail at a gate. Go left (north, then northeast) on the paved roadway.

2.2 A singletrack path leads left (north) toward the dam overlook.

2.3 Reach the overlook, take in the views, then retrace your steps to the trailhead.

4.6 Arrive back at the trailhead.

Hike Information

Local information: The City of Auburn, 1225 Lincoln Way, Auburn 95603; (530) 823-4211; www.auburn.ca.gov. The city site offers information for residents as well as visitors. Information about Auburn and its environs can also be found at the Auburn Visitor Center and through the Old Town Auburn Business Association. Call (530) 451-6822 or visit https://oldtownauburnca.com.

Local events/attractions: Both the 100-mile Western States Endurance Run and the 100-mile Western States Endurance Ride/Tevis Cup (an equestrian event) are staged in the foothills surrounding Auburn each year. For more information on the run, visit www.wser.org. For information about the ride, go to www.teviscup.org.

Hike tours: Docent-led interpretive hikes are conducted throughout the Auburn SRA. Contact the Auburn State Recreation Area Canyon Keepers (www.canyon keepers.org) for more information.

Restaurants: Ikeda's California Country Market, 13500 Lincoln Way, Auburn; (530) 885-4243; www.ikedas.com. The diner serves up delicious burgers and a BLT to die for; the pies are out of this world, and the market is stocked with fresh local produce and munchies for the trail.

Organizations: Volunteers with the Auburn State Recreation Area Canyon Keepers help with a variety of programs in the recreation area, from leading hikes to supporting the ranger staff. Visit www.canyonkeepers.org for more information, or contact the Auburn SRA ranger station.

Other resources: *American River Canyon Hikes*, a guide to trails along the Middle Fork and North Fork American River, is a wonderful compendium of hiking options. Compiled by members of the Auburn SRA Canyon Keepers, it is available locally and from online retailers.

41 Olmstead Loop

The terrain covered on this long foothills loop encompasses oak woodlands, hollows, and ranchlands, including a verdant drainage where Knickerbocker Creek waters bay laurels, maples, and other stalwarts of riparian zones. Plan to be out in the backcountry all day.

Start: Olmstead/Knickerbocker Trailhead behind the fire station in Cool

Distance: 8.6-mile loop

Hiking time: 4–5 hours

Difficulty: Challenging due to trail length and elevation changes

Trail surface: Dirt singletrack, dirt and gravel roadways

Best season: Spring, for wildflower blooms and cool temperatures

Other trail users: Mountain bikers, equestrians

Amenities: Picnic sites, restrooms, information kiosk at the trailhead. Other amenities, including gas stations and cafes, are just up CA 49 in Cool.

Canine compatibility: Leashed dogs permitted

Fees and permits: Day-use fee

Schedule: Open for day use from 7 a.m. to sunset year-round

Maps: USGS Auburn CA and Pilot Hill CA; Auburn State Recreation Area brochure available at the recreation headquarters on CA 49 and online at www.parks.ca .gov/?page_id=502

Trail contact: Auburn State Recreation Area, 501 El Dorado St., Auburn 95603-4949; (530) 885-4527; www.parks.ca.gov/ ?page_id=502

Finding the trailhead: From Sacramento, follow I-80 west for about 24 miles to the CA 49 exit (for Placerville / Grass Valley) in Auburn. Exit and head right on CA 49, toward Placerville, following signs that lead through downtown Auburn to where CA 49 dives into the American River canyon. Drop 2.5 miles to the junction of Old Foresthill Road and CA 49. Turn right on CA 49, heading south. Climb out of the canyon to St. Florian Court, which is at the fire station just before you arrive in the little town of Cool, about 3.4 miles from the bridge over the American River. Turn right on St. Florian Court and go about 0.1 mile to the signed Knickerbocker Area parking lot and fee station. The trailhead is in the southeast corner of the larger parking lot (used by equestrians for their trailers). **GPS:** N38 53.346' / W121 01.044'

The Hike

The Olmstead Loop begins amid the mixed evergreen forest and rolling grasslands that characterize the Sierra foothills at Auburn's elevation (about 1,500 feet). It drops through a shady canyon cradling Knickerbocker Creek, then climbs back into more oak woodland and meadowlands at the finish. Toss in wonderful vistas looking west toward the Sacramento Valley, a couple of relatively steep descents and climbs, and a feeling of seclusion, and Olmstead supplies just about everything a hardy hiker seeks.

Once known as the Knickerbocker Loop, the trail was renamed for hiker and mountain biker Dan Olmstead, who championed the trail's construction and promoted cooperative trail use among equestrians, mountain bikers, and hikers. He died in 1993 of cancer, but his legacy is a route that satisfies and delights adventurers on wheels, heels, and hooves.

That said, unless a large group of cyclists have chosen the Olmstead route for a day's outing, you're more likely to see equestrians on the trail than mountain bikers. And once you are a mile or two down the trail, it's a good bet you won't encounter another user at all—the route's length and the variety of terrain virtually guarantees plenty of space between you and anyone else.

You can travel the loop in either direction; it's described here circling clockwise. Olmstead trail markers are generally pale green, and while they may not be present at every junction, sighting a marker is reassurance that you're on the right track. Still, keep a map and/or directions handy as you hike.

Pass through the fence at the trailhead; the dirt path immediately splits. Go left at that initial split on the wide dirt track that roughly parallels CA 49 for a couple of miles or so. The trail rolls through grassy former ranchland studded with spreading oaks, passing country homes and sometimes within sight of the highway itself. It swings away from civilization for a brief stretch, devolving into narrow singletrack

From open meadows to oak woodlands to riparian stream corridors, the Olmstead Loop offers variety and challenge.

overgrown with blackberry as it crosses the marshy upper reach of Knickerbocker Creek. A small footbridge enables you to cross the creek without getting your shoes too wet, though the path through this section can be boggy in spring and after rain. At the unsigned junction above the footbridge, go right; the trail widens and the surroundings dry out as you leave the creek behind.

> Endurance seems to be the name of the athletic game in the foothills. There's the Western States 100-Mile Endurance Run and the Tevis Cup, a 100-mile equestrian challenge that incorporates long sections of trail in the Auburn State Recreation Area. Parts of the Olmstead Loop have been included in the Way Too Cool 50K Endurance Run and the American River Classic, an equestrian endurance ride that dates back to 1972 and typically spans the distance between Folsom Lake and the foothills town of Cool.

Reach a trail access point at the Cave Valley Gate behind Northside Elementary School. Stay straight on the Olmstead track, which continues to roll through scenic oak woodland; though climbing and falling, at one point, trail posts line up like beacons ahead, straight and sure amid the waving grasses.

Cross another stream, wet even in the dry season, via a footbridge. Wind past a last home on the left, then the trail bends southwest into former ranchland. Barbwire fences split the hillsides into pastures, and an old watering trough rests beside the route. Views open out across the foothills to the Sacramento Valley, and the trail itself is an open red-dirt roadway—clear, unshaded, and unobstructed. The last signs of civilization you'll see for a while are on the left—cell towers that clearly were placed here for the same wide-open reasons the views are so good.

The vistas disappear as you enter a woodland. Now descending, the trail intersects a couple of old ranch roads, but the signage is good and it's easy to stay on track. Slip through a gentle hollow watered by a seasonal stream, then drop into the cool, densely shaded drainage that cradles Knickerbocker Creek.

Water is a powerful force in the Sierra foothills, evidenced spectacularly in the American River's canyons. But water's power can also be quiet, as at Knickerbocker Creek. The drainage is deep, but it's softened by the lush greenery thriving on moisture from the waterway. Bay laurel, maples, madrone, manzanita, and oaks comingle, with an understory of blackberries (not native but producing tasty fruits in August), ferns, poison oak, and coffeeberry. It's lovely and cooling, features to be savored considering the climb to come.

A stonework dam/walkway assists passage across the creek when the water is high; when it's low in late summer and autumn, you can walk across without getting the tops of your shoes wet. A steep climb leads to a traverse across a grassy slope to the junction with the paved road. An extension of St. Florian Court, the roadway begins behind the gate at the trailhead in Cool and descends toward the canyon rim of the American River; this is an optional return route if you want to carve a

On a warm day, provided the water is flowing, Knickerbocker Creek offers hikers a nice spot to chill out.

few miles off the loop. Otherwise, head straight onto the dirt Olmstead track, then through an intersection with the Auburn–Cool Trail.

A rather steep descent takes you past the junction with the Coffer Dam / Salt Creek Loop Trail and then down into the Salt Creek drainage. Follow the stream, which rambles in its rocky bed to the right of the trail, for a short distance, then climb through more oak woodland. At the top of the climb, the path reenters the grasslands of ranch country and commences a rolling run through a pastoral landscape lush with wildflowers in spring.

Take a sharp right at the junction with the Training Hill Trail/Pointed Rocks Trail, which drops steeply to the left, down to the Western States Trail and other routes in the Auburn State Recreation Area. The Olmstead route is well defined and signed from this point on. As you complete the hike, pass junctions with the Wendell T. Robie and Quarry Trails, then drop down to a short section that borders busy CA 49. The roadside stretch ends at St. Florian Court, then curves back to the trailhead.

Miles and Directions

0.0 Start by passing through the break in the fence. The trail splits immediately; stay left.

0.5 Pass a trail marker. Country homes border the route on the left.

0.8 Cross the footbridge over upper Knickerbocker Creek. At the trail junction above the bridge, go right.

0.9 A trail joins from the right as the main route widens into a rough dirt road. Stay left.

1.0 Climb past a trail marker.

1.25 Reach the Cave Valley Gate (#156) at a trail access point behind a schoolyard. Stay straight on the Olmstead Loop. Do not go right on the Cave Valley roadway.

1.4 At the top of a hill, the trail splits. Stay left (straight) on the main path. At the junction at the base of the hill, stay left (straight) again.

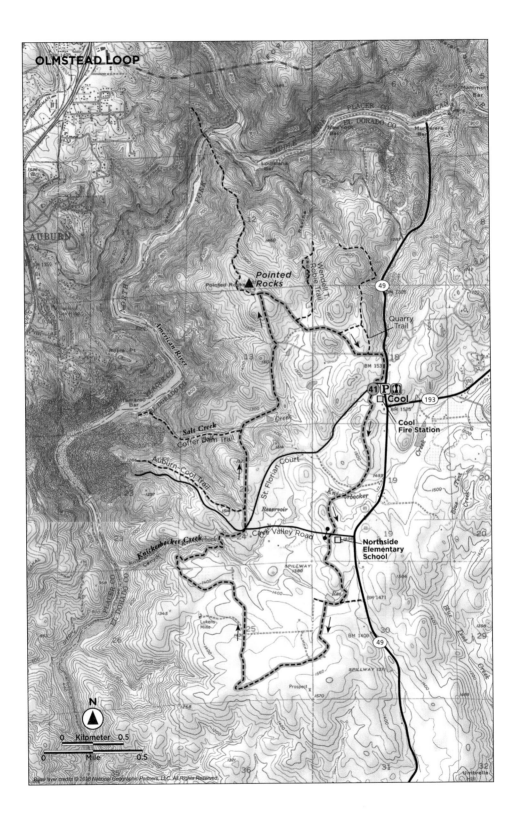

OLMSTEAD LOOP

Pointed Rocks

Cool

Cool Fire Station

Northside Elementary School

Quarry Trail

Wendell T. Robie Trail

Salt Creek

Coffer Dam Trail

Auburn-Cool Trail

Knickerbocker Creek

St. Florian Court

Cave Valley Road

Lukens Mine

American River

EL DORADO Rd

AUBURN

N

0   Kilometer   0.5

0   Mile   0.5

1.75 Cross a footbridge over a little stream.

2.0 Pass trail markers as the treadway narrows. Stay left, then pass the 2-mile marker.

2.25 Several trail markers direct you through a stand of oaks at the top of a climb. Descend past a roadway leading up to a ranch house on the left.

2.5 Pass a cement water basin for livestock. Where unsigned trails merge, stay on the red-dirt main track.

3.0 Pass the 3-mile marker. Look for the loop trail sign, which keeps you on the Olmstead Loop.

3.6 After passing the 3.5-mile marker, reach a junction and stay straight on the Olmstead Loop. Pass through a broken gate.

4.0 At the 4-mile marker, the track splits. Stay left, as the arrow on the trail marker indicates.

4.5 Descend past the 4.5-mile marker, then through a hollow watered by a tributary of Knickerbocker Creek.

5.3 A steep drop lands you beside Knickerbocker Creek. Cross the creek via stones or by wading, then climb out of the drainage and cross the paved road.

5.4 At the junction with the Auburn-Cool Trail, stay straight on the Olmstead Loop.

6.0 Reach the 6-mile marker and the junction with the Coffer Dam / Salt Creek Loop Trail to Auburn. Turn sharply right on the Olmstead Loop and drop into the Salt Creek drainage.

6.4 At the junction with a side trail, stay left on the rocky roadway, passing a trail marker.

7.25 At the junction beyond the 7-mile marker, the Training Hill Trail / Pointed Rocks Trail drops to the left. Go right; it is 1.7 miles to Cool.

7.5 Pass a junction; stay right on the Olmstead Loop.

7.7 Trails merge at a fence line. Go left and uphill on the Olmstead Loop.

7.8 At the junction with the Wendell T. Robie Trail, stay straight (right) on the Olmstead Loop.

7.9 At the junction, stay right on the Olmstead Loop.

8.1 Drop through a meadow to a junction. Go left on the well-used roadway along the fence line.

8.4 Pass the Quarry Trail junction as you climb the hill. The trail drops from here to CA 49.

8.5 Take a sharp right to follow the trail as it runs parallel to the highway.

8.6 Arrive back at the trailhead.

Hike Information

Local information: Historic Hwy 49.com is an online resource for all the gold country hamlets located along CA 49, from Cool to Coloma. Visit www.historichwy49.com.

The El Dorado County Visitors Authority is another source of information about activities in Placerville and along CA 49. The address is 542 Main St., Placerville, CA 95667; call (530) 621-5885; visit http://visit-eldorado.com/#3.

Local events/attractions: The annual Way Too Cool 50K Endurance Run begins and ends in tiny Cool—as if hiking more than 8 miles over hill and dale wasn't enough. For more information visit www.wtc50k.com.

42 Codfish Falls

The trail to Codfish Falls has the flavor of adventure, skimming through a hard-to-reach section of the North Fork American River canyon to a pretty cascade tucked away in a narrow gorge.

Start: North abutment of the bridge over the American River at the bottom of Ponderosa Way

Distance: 3.2 miles out and back

Hiking time: About 2 hours

Difficulty: Moderate

Trail surface: Dirt singletrack

Best season: Spring and fall. The summer sun can be blistering (though you can cool off in the river), and winter rain and snow may render the trail (and the road down into the canyon) inhospitable.

Other trail users: Hikers only

Amenities: Roadside parking for about 10 cars; portable toilets. Bring drinking water.

Canine compatibility: Leashed dogs permitted

Fees and permits: None

Schedule: Open for day use from 7 a.m. to sunset year-round

Maps: USGS Colfax CA and Greenwood CA; Auburn State Recreation Area brochure available at recreation headquarters on CA 49 and online at www.parks.ca.gov/?page_id=502

Trail contact: Auburn State Recreation Area, 501 El Dorado St., Auburn 95603-4949; (530) 885-4527; www.parks.ca.gov/?page_id=502

Special considerations: The trailhead is remote, reached via a steep, winding country road. The final 2.4 miles of the road are unpaved; a high-clearance vehicle is recommended.

Finding the trailhead: Follow I-80 east to the town of Weimar in the Sierra foothills (about 11 miles east of Auburn). Take the Weimar Cross Road exit. Turn right (west, then southwest) on Ponderosa Way. Follow Ponderosa Way to the end of the pavement at 3.2 miles, then drive 2.4 miles down the steep, rutted dirt road into the canyon, to the bridge over the North Fork American River (5.6 miles total). Park along the wide stretch of road just northeast of the bridge. The trail is beyond the metal guardrails at the bridge's north abutment. **GPS:** N39 00.028' / W120 56.391'

The Hike

The trail leading to secluded Codfish Falls follows the North Fork American River, skirting cool pools that, especially as the sun strengthens in summertime, invite side trips to sandbars and rocky beaches along the riverbank. The falls flow down a jumble of dark rocks in a shady enclave just north of the river valley. It's a year-round cascade watering a pocket of verdant mosses, oaks, and grasses in an environment parched for several months each year.

Ponderosa Way, which dives into the American River canyon from Weimar, offers a huge hint at how out-of-bounds this stretch of trail in the Auburn State Recreation Area is. The dirt road falls steeply into the gorge, requiring a driver's full concentration and heightening anticipation as the terrain grows more rugged and remote.

The narrow trail departs from the north abutment of the rustic metal-trussed Ponderosa Way bridge, which spans the river at the bottom of the canyon. A beach spreads below the trailhead, offering access to the cooling waters—the first of several such opportunities along the trail where you can take a break and dip your toes.

The dirt path traces the watercourse for about 1 mile before curving north into the Codfish Creek canyon. River views dominate, a lovely and classic tableau of water and rock walls. The trail is sometimes uneven and sometimes exposed, but always easy to negotiate. Straddling the interface between oak woodlands that dominate at lower elevations and evergreen forests that flourish higher up, the mixed forest insulating the trail includes live and black oaks, red-barked mountain manzanita, bay laurel, redbud (gorgeous in spring), the occasional madrone, and ponderosa pines. Pause at the golden-barked pines to sniff their vanilla scent—hugging a tree has never smelled so sweet.

Though the river is placid and clear in late season, it swells with snowmelt in spring and early summer. Wait for the flow to mellow before you dip your toes into the water. Fishing and rafting are also popular riverine pastimes.

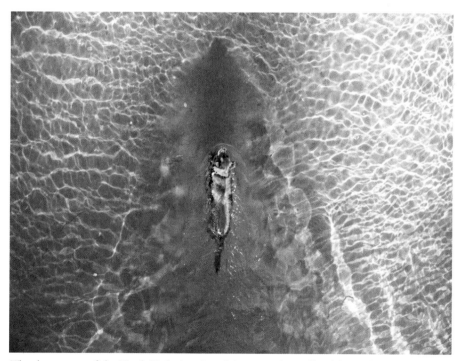

The clear waters of the North Fork American River near the trailhead for Codfish Falls make for cool swimming on a hot summer day.

As you pass the 1-mile mark, curve away from the river and into the Codfish Creek canyon. The falls themselves are about 25 feet high, vigorous when fed by winter rains and thinning to a trickle in summer. Still, they provide enough moisture to support a healthy coat of moss for the dark rocks on either side of the waterfall.

After your visit, retrace your steps to the trailhead.

Miles and Directions

0.0 Start on the singletrack trail on the north side of the Ponderosa Way bridge.

0.4 Flat sheets of shale pave a patch of trail.

0.8 The trail narrows in a gully, showing signs of erosion.

1.0 A narrow social trail breaks left (southeast) to the river. Stay straight on the obvious Codfish Falls Trail.

1.1 The trail curls northwest, away from the river. The trail splits just beyond, with a couple of social tracks heading left (southeast) back toward the river. Stay right (northwest), heading up the side canyon toward the falls.

1.4 Cross a seasonal stream, dry in the late season. The trail gently climbs through the mixed evergreen forest.

1.6 Reach Codfish Falls. Enjoy the cascade, then return as you came.

3.2 Arrive back at the trailhead.

The trail to Codfish Falls begins along the American River and offers several opportunities to drop off the path to swimming holes in summer and fall (after runoff).

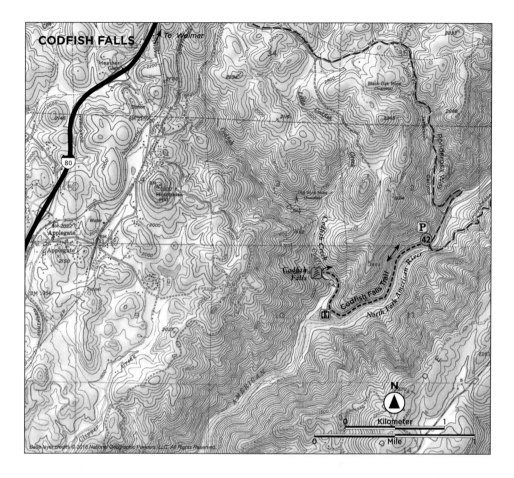

Hike Information

Local information: The city of Colfax, located about 5 miles east of Weimar on I-80, offers a variety of services, restaurants, and community events. The municipal website (www.colfax-ca.gov) includes links to visitor information and recreational and historical resources. The Colfax Area Chamber of Commerce is another source for information about the area; visit www.colfaxchamber.com/colfax-area-1.html or call (530) 346-8888.

Organizations: Protect American River Canyons (PARC) is an organization "dedicated to the protection and conservation of the recreational, cultural, and historical resources" of the North and Middle Fork American River canyons. Visit www.parc-auburn.org for more information; you'll also find links to area guides and maps on the website.

43 Cronan Ranch Regional Trails Park Loop

In Cronan Ranch, winding gravel roads sweep through meadows thick with wildflowers in spring, drop to beaches along a rumbling stretch of the South Fork American River, and ramble past a cluster of old ranch buildings.

Start: Trailhead on the east side of Cronan Ranch's parking area
Distance: 4.4-mile lollipop
Hiking time: 2-3 hours
Difficulty: Challenging, with steep pitches on the descent to riverside
Trail surface: Dirt ranch roads
Best season: Spring for wildflowers; fall for cool weather and great color
Other trail users: Equestrians, mountain bikers, trail runners
Amenities: Restrooms, trash cans, information board with maps
Canine compatibility: Leashed dogs permitted; however, dogs commonly run off-leash. If you allow your dog to run off-leash, keep him/

her under voice control to avoid conflicts with equestrians. Unleashed dogs also risk encountering unfriendly wildlife, including rattlesnakes.
Fees and permits: None
Schedule: Open daily, sunrise to sunset, year-round
Maps: USGS Coloma CA; trail map and brochure available at www.coloma.com/recreation/riverside-parks/cronan-ranch-trails-park/
Trail contact: Bureau of Land Management, Mother Lode Field Office, 5152 Hillsdale Circle, El Dorado Hills 95762; (916) 941-3101; www.blm.gov/visit/american-river-north-middle-south-forks

Finding the trailhead: From I-80 in Auburn, take the CA 49/Placerville exit and head south toward Placerville. Follow CA 49 for 11.5 miles, through Auburn, into the American River canyon, then through the hamlets of Cool and Pilot Hill to Pedro Hill Road on the right (west). Follow Pedro Hill Road south for 0.1 mile to the signed parking area on the left (south) side of the road.
Alternatively, take US 50 east out of Sacramento to the junction with CA 49 in Placerville. Turn left (north) on CA 49 and follow it for 14.2 miles, through Marshall Gold Discovery State Historic Park, to Pedro Hill Road on the left (west). **GPS:** N38 49.620' / W120 59.350'

The Hike

On cool autumn afternoons, with the sun low in the sky, the hills of Cronan Ranch Regional Trails Park take on smoky hues, darker where the forests grow thick on north slopes and lighter where the sun catches the golden annual grasses. The scene is arresting.

A wonderful network of about 12 miles of trails laces through Cronan Ranch, spreading equestrians, mountain bikers, and hikers along ridges and tucking them into long valleys. All roads eventually lead down to the South Fork American River, which defines portions of the property's southern and eastern boundaries. The river, even when the flow is low, rumbles swiftly over its bed, more inviting to rafters and anglers than to swimmers and waders. Still, spread a picnic on the rocky shore, with the music of the water rushing by, and you'll enjoy a restful and invigorating break. The steep descent to the riverside almost requires rest and regrouping; it's a steep climb back up to the trailhead.

The grasses coating the hills of Cronan Ranch—and most of California, for that matter—are nonnative annuals, many species inadvertently brought to the New World by Spanish conquistadors and missionaries in the late 1700s. The grasses grow green in the rainy season and are painted with a succession of native wildflowers— orange fiddlenecks, purple lupines, orange poppies, white yarrow, purple asters, red Indian paintbrush—as spring passes into summer. By the time the dog days roll around in late August, the wildflower blush has faded, and the meadowlands have been fried golden by the summer sun. The grasses have long supported grazing animals, including cattle raised by the Cronan family after purchasing the property from the Central Pacific Railroad in 1891. A cluster of ramshackle ranch buildings, in a meadow at the junction of the Long Valley Trail and Cronan Ranch Road, harken back to what must have been a monastic occupation for the Cronans and the ranching families that followed them.

Today the property is part of a plan to create a South Fork American River trail corridor that would stretch from Greenwood Creek to Salmon Falls. Equestrians, mountain bikers, and hikers easily share the trails—and also make room for paragliders, who climb to high launching points within the park then ride the thermals with the hawks and vultures.

The loop through Cronan Ranch Regional Trails Park traverses foothills meadowlands that blush green in winter and dry to gold in summer.

This route descends into the river canyon via the Down and Up and East Ridge Trails, easy-to-follow ranch roads that drop steeply in sections. Once beside the river, you'll walk downstream past rocky bars and picnic sites, any of which makes a perfect place to stop, rest, and enjoy.

The climb back to the trailhead follows the more gently inclined Long Valley Trail, which leads past the ranch buildings and up along a seasonal stream that blushes green even when the surrounding landscape is brown and dry. You can do the loop in the opposite direction, but the climb up the East Ridge Trail is punishing.

The forested north-facing slope of the river canyon on the opposite side of the south fork hosts dirt tracks used by off-road vehicles; the whine of motorcycle engines sometimes rips through the otherwise quiet canyon. No motorized vehicles are allowed in the regional park itself, but seasonal hunting is permitted.

Miles and Directions

0.0 Start from the parking area on Cronan Ranch Road, heading uphill through the grassland.

0.1 At the junction with the West Ridge Trail, stay straight (south) on Cronan Ranch Road.

0.2 Arrive at an information board and the junction with the Down and Up Trail. Go left (east) on the Down and Up Trail, also a former ranch road.

0.6 Pass the windsock used by paragliders launching off the hilltop to the left (north) of the trail.

0.8 At the intersection of the Down and Up and East Ridge Trails, go right (southwest) on the East Ridge Trail. Views open down toward the river valley.

1.0 Pass the junction with the Hidden Valley Cutoff, staying left (south) on the East Ridge Trail.

1.5 A side trail leads to an observation platform; the vistas are great. The trail steepens as you continue.

1.8 Arrive at the lower junction of the Down and Up and East Ridge Trails. Go right (southwest) on the Down and Up Trail, passing through a fence line.

2.1 At the next junction, stay left (south/downhill) into the riverside bottomlands.

2.3 Ignore side trails that lead left as you reach the river. Continue right (downriver) until you find the perfect spot to soak your feet, eat your lunch, and let the dog go for a swim. Restrooms are available along the riverfront, but there's no potable water.

2.6 Pass the first road/trail that climbs right (north/uphill) out of the river valley. Stay straight (west) on the riverside track. About 0.1 mile farther, cross a seasonal stream, then take the second trail leading uphill (north). This is Cronan Ranch Road.

2.9 Climb past an intersection with the Down and Up Trail. Stay left (uphill/west) on Cronan Ranch Road.

3.1 Bear right on the ranch road through a cluster of old ranch buildings to a three-way trail intersection. Cronan Ranch Road is the middle track; the Long Valley Trail departs to the right (north). You can follow either Cronan Ranch Road or Long Valley to the trailhead. The Long Valley Trail is described, traveling up the valley floor alongside the seasonal stream.

3.7 Cross a culvert that channels an intermittent stream.

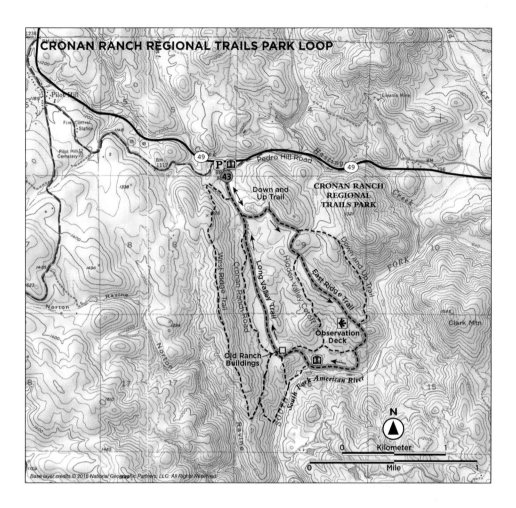

4.0 The Long Valley Trail ends on Cronan Ranch Road. Stay right (north) on Cronan Ranch Road.

4.2 Reach the end of the loop at the junction with the Down and Up Trail. From here, retrace your steps to the trailhead.

4.4 Arrive back at the trailhead and parking area.

Hike Information

Local information: Historic Hwy 49.com is an online resource for all the gold country hamlets located along CA 49, from Cool to Coloma. Visit www.historichwy49.com.

The El Dorado County Visitors Authority is another source of information about activities in Placerville and along CA 49. The address is 542 Main St., Placerville, CA 95667; call (530) 621-5885; visit http://visit-eldorado.com/#3.

44 Dave Moore Nature Trail

This sweet little route meanders through oak woodlands down to a rocky beach on the South Fork American River, offering the wheelchair-bound, stroller-bound, and able-bodied easy access to a backcountry experience.

Start: Behind the restroom at the north end of the parking lot
Distance: 1.1-mile loop
Hiking time: About 1 hour
Difficulty: Easy
Trail surface: Wheelchair-accessible decomposed granite path, dirt singletrack
Best season: Spring through fall
Other trail users: Hikers only
Amenities: Vault toilet, picnic tables; no drinking water
Canine compatibility: Leashed dogs permitted
Fees and permits: None

Schedule: Open daily, 8 a.m. to sunset, year-round
Maps: USGS Coloma CA. The trail is straightforward enough that no map is needed.
Trail contact: Bureau of Land Management, Mother Lode Field Office, 5152 Hillsdale Circle, El Dorado Hills 95762; (916) 941-3101; www.blm.gov/visit/dave-moore-nature-area
Other: The first 0.5 mile of the trail is wheelchair and stroller accessible. For those traveling on wheels, the trail must be taken out and back. Bring your own drinking water.

Finding the trailhead: From I-80 in Auburn, take the CA 49 / Placerville exit and head south. Follow CA 49 for about 15.7 miles, through Auburn and the American River canyon, then through the hamlets of Cool and Pilot Hill, to the nature area's entrance on the right (west). The entry is well signed and bordered by large cobblestone walls. Follow the dirt access road west for 0.1 mile to the parking area.

Alternatively, you can take US 50 east out of Sacramento to the junction with CA 49 in Placerville. Turn left (north) on CA 49 and follow it for about 10 miles, through Marshall Gold Discovery State Historic Park, to the trailhead access road on the left (west). **GPS:** N38 48.923' / W120 55.246'

The Hike

Following the sweeping curves of the Dave Moore Nature Trail is reminiscent of walking a labyrinth. The first 0.5 mile curls through oak woodlands, offering travelers ample chance to contemplate what draws them outdoors—how the sun filters through a forest canopy, the unique shapes of rocks and boulders, how fleeting glimpses of a nearby river quicken the senses.

Surfaced in decomposed granite, the wheelchair-accessible portion of the route spans seasonal streams via sturdy bridges and handles grades via gentle switchbacks that sweep past, among other things, a huge old madrone ring, a boulder that pops from the forest floor like a button mushroom, and the handiwork of Chinese laborers who, during the gold rush, carved ditches and built rock walls to aid miners in their quest to recover precious nuggets.

The trail is dedicated to the memory of a Bureau of Land Management (BLM) conservation ranger who was stricken with multiple sclerosis at a young age. David Moore was an avid outdoorsman, and his disability heightened awareness among his BLM colleagues of the challenges faced on trails by the wheelchair-bound. This trail was designed with his needs—and the needs of other physically impaired individuals—foremost.

▶ **Rafting is popular on all three forks of the American River. Rafting outfits, which can be recommended by local management agencies including the BLM and the Auburn State Recreation Area, offer guide services on the river.**

A mushroom-shaped boulder lies just off the wheelchair-accessible portion of the Dave Moore Nature Trail.

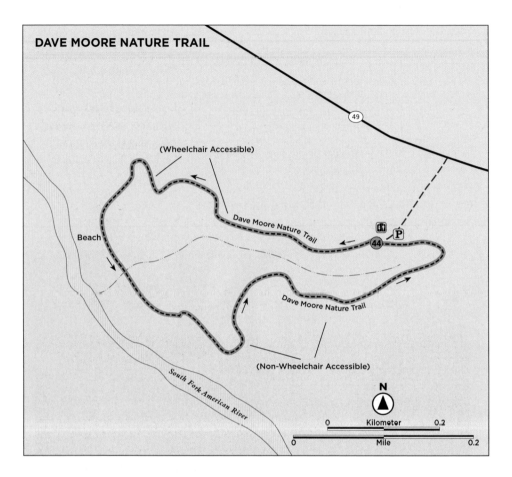

DAVE MOORE NATURE TRAIL

(Wheelchair Accessible)

Dave Moore Nature Trail

Beach

49

44

Dave Moore Nature Trail

(Non-Wheelchair Accessible)

South Fork American River

N

Kilometer
0   0.2
Mile
0   0.2

The wheelchair-accessible stretch ends on a rocky little riverside beach. The South Fork American River is shallow here in summer and fall, skipping over a pebbly bed. Willows and oaks shade the spot, which is perfect for picnicking and wading. Fed by snowmelt from the high country, the river is higher in spring, and may push recreationalists back into the woodland for rest and a snack.

The second half of the loop is decidedly not wheelchair accessible. Wildflowers, willows, and reeds encroach on the path, which narrows and becomes rocky as it skirts trees and rock outcrops parallel to the river. This stretch is a habitat restoration area, so stay on the path to minimize impacts.

The trail bends back through the woodlands toward the trailhead. You'll find seclusion on this segment, as many visitors return down the gravel path. But the woodlands are serene and worth the walk-through, especially a parklike grove of oaks that line the trail like an avenue. A final bridge crossing, and you arrive back at the trailhead.

Miles and Directions

0.0 Start at the trailhead on the north side of the parking area, just behind the restroom.

0.1 At the trail fork stay left on the rock-lined path toward a picnic table, then switchback down to where the paths merge and cross the bridge.

0.2 Cross another bridge amid blackberry brambles, then pass the mushroom rock and a picnic table on the left. The path narrows through a gully where the treadway is softened by pine needles. A broad switchback leads down to and across another bridge and rambles alongside a rock wall built by Chinese workers, who created the channels and earthworks to aid gold miners.

0.4 Switchback down and across two bridges, then arrive on a rocky little beach on the South Fork American River. The wheelchair-accessible portion of the trail ends here. Picnic and play, then return to the trail and go right (southeast) on the dirt path. (*Option:* To stay on the accessible path, return as you came for an 0.8-mile trek.)

0.5 Continuing on the non-wheelchair-accessible portion of the trail, cross a bridge spanning a seasonal stream.

0.7 Swing left (north), away from the river, into a cut in the bank. A split-log bridge spans a seasonal stream. Stay on the maintained trail along the streambed, avoiding social paths.

0.9 Climb into a parklike grove of oaks, then circle northeast toward the parking lot.

1.1 Cross a bridge over a seasonal stream, pass a trail that leads right (east) to a picnic spot, and arrive back at the trailhead parking area.

Hike Information

Local information: Historic Hwy 49.com is an online resource for all the gold country hamlets located along CA 49, from Cool to Coloma. Visit www.historichwy49.com.

The El Dorado County Visitors Authority is another source of information about activities in Placerville and along CA 49. The address is 542 Main St., Placerville, CA 95667; call (530) 621-5885; visit http://visit-eldorado.com/#3.

45 El Dorado Trail from Missouri Flat to Forni Road

This section of the El Dorado Trail, which extends from the western El Dorado County line east to Camino in the foothills, winds through the woodlands south of central Placerville.

Start: Trailhead in the small parking lot on Missouri Flat Road in Placerville
Distance: 5.4 miles out and back
Hiking time: 2-3 hours
Difficulty: Easy
Trail surface: Pavement
Best season: Year-round
Other trail users: Cyclists
Amenities: Trash cans, information signboards at trailheads
Canine compatibility: Leashed dogs permitted
Fees and permits: None

Schedule: Open daily, sunrise to sunset, year-round
Maps: USGS Coloma CA; online at http://eldoradotrail.com/trail-map/; no map needed for the obvious route
Trail contact: El Dorado County Transportation Commission, 2828 Easy Street, Ste. 1, Placerville 95667; (530) 642-5260; www.edctc.org/3/ElDoradoTrail.html. Friends of El Dorado Trail; PO Box 1388, Placerville 95667; http://eldoradotrail.com.

Finding the trailhead: From Sacramento, take US 50 west to Placerville. Take the Missouri Flat Road exit and go right on Missouri Flat Road for about 0.8 mile, past the shopping centers on the right, to the fenced parking area for the Missouri Flat trailhead, on the left. There is parking for about fifteen cars. **GPS:** N38 42.217' / W120 49.551'

The Hike

Midway across the trestle bridge that spans Weber Creek on this scenic stretch of the El Dorado Trail, the guardrails are secured with dozens of locks. They are inscribed with the names of lovers who have come to this high place to declare their devotion to each other and secure it with lock and key—or a combination, as the case may be.

The setting of the high trestle is the main draw along this section of rail trail in Placerville, captivating hikers and cyclists as well as the romantically inclined. The span towers above the forested gorge, with the stream running out of sight and out of earshot far below.

This is but a short section of a much longer trail that occupies the former rights-of-way of two defunct lines: the Sacramento-Placerville Transportation Corridor and the Michigan-California rail corridor. The hike- and bikeway currently stretches from the El Dorado County line on the west to Camino, about 7 miles east of Placerville. The hope is that one day the trail will reach over the crest of the Sierra into the Lake Tahoe basin, creating yet another long-distance walkway/bikeway in the region.

The keys to their hearts: Lovers have affixed locks to the trestle crossing on the El Dorado Trail.

The 2.7-mile stretch included in this guide is essentially an urban route in a mostly rural setting, a paved lane that winds through woodland and grassland but is never far from development and never truly free of road noise from nearby highways. Nonetheless, it offers walkers and cyclists a chance to stretch their legs and clear their minds, whether they've got just enough time to make it to the bridge and back or can spend all day following the route for miles and miles. Parcourse installations add an alternative fitness option to the walk. And you might be pleasantly surprised to find yourself alone for long stretches, particularly if you take to the trail on a weekday.

Begin at the trailhead on Missouri Flat Road, which is a busy thoroughfare offering access to shopping and other services. Though development is obvious on either side of the path, it is gradually screened by thicker and thicker curtains of brush and woodland.

By the time you reach the Weber Creek trestle, obvious signs of civilization have thinned out considerably. On the far side of the bridge, countryside dominates, with meadows and stands of oaks bordering the route. As for the climbing, even as the pitch increases it remains minimal; this is a rail trail, after all.

The trail is bisected by a roadway not far beyond the halfway point, and the incline increases by a few degrees. Signs of civilization—parcourse installations, houses, and finally commercial lots—slowly creep back into the picture as you approach the Forni Road trailhead, the turnaround point. Retrace your steps to the trailhead.

Miles and Directions

0.0 Start by passing the information signboard. Restrooms are located a short distance up the paved route.

0.5 A short up-and-down stretch transitions from the more urban setting to the more rural, with a pasture to the left.

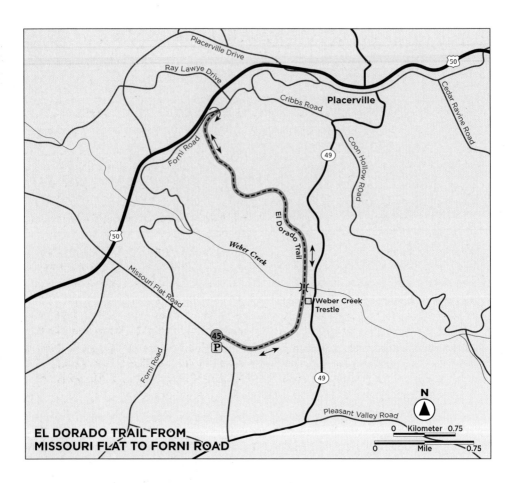

**EL DORADO TRAIL FROM
MISSOURI FLAT TO FORNI ROAD**

0.9 Reach the Weber Creek trestle bridge. It's a long one, with a viewpoint in the middle; locks have been fastened to the wire railing.

1.6 Cross a roadway; the trail has been steadily climbing, but the incline steepens at this point.

2.2 Signs of civilization begin to encroach again, with houses backing up to the trail corridor.

2.4 Pass a pair of parcourse installations; a commercial parking lot abuts the trail.

2.7 Reach the Forni Road trailhead, the turnaround point. Retrace your steps.

5.4 Arrive back at the Missouri Flat trailhead.

Hike Information

Local information: Historic Hwy 49.com is an online resource for all the gold country hamlets located along CA 49, from Cool to Coloma. Visit www.historichwy49.com.

The El Dorado County Visitors Authority is another source of information about activities in Placerville and along CA 49. The address is 542 Main St., Placerville, CA 95667; call (530) 621-5885; visit http://visit-eldorado.com/#3.

46 Monroe Ridge-Marshall Monument Trail Loop

Climb through oak woodlands to viewpoints above the South Fork American River, then tour a historic gold rush town, including the site where the precious metal was first discovered in 1848.

Start: North Beach parking area, Marshall Gold Discovery State Historic Park
Distance: 3.8-mile loop
Hiking time: 2–3 hours
Difficulty: Moderate
Trail surface: Dirt singletrack, some paved roadways and rustic sidewalks, gravel paths
Best season: Year-round, though winter storms and cold may render the trail inhospitable.
Other trail users: Hikers only
Amenities: Restrooms, water, and picnic facilities at the North Beach trailhead; drinking fountain located at the Marshall Monument site
Canine compatibility: Leashed dogs permitted

Fees and permits: Day-use fee, payable at visitor center
Schedule: Open daily, 8 a.m. to sunset, year-round
Maps: USGS Coloma CA; state historic park map available at the visitor center / museum and online at www.parks.ca.gov/?page _id=484
Trail contact: California State Parks, 1416 9th St. (PO Box 942896), Sacramento 94296; (800) 777-0369; www.parks.ca.gov. The park address is 310 Back Street (PO Box 265), Coloma 95613; (530) 622-3470; www.parks .ca.gov/?page_id=484.

Finding the trailhead: From downtown Sacramento, head east on US 50 to Placerville and the junction with CA 49. Turn left (north) on CA 49 and follow the scenic road for 9 miles, through the town of Coloma and past the Marshall SHP visitor center, to the North Beach picnic and parking area on the right (east). Park in the southernmost part of the parking lot; the trailhead is across CA 49, at a break in the split-rail fence near the old mining cabin. **GPS:** N38 48.245' / W120 53.698'

The Hike

You can still pan for gold along the South Fork American River in Marshall Gold Discovery State Historic Park, but, arguably, gold is not the most valuable thing that can be gleaned from these hills in modern times. The state park celebrating James Marshall's fateful discovery is a treasure chest of historic sites and stories, and the canyon walls hovering over Sutter's Mill offer spectacular views up and down the river valley.

The origins of the gold rush are familiar to most Californians, but here's a quick and dirty recap: In 1848 Marshall, who ran a Coloma lumber mill in partnership with John Sutter, was checking the mill's tailrace and discovered gold flakes in the detritus that had backed up there. One of the largest gold rushes in history followed, with thousands of fortune-seekers from all over the world racing to the foothills of the Sierra Nevada hoping to get rich quick. The rush itself was short-lived, but in its aftermath California, acquired from Mexico in the same year Marshall made his discovery, became America's "Golden State." That legacy of adventure, invention, hard work, luck (good and bad), and greed informs the state's psyche into modern times.

The town of Coloma and the state historic park are pretty much one and the same. Some old miners' cabins, including that of James Marshall, are preserved intact; other historic homes have been transformed into bed-and-breakfasts and private residences. Storefronts dating back to gold rush days now house historic exhibits, restaurants, and gift shops. Along the Gold Discovery Loop Trail, which meanders down by the river, a reproduction of Sutter's Mill overlooks picnic grounds, and a striking river rock monument marks the original mill site. A bronze statue of James

Re-creations of historic structures such as Sutter's Mill, as well as a great museum and the chance to pan for gold yourself, are among the highlights of an exploration of the Monroe Ridge–Marshall Monument Trail Loop.

THE GOLD DISCOVERY MUSEUM

Every hike in Marshall Gold Discovery State Historic Park should begin at the Gold Discovery Museum and Visitor Center. It's not just a matter of paying the day-use fee; it's also about the exhibits inside, which offer insights into the discovery that turned a sleepy Mexican frontier into the Golden State.

The museum houses dioramas depicting the lifestyles of native tribes that hunted and gathered in the area before the arrival of the forty-niners, as well as the area's natural history. But it's the artifacts of the gold rush that mesmerize: reproductions of gold nuggets; collections of old bottles, assay instruments, household items—even an old stagecoach.

The museum is open daily from 10 a.m. to 5 p.m. Mar through Oct, and from 9 a.m. to 4 p.m. Nov through Feb. The address is 310 Back St., Coloma 95613; call (530) 622-3470.

Marshall himself stands on a pedestal on the southwest side of the canyon, overlooking the entire scene.

This route, while saturated in history, also rises above it. It begins and ends at the Monroe homesite: The matriarch of the Monroe family was a former slave who purchased her son's freedom with money earned working for miners. The family remained in Coloma for more than a century before selling their property to the state.

The trail climbs the steep canyon wall via several switchbacks, winding through stands of red-barked mountain manzanita, oaks, and, in its upper reaches, ponderosa pines. Road noise from CA 49 filters up through the trees, but fades as you gain altitude and distance.

The route tops out on a forested ridge, where a picnic table overlooking the river valley offers a comfortable place to rest. Pass remnants of mining operations as you continue across the ridge. Beyond a second picnic table and overlook, the trail begins its descent, dropping around more switchbacks through the mixed woodland toward the town below. Pass a cistern then meet up with a paved park road, which leads down to the Marshall Monument, where you can enjoy the same views the bronze man enjoys. Take in the sights, read the interpretive signs, drink the sweet water from the fountain, then continue down into town.

The path back to the Monroe homesite meanders along peaceful roads lined with historic buildings, including Marshall's cabin, a tiny Catholic church, and the old jailhouse. An interpretive trail winds through an exhibit of mining equipment outside the park's museum.

Cross the highway, and head toward the banks of the American River. Here the Gold Discovery Loop Trail leads past the original mill and discovery site. The discovery site is simple and provocative: a pond of still water where even the most skeptical visitor can't help but hope she'll spot a precious nugget.

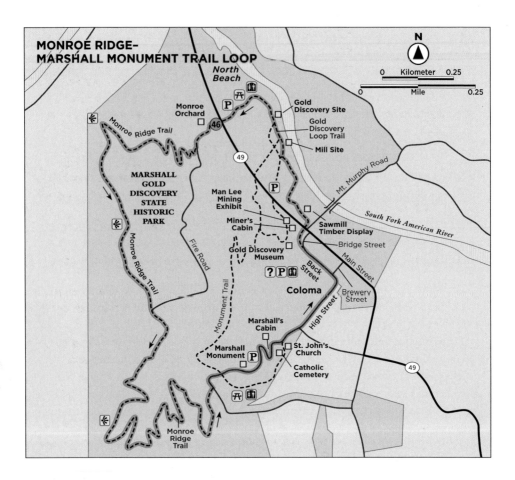

Back at North Beach you can rest on the riverbank and mull the possibilities. Outfitted with a pan, a red flannel union suit under your dungarees, a little elbow grease, and optimism, you too could be a placer miner.

Miles and Directions

0.0 Start on the Monroe Ridge Trail, climbing past a mining cabin and through the remnants of the Monroe family orchard.

0.1 Stay right (uphill/southwest) on the singletrack Monroe Ridge Trail, avoiding the fire road on the left.

0.2 Switchbacks lead to a staircase and bridge across a flume once used for mining and irrigation.

0.6 Round a switchback where views open to the north. Keep up!

0.8 A long ascending traverse attains the ridgetop then follows its spine south to a picnic table in a stand of oaks. Spectacular views drop hundreds of feet to the river and Coloma.

1.1 Pass a side trail to a fenced-off pit on the left. Stay right on the Monroe Ridge Trail.

1.2 Reach a saddle with low-slung power lines overhead.

1.5 Arrive at a second picnic bench and overlook. Enjoy a rest before continuing on the now-descending Monroe Ridge Trail. Switchbacks drop across sunny south-facing slopes that bloom with wildflowers in season, passing a short path and another viewpoint.

2.1 More than a half-dozen switchbacks lead down to a trail marker at a clearing in the woodland. A covered cistern sits uphill to the right (south). Stay left (east), heading toward the Marshall Monument.

2.2 The path meets the paved park road at a picnic area. Walk left (uphill) on the road toward a park residence, then go right (east) on the signed Marshall Monument path (also paved). Stairs lead up to the monument site, where Marshall's bronzed likeness stands atop a marble-and-granite pedestal. Descend the steps to the paved roadway and go left (east), heading down into the historic district.

2.8 Reach Marshall's Cabin and St. John's Catholic Church and cemetery. Continue northeast on High Street.

3.0 At the corner of Back and Brewery Streets, turn left (north), passing the ruins of the El Dorado County Jail.

3.1 Back Street leads to Bridge Street and the visitor center / museum. Follow the interpretive trail through the mining equipment exhibit. Cross CA 49 and turn left (north), passing the Gold Trail Grange building, to the Gold Discovery Loop Trail.

3.3 Visit the Sutter's Mill replica, then follow the crushed granite riverside path left (north).

3.5 Pass the original site of Sutter's Mill and the gold discovery site in quick succession.

3.8 Arrive back at the North Beach trailhead and parking lot.

Hike Information

Local information: Recreational opportunities, dining options, entertainment, and more are listed on the Coloma-Lotus Valley website: www.coloma.com.

The El Dorado County Visitors Authority is another source of information about activities in Placerville and along CA 49. The address is 542 Main St., Placerville, CA 95667; call (530) 621-5885; visit http://visit-eldorado.com/#3.

Organizations: The nonprofit Gold Discovery Park Association works to promote and support educational and historical programs at the state historic park, including gold-panning demonstrations. The association also runs annual events at the park, such as Christmas in Coloma. For more information call (530) 622-6198 or visit http://marshallgold.org.

47 Jenkinson Lake Loop

Circumambulating Jenkinson Lake, in the Sierra foothills east of Placerville, you'll meander through a restored meadowland at the mouth of Hazel Creek, visit a waterfall near the outlet of Park Creek, and enjoy long roller-coaster stretches of easy woodland walking with great lake views.

Start: Stonebraker boat launch parking area
Distance: 8.9-mile loop
Hiking time: 5-6 hours
Difficulty: Challenging
Trail surface: Dirt singletrack, with short sections of paved roadway, dirt roadway, and boardwalk
Best season: Early summer for wildflowers; late fall and winter for serenity
Other trail users: Mountain bikers, equestrians on some sections
Amenities: Restrooms, picnic sites, trash cans, boat launches, camping
Canine compatibility: Leashed dogs permitted
Fees and permits: Day-use fee

Schedule: The Sly Park Recreation Area is open daily, sunrise to sunset, year-round. If you are camping at the lake and enjoy hiking in the dark, the trail is accessible 24 hours a day.
Maps: USGS Sly Park CA; available at the park entrance station and online at www.eid.org/home/showdocument?id=5256
Trail contact: Sly Park Recreation Area / Jenkinson Lake, 4771 Sly Park Rd., Pollock Pines 95726; (530) 295-6810; www.eid.org/recreation/sly-park-recreation-area-spra-at-jenkinson-lake
Other: Jenkinson Lake offers a variety of recreational opportunities, including camping, boating, and fishing. Visit www.webreserv.com/eldoradoirrigationdistrictca for details.

Finding the trailhead: From Sacramento, head east on US 50 for about 50 miles, traveling through Placerville, to Pollock Pines. Take the Sly Park Road exit and go right (south) on Sly Park Road. Drive 4.2 miles to the Sly Park Recreation Area entrance, on the left. **GPS:** N38 43.857' / W120 32.589'

The Hike

In a very nice way, Jenkinson Lake is two-faced. The north shore, you might say, is the prom queen: all gussied up with campgrounds and boat launches and picnic areas—a little flashy, a little loud, and a load of fun. The south shore is the tomboy: rugged and challenging, dressed down but beautiful, and just as much fun. That's the one thing the two shorelines have in common—they both will show you a good time.

You can pick up the trail almost anywhere along the north shore. The challenge on busy summer days will be finding a place to park and get on the trail. Regardless of where you start, or which direction you travel (the route is described here in a clockwise direction), you'll hike a good distance on well-maintained footpaths, with a few sections of gravel road, some campground road, and a sliver of boardwalk in the mix.

Beginning at the Stonebraker boat launch and picnic area, located toward the northeast corner of the reservoir, descend a flight of steps to the Sierra-Chimney Trail. Head left (east) on the singletrack, enjoying great lake views. Here, and for most of the loop, you'll pass plenty of places where you can drop off the trail to the lakeshore for a rest, a snack, or a swim.

The Sierra-Chimney Trail empties onto the paved lake service road at the Chimney campground. Aptly named, two stone chimneys are on the beach—one still upright, the other little more than a heap of broken rock.

▶ **The resident bats in Sly Park are capable of consuming 1,000 insects each per night. Bad news for pesky mosquitoes; good news for hikers. But sometimes they just can't keep up, so visitors should still bring along insect repellent.**

Follow the paved road east to Hazel Meadow, where you'll drop onto a boardwalk lined with interpretive signs describing the flora and fauna of the restored wetland

A waterfall spills into a pool on Park Creek.

surrounding one of Jenkinson Lake's inlet streams. The viewing platform affords great views down the length of the lake to one of its distant dams, and interpretation describes the importance of water conservation, the different species of bats in the park, and the annual ladybug migration in spring, when the bright red, lucky bugs swarm on the trunks of evergreens lining the meadow.

> **Jenkinson Lake is a water supply. Please don't let your pet swim in the lake, and young children should wear swim diapers if they go in the water.**

Hazel Creek camp is behind the meadow, with picnic areas and restrooms. For a shorter hike of about 2.2 miles, you can turn around here and retrace your steps to the trailhead.

The loop resumes on the signed South Shore Trail, at the bridge over Hazel Creek. On this side of the lake, the path forks repeatedly, with horses directed onto one path and hikers and bikers onto another (and sometimes bikers onto a separate trail of their own). Follow the signs, and don't worry if you make a "wrong turn"; the trails always merge again.

At about the 2-mile mark, the path leads into the Park Creek drainage. Take a detour before you cross the bridge over Park Creek to visit the waterfall, following a side trail that leads back along the creek for less than 0.1 mile to the falls. The white-

A pair of stone chimneys, one little more than a heap of rock, stands sentinel at Chimney Camp on the shores of Jenkinson Lake.

water spill of about 25 feet lands in a clear pool, where you can wet your feet (or more), depending on the season. The pool is surrounded by a smooth rock outcrop perfect for sunning and picnicking. Again, this is a great turnaround point (about 4 miles out and back) if you don't want to make the full loop.

From Park Creek the trail begins a roller-coaster ramble through mixed evergreen forest, with occasional side trails leading down to the lakeshore. It's an easy walk despite the ups and downs, with good lake views through the trees. Circle into another drainage, passing some excellent lakefront picnic beaches. Again, where trails merge and diverge, stay mostly to the right, near the water. You'll pass through another drainage about 1 mile on—more side trails, more keeping to the right . . .

As you near the first dam, the trail widens. A brief ascent, then descent, drops you to the paved Mormon Emigrant Trail (not a trail, but a two-lane roadway). Go right, across the dam, to the signed trail on the far side.

Welcome back to civilization. The route parallels the road for a stretch, then crosses it again and switchbacks down to the spillway below the second dam. Follow the steep horse trail up to the roadway and cross again to regain the lakeside path, which is now back on the north side of the lake. Be sure to take advantage of the views from the boat launch parking area. Looking east across Jenkinson Lake, the Sierra crest—snowbound into summer if winter's snowfall was average or above—is visible. Beyond the boat launch the wide path passes through a stately evergreen forest, with the trees lined up in columns on either side.

The last few miles of the loop pass through the developed areas of the Sly Park Recreation Area, with campgrounds and picnic areas bordering the route. Occasionally the trail follows a stretch of paved campground road; sometimes it grows rugged again, circling through drainages and crossing bridges and boardwalks that span seasonal inlet streams. The final leg, back on the Sierra-Chimney Trail, echoes the wild feel of the south shore, passing close to the water at the lake's narrow point before cruising back into the Stonebraker boat launch area. Climb the stairs back to the trailhead and parking area.

Miles and Directions

0.0 Start by dropping from the Stonebraker parking area via a staircase to the Sierra-Chimney Trail. Go left on the dirt footpath.

0.25 Cross a little bridge in a wooded drainage.

0.6 Arrive at the paved road at the Chimney campground. Go right on the road, following "Trail" signs painted on the pavement.

1.1 Reach Hazel Meadow and the Hazel Creek campground. Cross the boardwalk and the bridge over Hazel Creek, now on the South Shore Trail.

1.3 The trail splits. Stay right on the signed hiking trail (cyclists and equestrians are directed onto the left path). Social trails break right to the lakeshore; stay on the loop trail.

1.75 The horse/bike and hiking trails merge. Stay right on the main path.

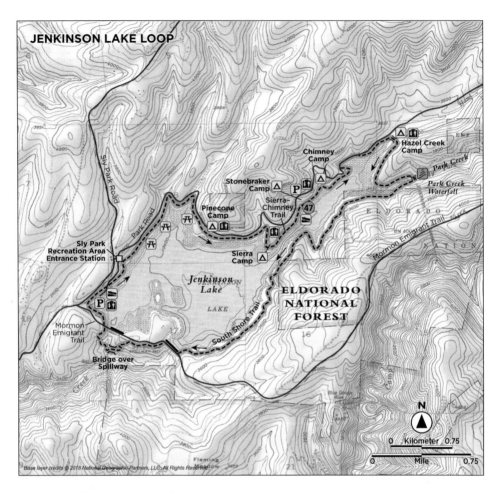

2.0 Arrive at the bridge over Park Creek. Go straight on the path headed upstream to reach the waterfall; then return to the bridge and go left, continuing the loop.

2.3 The horse trail splits to the left, followed by a second split with mountain bikers directed left. The hiking trail stays right, then climbs a flight of stone steps to rejoin the bike trail.

3.0 Different social trails merge as the main path curves through another creek drainage. Stay right along the lakeshore.

4.0 Reach another stream drainage, where social trails merge again. Go right on the hike/bike trail.

4.6 The horse trail meets the hike/bike trail. Stay right on the main path, which widens to roadway width.

4.75 Drop to the paved Mormon Emigrant Trail roadway and the first dam. Turn right, cross the dam, and pick up the signed trail on the other side.

5.0 At the paved park road, head left for about 25 yards to pick up the signed hiking/biking trail. Do *not* continue on the gated road. At the second park road crossing, go straight on the trail.

5.2 The trail empties onto the two-lane Mormon Emigrant Trail roadway again, just above the main dam. Cross the road to the signed trail and descend switchbacks.

5.4 Cross the bridge over the dam spillway. Continue straight on the signed horse trail for about 100 yards to a trail Y. Go right and steeply uphill on the rugged horse trail.

5.6 Arrive at a junction with the Mormon Emigrant Trail again. Drop onto the road, cross it, and pick up the dirt anglers' trail on the other side, heading left. The lakeshore is on your right.

5.8 The anglers' trail merges into the formal hiking/biking trail at a stone staircase on the left. Continue straight on the trail.

6.0 Arrive at the boat launch parking area. Cross the lot to pick up the trail near the restroom. The path is bounded by a stone retaining wall on the left and the lake on the right.

6.8 Enter a picnic area that stretches for about 0.2 mile along the lakeshore. The tables (and trail) have wonderful views and access to the water.

7.0 Go right on the obvious path; the left track leads up to the park road.

7.3 The trail narrows to singletrack as it approaches the park road; the Miwok Nature Trail is across the road. Go left, across the bridge.

7.5 Enter Pinecone camp. Go right on the paved camp road / bike trail, along the lakeshore.

8.0 The camp road ends on the park road. A sign for the Sierra camp marks the resumption of the dirt singletrack on the right. Pick this up and continue the loop.

8.2 A fence line marks the boundary with the Sierra camp. Climb up along the fence to the camp road and go right on the paved campground road.

8.4 Pick up the signed Sierra-Chimney Trail on the right. Follow the dirt track toward the Chimney camp (1 mile ahead).

8.9 Arrive back at the Stonebraker trailhead.

Hike Information

Local information: El Dorado County Visitors Authority; 542 Main St., Placerville 95667; (530) 621-5885; http://visit-eldorado.com/#1. The Visit El Dorado website includes information about recreational and cultural opportunities in the region, as well as local restaurants and businesses.

Camping: Campgrounds line the north shore of the lake, including Pinecone, Sierra, Jenkinson, Stonebraker, Chimney, and Hazel Creek. To make reservations call the Sly Park Recreation Area reservations line at (530) 295-6810 or visit www.eid .org/recreation/imbeddedreservations.

Honorable Mention

Other Trails in the Auburn State Recreation Area

The canyons of the three forks of the American River are chock-full of hiking opportunities. Many of the trails lie within the Auburn State Recreation Area (SRA). To learn more about hiking in the Auburn SRA, visit www.parks.ca.gov/?page _id=502 or call the park office at (530) 885-4527. To learn more about specific hikes in the canyons of the Auburn SRA, visit the Auburn State Recreation Area Canyon Keepers website: www.canyonkeepers.org. The site includes links to individual hiking pages produced by the state parks department, which have route descriptions and directions to the various trailheads.

Be Prepared

Hiking in the Sacramento Valley and surrounding mountainous areas is generally safe. Still, hikers should be prepared, whether they are out for a short stroll along the Sacramento River waterfront or venturing into the secluded American River canyon. Some specific advice:

Know the basics of first aid, including how to treat bleeding; bites and stings; and fractures, strains, or sprains. Pack a first-aid kit on each excursion.

Familiarize yourself with the symptoms of heat exhaustion and heat stroke. Heat exhaustion symptoms include heavy sweating, muscle cramps, headache, dizziness, and fainting. Should you or any of your hiking party exhibit any of these symptoms, cool the victim down immediately by rehydrating and getting him or her to an air-conditioned location. Heat stroke is much more serious: The victim may lose consciousness, and the skin is hot and dry to the touch. In this event, call 911 immediately.

Regardless of the weather, your body needs a lot of water while hiking. Consuming a full 32-ounce bottle is advisable for hikes less than 5 miles long. Add more for longer distances. Bring water with you, regardless of whether water is available at the trailhead or along the route.

Don't drink from streams, rivers, creeks, or lakes without treating or filtering the water first. Water from these sources may host a variety of contaminants, including giardia, which can cause serious intestinal distress.

Carry a backpack in which you can store extra clothing, ample drinking water and food, and whatever goodies, like guidebooks, cameras, and binoculars, you might want.

Many area trails have cell phone coverage. Bring your device, but make sure you've turned it off or got it on the vibrate setting while hiking.

Keep children under careful watch. The bigger rivers have dangerous currents and are not safe for swimming. Hazards along some of the trails include poison oak, uneven footing, and steep drop-offs. Make sure children don't stray from the designated route. Children (really, all hikers) should carry a plastic whistle. If they become lost, they should stay in one place and blow the whistle to summon help.

Hike with a partner. There is safety in numbers, even if that number is only two.

LEAVE NO TRACE

Trails in the Sacramento area and neighboring foothills are heavily used year-round. We, as trail users and advocates, must be especially vigilant to make sure our passage leaves no lasting mark. Here are some basic guidelines for preserving trails in the region:

- Pack out all your own trash, including biodegradable items like orange peels. You might also pack out garbage left by less-considerate hikers.

- Don't approach or feed any wild creatures—the ground squirrel eyeing your snack food is best able to survive if it remains self-reliant.

- Leave wildflowers, rocks, antlers, feathers, and other treasures where you find them. Removing these items degrades natural values and takes away from the next explorer's experience.

- Remain on the established route to avoid damaging trailside soils and plants. This is also a good rule of thumb for avoiding poison oak and stinging nettle, common regional trailside irritants.

- Don't cut switchbacks, which can promote erosion.

- Be courteous by not making loud noises while hiking. This extends to your cell phone. Make sure it is on mute, and use it only in case of emergency. If you must listen to music, conduct business, or help solve your best friend's romantic issues while on the trail, use ear buds and not the speaker function.

- Many of these trails are multiuse, which means you'll share them with other hikers, trail runners, mountain bikers, and equestrians. Generally, hikers yield to equestrians, and mountain bikers yield to all trail users. Familiarize yourself with the proper trail etiquette, but use common sense. It's often easier for a hiker to step aside than for a mountain biker to dismount and move off the path.

- Use outhouses at trailheads or along the trail.

For more information, visit www.LNT.org.

Organizations, Hiking Clubs, and Other Associations

The following government and private organizations manage, provide interpretation or tours on, or otherwise support public lands described in this guide. They can provide further information on these hikes and other trails in the region.

Auburn State Recreation Area Canyon Keepers; www.canyonkeepers.org. A clearinghouse for all things recreational in the Auburn State Recreation Area, this group publishes a wonderful guide to hiking trails in the North Fork and Middle Fork American River and leads guided hikes.

Bureau of Land Management, Mother Lode Field Office, 5152 Hillsdale Circle, El Dorado Hills 95762; (916) 941-3101; www.blm.gov.

California State Parks, Department of Parks and Recreation, 416 9th St., Sacramento 95814 (PO Box 942896, Sacramento 94296); (800) 777-0369 or (916) 653-6995; www.parks.ca.gov; e-mail: info@parks.ca.gov. A complete listing of state parks is available on the website, along with park brochures and maps.

Cosumnes River Preserve, 13501 Franklin Blvd., Galt 95632; (916) 684-2816; www.cosumnes.org. This organization provides information about both the Cosumnes River Preserve and the Howard Ranch Trail outside Galt.

Middle Mountain Interpretive Hikes; www.middlemountainhikes.org. This nonprofit provides educational programs and interpretive journeys in the Sutter Buttes.

Protect American River Canyons (PARC); www.parc-auburn.org. Dedicated to promoting conservation, recreation, and education about the canyons of the American River.

Sacramento Audubon Society, PO Box 160694, Sacramento 95816; www.sacramentoaudubon.org.

Sacramento County Regional Parks Department, (916) 875-PARK (7275); www.regionalparks.saccounty.net; e-mail: parksinfo@saccounty.net. The park office is open from 8 a.m. to 5 p.m. daily.

Sacramento Valley Conservancy, PO Box 160694, Sacramento 95816-0694; www.sacramentovalleyconservancy.org.

Regional Trails

Regional trails in the area include the Jedediah Smith National Recreation Trail and the Western States Pioneer Express Trail. Portions of these regional trails are described in this guide. More information on the Jedediah Smith National Recreation Trail can be found at www.regionalparks.saccounty.net/Parks/Pages/JedediahSmith.aspx. For the Western States trail, visit www.teviscup.org, www.wser.org, or wstrail.org.

Acknowledgments

I am indebted to the lovers of parks and open spaces who have worked over the years to preserve pockets of wildland throughout the Sacramento area. A guidebook like this wouldn't be possible without their efforts.

Thanks to the land managers who have taken the time to review the hikes described in this guide, and to other writers who have shared their impressions of and experiences on Sacramento-area trails both in books and online.

Thanks to all the kind folks I met on the trails who pointed me in the direction of their favorite regional hikes. I hope I've done justice to their recommendations, and that this guide helps them find new favorites.

Thanks to the expert team of editors and production staff at FalconGuides for helping make this guide the best it can be, including David Legere and Julie Marsh.

Thanks also to family and friends who support my work as a guidebook writer. I never would have pulled together the first edition of this guide without the support of Karen Charland, Kelly Knappe, Kerin McTaggart, Julie Roth, and Sara Hesse Bergendahl. My cousin, Meg Sayles, gave me nice tips about where to eat in the Sacramento region. Family is my backbone, whether they are jealous of my frequent escapes into the woods or merely tolerate them. My gratitude always to my parents, Jesse and Judy Salcedo; my brothers, Nick and Chris Salcedo; and Sarah Chourré and the rest of the Chourré clan.

Finally, to my sons, Jesse, Cruz, and Penn: Whether on the trail or not, I'm very lucky to be able to share my journey with you.

Further Reading

Alden, Peter, and Fred Heath. *National Audubon Society Field Guide to California*. New York: Alfred A. Knopf, Inc. (Chanticleer Press), 1998.

Avella, Steven M. *Sacramento: Indomitable City*. Charleston, SC: Arcadia Publishing, 2003.

Evans, Steven L. *Top Trails Sacramento: Exploring Valley, Foothills, and Mountains in the Sacramento Region*. Berkeley, CA: Wilderness Press, 2008.

Ferris, Jim, Michael Lynch, and Sheila Toner. *American River Canyon Hikes: Practical Guides to Trails in the Canyons of the North and Middle Forks American River*. Audubon State Recreation Area Canyon Keepers, 2005.

Lawton, Rebecca, and Gary Fricker. *Sacrament: Homage to a River*. Berkeley, CA: Heyday Books, 2013.

Summers, Jordan. *60 Hikes within 60 Miles: Sacramento*. Birmingham, AL: Menasha Ridge Press, 2008.

Index

About the Author

Tracy Salcedo has written guidebooks to a number of destinations in California and Colorado, including *Hiking Through History San Francisco*, *Hiking Waterfalls in Northern California*, *Hiking Lassen Volcanic National Park*, *Best Hikes Near Reno–Lake Tahoe*, *Best Rail Trails California*, and Best Easy Day Hikes guides to San Francisco's Peninsula, San Francisco's North Bay, San Francisco's East Bay, San Jose, Lake Tahoe, Reno, Sacramento, Fresno, Boulder, Denver, and Aspen. She's also the author of *Historic Yosemite National Park* and *Historic Denali National Park and Preserve*. She lives with her family in California's Wine Country. You can learn more by visiting her website at www .laughingwaterink.com.

*The walls of Malakoff Diggins evoke
the color schemes of the desert.*